My Samsung
Galaxy S®7

Craig James Johnston
Eric Butow

800 East 96th Street,
Indianapolis, Indiana 46240 USA

My Samsung Galaxy S®7

ISBN-13: 978-0-7897-5763-0
ISBN-10: 0-7897-5763-X

Library of Congress Control Number: 2016939724

Printed in the United States of America

3   16

Trademarks

All terms mentioned in this book that are known to be trademarks or service marks have been appropriately capitalized. Que Publishing cannot attest to the accuracy of this information. Use of a term in this book should not be regarded as affecting the validity of any trademark or service mark.

All Galaxy S7 images are provided by Samsung Electronics America.

Warning and Disclaimer

Every effort has been made to make this book as complete and as accurate as possible, but no warranty or fitness is implied. The information provided is on an "as is" basis. The author and the publisher shall have neither liability nor responsibility to any person or entity with respect to any loss or damages arising from the information contained in this book.

Bulk Sales

Que Publishing offers excellent discounts on this book when ordered in quantity for bulk purchases or special sales. For more information, please contact

U.S. Corporate and Government Sales
1-800-382-3419
corpsales@pearsontechgroup.com

For sales outside of the U.S., please contact

International Sales
intlcs@pearson.com

Editor-in-Chief
Greg Wiegand

Acquisitions Editors
Michelle Newcomb
Laura Norman

Development Editor
Charlotte Kughen

Managing Editor
Sandra Schroeder

Project Editor
Mandie Frank

Copy Editor
Charlotte Kughen

Indexer
Ken Johnson

Proofreader
Debbie Williams

Technical Editor
Christian Kenyeres

Editorial Assistant
Cindy Teeters

Designer
Chuti Prasertsith

Compositor
Trina Wurst

Contents at a Glance

Table of Contents

My Samsung Galaxy S7

About the Authors

Craig James Johnston has been involved with technology since his high school days at Glenwood High in Durban, South Africa, when his school was given some Apple][Europluses. From that moment, technology captivated him, and he has owned, supported, evangelized, and written about it.

Craig has been involved in designing and supporting large-scale enterprise networks with integrated email and directory services since 1989. He has held many different IT-related positions in his career, ranging from sales support engineer to mobile architect for a 40,000-smartphone infrastructure at a large bank.

You can see Craig's previously published work in his books *Professional BlackBerry*, *My iMovie*, and many other *My* series books that cover devices by BlackBerry, Palm, HTC, Motorola, Samsung, and Google.

Craig also enjoys high-horsepower, high-speed vehicles and tries very hard to keep to the speed limit while driving them.

Originally from Durban, South Africa, Craig has lived in the United Kingdom, the San Francisco Bay Area, and New Jersey, where he now lives with his wife, Karen, and a couple of cats.

Craig would love to hear from you. Feel free to contact Craig about your experiences with *My Samsung Galaxy S7* at http://www.CraigsBooks.info.

All comments, suggestions, and feedback—both positive and negative—are welcome.

Eric Butow began writing books in 2000 when he wrote *Master Visually Windows 2000 Server*. Since then, Eric has authored or coauthored 26 other books. Those books include Addison-Wesley's *User Interface Design for Mere Mortals*, Amacom's *How to Succeed in Business Using LinkedIn*, Wiley Publishing's *Droid Companion*, Wiley Publishing's *Google Glass For Dummies*, Que Publishing's *Blogging to Drive Business,* Second Edition, and Que Publishing's *My Samsung Galaxy Tab S2*.

Eric lives in Jackson, California. He has a master's degree in communication from California State University, Fresno, and is the owner of Butow Communications Group (BCG), an online marketing ROI improvement firm.

Website: http://butow.net

LinkedIn: http://linkedin.com/in/ebutow

Dedication

"I love deadlines. I like the whooshing sound they make as they fly by."
—Douglas Adams

To everyone who never gave up on me.
—Eric Butow

Acknowledgments

We would like to express our deepest gratitude to the following people on the *My Samsung Galaxy S7* team who all worked extremely hard on this book:

- Michelle Newcomb, our acquisitions editor, who worked with us to give this project an edge

- Christian Kenyeres, our technical editor, who double-checked our writing to ensure the technical accuracy of this book

- Charlotte Kughen, who edited the manuscript skillfully

- Mandie Frank, who kept the book project on schedule

- Trina Wurst, who combined the text and art into colorful pages

We Want to Hear from You!

As the reader of this book, *you* are our most important critic and commentator. We value your opinion and want to know what we're doing right, what we could do better, what areas you'd like to see us publish in, and any other words of wisdom you're willing to pass our way.

We welcome your comments. You can email or write to let us know what you did or didn't like about this book—as well as what we can do to make our books better.

Please note that we cannot help you with technical problems related to the topic of this book.

When you write, please be sure to include this book's title and author as well as your name and email address. We will carefully review your comments and share them with the authors and editors who worked on the book.

Email: feedback@quepublishing.com

Mail: Que Publishing
            ATTN: Reader Feedback
            800 East 96th Street
            Indianapolis, IN 46240 USA

Reader Services

Register your copy of *My Samsung Galaxy S7* at quepublishing.com for convenient access to downloads, updates, and corrections as they become available. To start the registration process, go to quepublishing.com/register and log in or create an account*. Enter the product ISBN, 9780789757630, and click Submit. Once the process is complete, you will find any available bonus content under Registered Products.

*Be sure to check the box that you would like to hear from us in order to receive exclusive discounts on future editions of this product.

Samsung Galaxy S7

Samsung Galaxy S7 edge

In this chapter, you become familiar with the external features of the Galaxy S7 and the basics of getting started with the Android operating system. Topics include the following:

→ Getting to know your Galaxy S7's external features
→ Learning gestures and motions
→ Setting up your Galaxy S7 for the first time
→ Learning the fundamentals of Android 6.01 (Marshmallow) and TouchWiz
→ Installing desktop synchronization software

Getting to Know Your Galaxy S7

Before you start customizing your Galaxy S7 and working with apps, you should examine the external features, device features, and the Android 6.01 operating system.

In addition to Android 6.01 (Marshmallow), this chapter covers the Samsung TouchWiz interface, which is overlaid on top of Android to adjust the way things look and function.

Your Galaxy S7's External Features

Becoming familiar with the external features of your Galaxy S7 is a good place to start because you will be using them often. This section covers some of the technical specifications of your Galaxy S7, including the touchscreen and camera. There are two versions of the Samsung Galaxy S7: the S7 and the S7 edge. With the exception of a few extra features provided by the curved screen on the S7 edge, the functionality and look and feel of the interface on the two phones are exactly the same.

Getting to Know Your Galaxy S7
Front

Indicator light

Light sensor

Proximity/gesture sensor

Front camera

Earpiece

Touchscreen

Home button/ fingerprint reader

Recent Apps button

Back button

- **Proximity/gesture sensor**—Detects when you place your Galaxy S7 against your head to talk, which causes it to turn off the screen so that your ear doesn't inadvertently activate any onscreen items. This sensor also allows you to use gestures (in conjunction with the accelerometer). Gestures are covered later in the Prologue.

- **Light sensor**—Adjusts the brightness of your Galaxy S7's screen based on the brightness of the ambient light.

- **Earpiece**—The part you hold against your ear while on a call.

- **Indicator light**—Indicates new events (such as missed calls, new Facebook messages, and new emails). This indicator light is invisible until it illuminates.

- **Front camera**—A 5.0-megapixel front-facing camera that you use for video chat, taking self-portraits, and even unlocking your Galaxy S7 using your face.

- **Touchscreen**—On the Galaxy S7, a 5.1" 1440x2560 pixel Quad HD Super AMOLED (Super Active-Matrix Organic Light-Emitting Diode) screen that incorporates capacitive touch. On the Galaxy S7 edge, a 5.5" 1440x2560 pixel Quad HD Super AMOLED (Super Active-Matrix Organic Light-Emitting Diode), dual-edge screen that incorporates capacitive touch.

- **Back button**—Takes you back one screen when you're using an application or menu. This is a touch-sensitive button.

- **Recent Apps button**—Shows you a list of apps you recently used. You can then touch to jump to them or swipe them off the screen to close them. Touch and hold to see additional options for the current screen. The Recent Apps button replaces the Menu button on previous Galaxy S series phones.

- **Home button/fingerprint reader**—Takes you to the Home screen. The application that you are using continues to run in the background. Press twice to launch the Camera app. Press and hold to launch Google Now. A fingerprint reader is built in to the Home button; you can read more about it in Chapter 1, "Making the S7 Your Own."

Back

Noise-canceling microphone

SIM card and microSD card tray

LED camera flash

Rear camera

Heart rate sensor

Volume up/down buttons

Power button

- **Volume up/down buttons**—Enable you to control the audio volume on calls and while playing audio and video.

- **Power button**—Allows you to wake up your Galaxy S7 by pressing once. Press and hold for one second to reveal a menu of choices. The choices enable you to power off your S7, restart your S7, or put it into Emergency mode. In Emergency mode, your S7 greatly reduces battery usage and starts reporting its location to a chosen contact.

- **Rear camera**—A 12-megapixel camera with autofocus and Optical Image Stabilization (OIS) that takes clear pictures close up or far away.

- **LED (light-emitting diode) camera flash**—Helps to illuminate the surroundings when you're taking pictures in low light.

- **Heart rate sensor**—While using the S Health app, place your finger over the heart rate sensor to allow S Health to detect your heart rate.

- **SIM card and microSD card tray**—Use the SIM card tray ejection tool provided in the box to eject the SIM card tray and insert a new or replacement SIM card. The SIM card tray also includes a place to insert a microSD memory card. This allows you to expand the memory on your S7 up to 200 Gigabytes.

- **Noise-canceling microphone**—Use in conjunction with the regular microphone to reduce background noise during phone calls. This microphone is also used when you record videos.

Bottom

Speaker
Microphone
Micro USB 2 port
3.5mm headphone jack

- **Micro USB 2 port**—You can use the Micro USB 2 port to synchronize your Galaxy S7 to your desktop computer and charge it.

- **Microphone**—You use the microphone when you are on a call and holding your Galaxy S7 to your ear.

- **Speaker**—The speaker is used when you use the speakerphone function while on a phone call, and it is also used to play all audio, including notifications, music, and audio from videos.

- **3.5mm headphone jack**—Plug in your Galaxy S7 or third-party headset to enjoy music and talk on the phone.

Gestures and Motions

Gestures and motions allow you to quickly use certain functions or features by making hand gestures or moving the S7 in a specific way.

- **Direct Call**—While you are looking at a missed call, reading an SMS (text message) from someone, or viewing someone's contact information, you can lift your S7 to your ear and hold it there to dial the phone number being viewed.

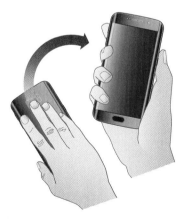

- **Smart Alert**—If you have missed calls or messages, when you pick up your S7 from a flat surface, it vibrates.

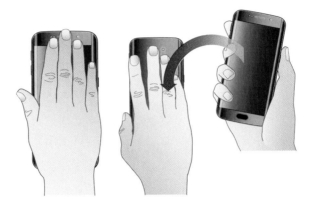

- **Easy Mute**—To mute incoming calls and alarms, either place your hand over the screen or turn your S7 over.

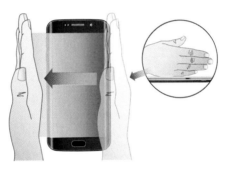

- **Palm Swipe to Capture**—You can capture a screenshot by holding your palm perpendicular to the screen, touching it on the screen and swiping it from left to right or right to left. The captured screenshot goes to the Screenshots album, which you can view using the Gallery or Photos app.

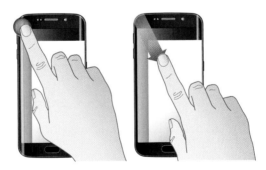

- **Pop-up View**—Swipe diagonally down from the top-left of the screen to make the app you are using switch the Pop-up view where it reduces in size to a smaller on-screen window. Read more about Pop-up view later in this Prologue in the "Run Multiple Apps on the Screen at the Same Time" section.

First-Time Setup

Before setting up your new Samsung Galaxy S7, you should have a Google account because your Galaxy S7 running Android is tightly integrated with Google. When you have a Google account, you can store your content—including any books and music you buy or movies you rent—in the Google cloud. If you do not already have a Google account, go to https://accounts.google.com on your desktop computer and sign up for one.

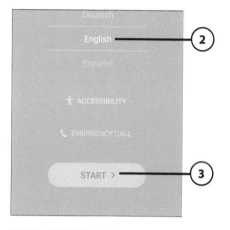

1. Press and hold the Power button until you see the animation start playing (not shown).

2. Tap to change your language if needed.

3. Tap Start to continue.

4. Tap a Wi-Fi network you want to connect to during setup. If you'd rather not connect to a Wi-Fi network, tap Next and continue at step 8.

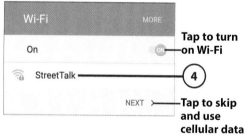

Tap to turn on Wi-Fi

Tap to skip and use cellular data

Why Use Wi-Fi During Setup?

As you go through the first-time setup of your S7, you may choose to restore a backup of a previous device to your S7, and at the end of the device setup, a number of apps may need to be updated. Both of these activities can use a lot of data. Using Wi-Fi speeds up these activities as well as saves you the cost of the cellular data charges. Although you do not have to connect to a Wi-Fi network for device setup, it is advisable.

5. Enter the password for the Wi-Fi network using the onscreen keyboard.

6. Tap Connect. Your Galaxy S7 connects to the Wi-Fi network.

7. Tap Next.

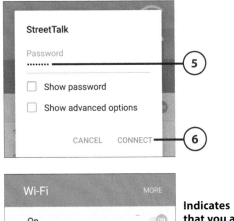

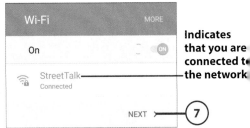

Indicates that you are connected to the network

>>>Go Further
SMART NETWORK SWITCH

Smart Network Switch is a feature that, once enabled, allows your S7 to seamlessly switch between the two Wi-Fi bands (2.4GHz and 5GHz) and cellular data to maintain a stable Internet connection. Your S7 constantly analyzes its connection to the Internet and switches between Wi-Fi networks operating on 2.4GHz and 5GHz to provide the best connection, and if the Wi-Fi connectivity becomes poor, it switches to the cellular data network. Bear in mind that with this option enabled you might start seeing higher cellular data usage, especially in areas where Wi-Fi is unstable, slow, or overcrowded. To enable Smart Network Switch, after your device is set up, tap Settings, Wi-Fi, More, Smart Network Switch.

8. Check the box to allow Samsung to collect diagnostic and usage data from your S7.

9. Tap Next.

10. Tap Agree after you have read and understood the End User License Agreement (EULA).

11. If you have another Android device (tablet or smartphone) running Android 5.0 (Lollipop) or later, and you want to transfer the data from it to your new phone, select Copy your Google Accounts, apps, and data from another device, tap Next, and follow the instructions on the following screens, or select No thanks, and tap Next to continue.

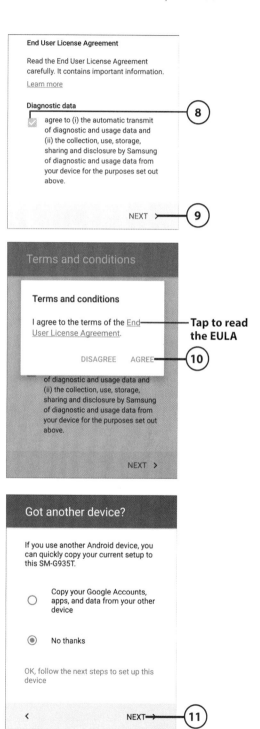

12. Enter your Google account email address (your Gmail address).

13. Tap Next.

14. Enter your Google account password.

15. Tap Next to continue.

16. Tap Accept to continue.

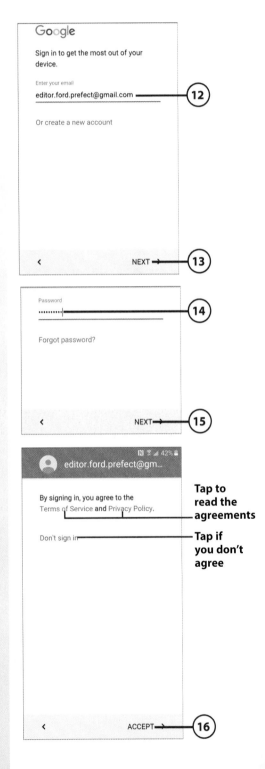

Tap to read the agreements

Tap if you don't agree

17. Check this box if you want to back up your phone's data so that it can be restored to a new Android phone or smartphone in the future.

18. Check this box if you are okay with Google collecting information about your geographic location at any time. Although Google keeps this information safe, if you are concerned about privacy rights, you should uncheck this box.

19. Check this box if you are okay with your phone scanning for Wi-Fi networks even if you have the Wi-Fi radio turned off. This helps improve location accuracy.

20. Tap Next to continue.

21. Select Not Now. Chapter 6, "Email and Text Messages," covers adding IMAP and POP accounts.

22. Tap Next.

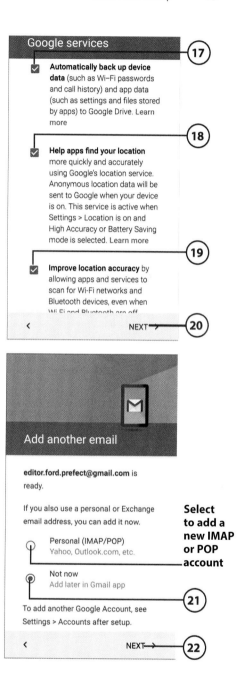

Select to add a new IMAP or POP account

23. Tap Set Up Fingerprint. If you choose not to set any phone protection (not recommended), tap No Thanks, and skip to step 32.

24. Tap Next.

25. Tap PIN to choose to use a numeric PIN as your fingerprint backup unlock method. This example uses a PIN; however, you can choose to use a pattern or password as your fingerprint backup unlock method.

Why Must I Use a PIN, Pattern, or Password When Choosing Fingerprint?

When you choose to use your fingerprint to unlock your Galaxy S7, you must first choose a backup unlock method. This method is used as the only method of unlocking your S7 after you restart it, or if your fingerprint cannot be read by the fingerprint sensor.

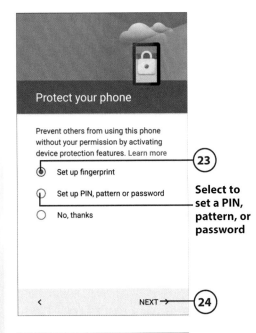

Select to set a PIN, pattern, or password

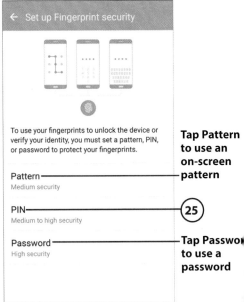

Tap Pattern to use an on-screen pattern

Tap Password to use a password

26. Enter a numeric PIN and tap Continue.

27. Re-enter the same numeric PIN and tap OK.

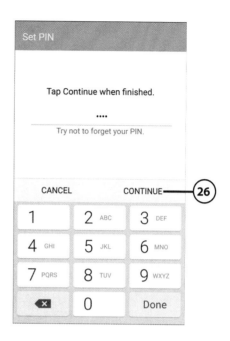

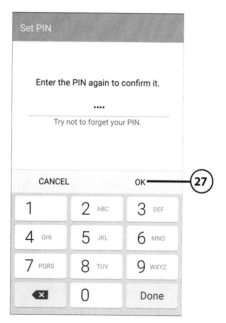

28. Follow the on-screen instructions that walk you through placing your finger on the Home key and then lifting it off the Home key repeatedly until your S7 has fully captured your fingerprint.

29. Choose whether you want notifications to be displayed on the Lock screen while your phone is locked. You can choose to show notifications and their content, notifications with no content, or to hide all notifications.

30. Tap Done.

31. Tap Next on the screen lock confirmation screen (not shown).

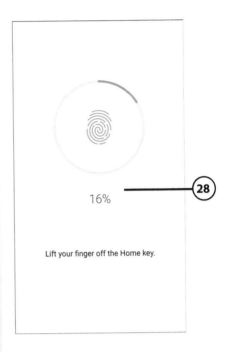

16%

Lift your finger off the Home key.

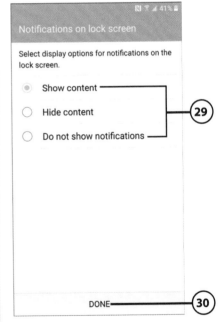

Notifications on lock screen

Select display options for notifications on the lock screen.

⦿ Show content

◯ Hide content

◯ Do not show notifications

DONE

32. Enter the email address you used for your Samsung account.

33. Enter your Samsung account password.

34. Tap Sign In.

35. Move the slider to on to enable automatically backing up your data to your Samsung account.

36. Tap Later. For this example we are not restoring a backup from a previous Samsung device. However, if you would rather restore a backup, tap Next and follow the steps, then continue at step 37.

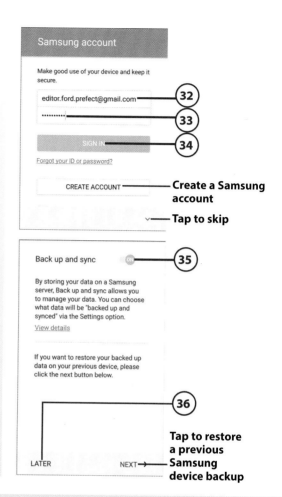

Samsung account

Make good use of your device and keep it secure.

editor.ford.prefect@gmail.com ——— **32**

·············· ——— **33**

SIGN IN ——— **34**

Forgot your ID or password?

CREATE ACCOUNT ——— **Create a Samsung account**

⌄ ——— **Tap to skip**

Back up and sync   ⬤ ——— **35**

By storing your data on a Samsung server, Back up and sync allows you to manage your data. You can choose what data will be "backed up and synced" via the Settings option.

View details

If you want to restore your backed up data on your previous device, please click the next button below.

——— **36**

LATER   NEXT → ——— **Tap to restore a previous Samsung device backup**

>>>Go Further

DO I NEED A SAMSUNG ACCOUNT?

Android was designed to be used with a Google account. That Google account enables you to access the Google ecosystem of Android apps, music, movies, and books; plus, your phone's settings are backed up to the Google cloud. If you change devices, your new device reverts to the way you had your old device set up. A Samsung account does a similar thing, but it uses the Samsung ecosystem. If you would like to take advantage of the extra Samsung services on your S7, such as the Galaxy app store, the ability to locate your lost device, or to keep track of your S Health diet and health information, you should sign up for a Samsung account.

37. Tap to turn the switch on if you want your S7 to use Easy mode. Easy mode uses a simplified Home screen layout and enlarges the text and size of the app icons. You can always disable Easy mode later if you decide it's not for you.

38. Tap Finish to complete your S7's setup. Depending on the wireless provider you are using, after you finish the device setup, you may see some extra screens that are specific to your wireless provider.

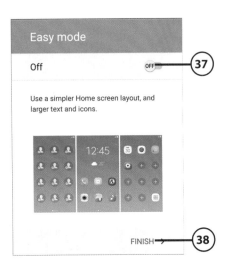

Fundamentals of Android 6.01 and TouchWiz

Your Galaxy S7 is run by an operating system called Android. Android was created by Google to run on any smartphone, and your Galaxy S7 uses a version called Android 6.01 (or Marshmallow). Samsung has made many changes to this version of Android by adding extra components and modifying many standard Android features. They call this customization TouchWiz.

The Lock Screen

If you haven't used your Galaxy S7 for a while, the screen goes blank to conserve battery power. This task explains how to interact with the Lock screen.

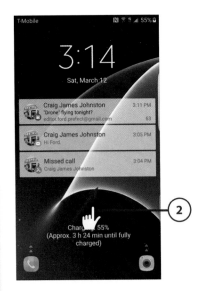

1. Press the Power button or Home button to wake up your Galaxy S7 (not shown). It is better to press the Home button, especially if you are making use of the fingerprint reader to unlock your S7.

2. Slide your finger across the screen in any direction to unlock your Galaxy S7.

Unlocking Your S7

Step 2 assumes that you are using the swipe-to-unlock method of unlocking your S7, which is why we direct you to swipe the screen; however, you may have chosen to use a more secure method of locking your S7 including using a pattern, a numeric PIN, a password, or even your fingerprint. If you are using your fingerprint to unlock your S7, and just want to see the notifications on your Lock screen without actually unlocking your S7, then you should either press the Power button or press the Home button using a finger that you have not scanned with the fingerprint reader.

3. Tap a notification, such as a missed call or new email notification, and then swipe the screen to unlock and go directly to the call log or email message.

4. Swipe up from the Camera icon to launch the Camera.

5. Swipe up from the Phone icon to launch the Phone.

6. Swipe the notifications down if you want to see more of them.

7. Swipe the notifications left or right to dismiss them.

Working with Settings on the Lock Screen

You can work with settings right on the Lock screen. Swipe down from the top of the screen to show the Quick Settings. You see the Quick Settings plus any notifications. Tap Clear to clear all notifications.

Swipe down to see settings

Tap to clear all notifications

Answering a Call from the Lock Screen

If your Galaxy S7 is locked when a call comes in, you have three choices: Drag the green icon to the right to answer the incoming call; drag the red icon to the left to reject the incoming call and send it straight to voicemail; or drag up from the bottom of the screen to reject the call and send a preset text message (SMS) to the caller.

Drag to answer.

Drag to reject.

Slide up to reject and send a text message.

The Home Screen

After you unlock your Galaxy S7, you are presented with the Home screen. Your Galaxy S7 has four Home screen panes (although you can create more). The Home screen panes contain application shortcuts, a Launcher icon, Notification bar, Shortcuts, Favorites Tray, and widgets.

- **Notification bar**—The Notification bar shows information about Bluetooth, Wi-Fi, and cellular coverage, as well as the battery level and time. The Notification bar also serves as a place where apps can alert or notify you using notification icons.

- **Notification icons**—Notification icons appear in the Notification bar when an app needs to alert or notify you of something. For example, the Phone app can show the Missed Calls icon, indicating that you missed a call.

- **Widgets**—Widgets are applications that run directly on the Home screens. They are specially designed to provide functionality and real-time information. An example of a widget is one that shows the current weather or provides a search capability. Widgets can be moved and sometimes resized.

- **App shortcut**—When you tap an app shortcut, the associated app launches.

- **App folders**—You can group apps together in a folder as a way to organize your apps and declutter your screen.

- **Favorites Tray**—The Favorites Tray is visible on all Home screen panes. You can drag apps to the Favorites Tray so that they are available no matter which Home screen pane you are looking at. You can rearrange or remove apps in the Favorites Tray.

Notification icons

Notification bar

Widgets

App shortcut

App folder

Swipe left and right to see all Home screen panes.

Launcher icon

Favorites Tray

- **Launcher icon**—Tap to show application icons for all applications that you have installed on your Galaxy S7.

The Special Home Screen Pane: Flipboard Briefing

If you swipe all the way to the left-most Home screen pane, you see the Flipboard app's Briefing view. The Flipboard app is a portal for news including business, technology, celebrity, science, entertainment, style, food, and travel. Your S7 provides you with the Flipboard app's Briefing view. Scroll up and down to see all news feeds. Tap the Menu icon to customize each news topic, rearrange the topic layout, and install the full Flipboard app. Swipe left to return to the first Home screen pane.

Tap to customize the Flipboard app

Swipe up to see more news topics

Work with Notifications

To interact with notifications that appear in the Notification bar, place your finger above the top of the screen and drag to pull down the Notification bar and reveal the notifications. Swipe individual notifications off the screen to the left or right to clear them one by one, or tap Clear to clear all of them at once. The Notification bar also includes Quick Settings, such as the ability to turn on or off Wi-Fi or Bluetooth.

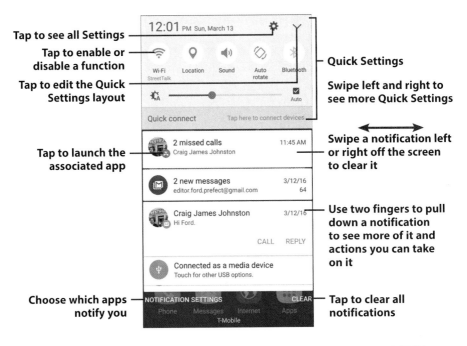

Tap to see all Settings

Tap to enable or disable a function

Tap to edit the Quick Settings layout

Tap to launch the associated app

Choose which apps notify you

Quick Settings

Swipe left and right to see more Quick Settings

Swipe a notification left or right off the screen to clear it

Use two fingers to pull down a notification to see more of it and actions you can take on it

Tap to clear all notifications

What Are Quick Settings?

Quick Settings are icons that allow quick on/off actions. Examples are turning Wi-Fi on or off and turning Bluetooth on or off. To change the settings of a particular function, touch and hold on the icon for that function. Tapping the down arrow enables you to see all of the possible Quick Settings icons, rearrange the Quick Settings icon positions, and choose which icons are visible.

Create App Shortcuts

Tap the Launcher icon to see all of your apps. (Refer to the figure in "The Home Screen" section for help identifying the Launcher icon.) Touch and hold on the app you want to make a shortcut for. After the Home screen appears, drag the app shortcut to the location you want the shortcut to be on the Home screen, drag it to an app folder, or drag it left or right off the screen to move between Home screen panes. Release the icon to place it.

Drag to where you want the icon and release it

Drag the icon to the right-most pane to create a new Home screen pane and place the icon on it

Touch and hold an app icon

Drag between Home screen panes

Create App Folders

To create a new app folder, touch and hold the first app shortcut you want in your folder and drag it on top of the second app shortcut you want in your folder. After you give your app folder a name, tap outside the folder to see the folder on your Home screen. Now you can drag other app shortcuts into that folder. To open the folder, tap it to reveal the shortcuts in that folder.

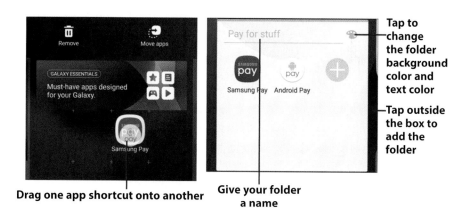

Tap to change the folder background color and text color

Tap outside the box to add the folder

Drag one app shortcut onto another

Give your folder a name

Drag other app shortcuts to the folder

Create a New Home Screen Pane and Remove an App Shortcut

If you want to create a new Home screen pane, touch and hold an app shortcut icon. Drag your app shortcut icon to the right-most pane, and the shortcut is placed on a brand-new Home screen pane. To remove an app shortcut icon, drag it to the Remove icon.

Drag an app shortcut icon to the Remove icon to delete it from the Home screen pane

Drag an app shortcut icon to the right-most pane to put it on a new Home screen pane

Use the Touchscreen

You interact with your Galaxy S7 mostly by touching the screen. You can tap, swipe, pinch, touch and hold, double-tap, and type.

 • **Tap**—To start an application, tap its icon. Tap a menu item to select it. Tap the letters of the onscreen keyboard to type.

 • **Touch and hold**—Touch and hold to interact with an object. For example, if you touch and hold a blank area of the Home screen, a menu pops up. If you touch and hold an icon, you can reposition it with your finger.

 • **Drag**—Dragging always starts with a touch and hold. For example, if you touch the Notification bar, you can drag it down to read all of the notification messages.

 • **Swipe or slide**—Swipe or slide the screen to scroll quickly. To swipe or slide, move your finger across the screen quickly. Be careful not to touch and hold before you swipe or you will reposition something. You can also swipe to clear notifications or close apps when viewing the recent apps.

- **Double-tap**—Double-tapping is like double-clicking a mouse on a desktop computer. Tap the screen twice in quick succession. For example, you can double-tap a web page to zoom in to part of that page.

- **Pinch**—To zoom in and out of images and pages, place your thumb and forefinger on the screen. Pinch them together to zoom out or spread them apart to zoom in (unpinching). Applications such as Browser, Gallery, and Maps support pinching.

- **Rotate the screen**—If you rotate your Galaxy S7 from an upright position to being on its left or right side, the screen switches from portrait view to landscape view. Most applications honor the screen orientation. The Home screens and Launcher do not.

Use the Keyboard

Your Galaxy S7 has a virtual or onscreen keyboard for those times when you need to enter text. You might be a little wary of a keyboard that has no physical keys, but you will be pleasantly surprised at how well it works.

Most applications automatically show the keyboard when you need to enter text. If the keyboard does not appear, tap the area where you want to type and the keyboard slides up, ready for use.

To make the next letter you type a capital letter, tap the Shift key. To make all letters capitals (or CAPS), double-tap the Shift key to engage CAPS Lock. Tap Shift again to disengage CAPS Lock.

Tap to capitalize the next character
Double-tap to engage CAPS Lock
Tap for numbers and symbols

Touch and hold to speak the text

As you type, your Galaxy S7 makes word suggestions. Think of this as similar to the spell checker you would see in a word processor. Your Galaxy S7 uses a dictionary of words to guess what you are typing. If the word you were going to type is the middle option in the list of suggestions, tap space or period to select it. If you can see the word in the list but it is not the middle word, tap the word to select it.

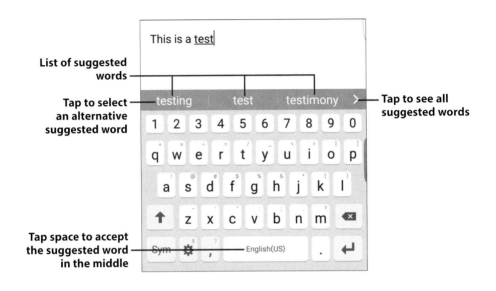

List of suggested words

Tap to select an alternative suggested word

Tap to see all suggested words

Tap space to accept the suggested word in the middle

>>>Go Further

NEXT WORD SUGGESTION

When you are between typing words, the keyboard tries to predict the next word you want to type. (In this example I typed "This is a test"; the keyboard is suggesting that the most obvious word I want to type next is "drive," but it is also showing that I might want to type "of" or "to.") All you need to do is tap the correct word, and the keyboard types it for you. If the keyboard is not showing a word that you want to use, simply continue typing. The more you type, the more the keyboard learns how you write and the better it will become at suggesting the next words you are likely to type.

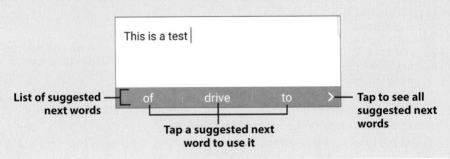

List of suggested next words

Tap a suggested next word to use it

Tap to see all suggested next words

To type numbers or symbols, tap the Symbols key. When on the Numbers and Symbols screen, tap the Symbols key to see extra symbols. There are two screens of symbols. Tap the ABC key to return to the regular keyboard.

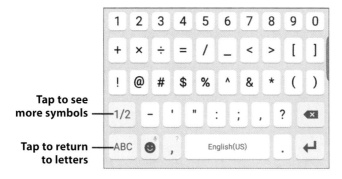

Tap to see more symbols —— 1/2

Tap to return to letters —— ABC

Quick Access to Symbols

If you want to type commonly used symbols, touch and hold the period key. A small window opens with those common symbols. Tap a symbol to type it.

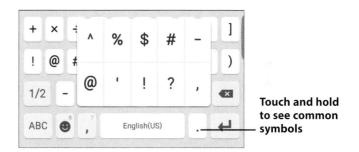

Touch and hold to see common symbols

To enter an accented character, touch and hold any vowel or the C, N, or S key. A small window opens enabling you to select an accented or alternative character. Slide your finger over the accented character and lift your finger to type it.

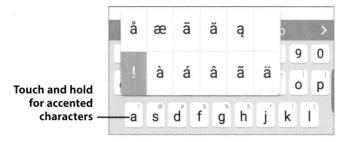

Touch and hold for accented characters

To reveal other alternative characters, touch and hold any other letter, number, or symbol.

Want a Larger Keyboard?

Turn your Galaxy S7 sideways to switch to a landscape keyboard. The landscape keyboard has larger keys and is easier to type on.

Landscape keyboard

Swipe to Type

Instead of typing on the keyboard in the traditional way by tapping each letter individually, you can swipe over the letters in one continuous movement. This is called Continuous Input. It is enabled by default; to use it, just start swiping your finger over the letters of the word you want to type. Lift your finger after each word. No need to worry about spaces because your Galaxy S7 adds them for you. To type a double letter (as in the word pool), loop around that letter on the keyboard. As you swipe, a blue line trails your finger.

Dictation—Speak Instead of Type

Your Galaxy S7 can turn your voice into text. It uses Google's speech recognition service, which means you must have a connection to the cellular network or a Wi-Fi network to use it.

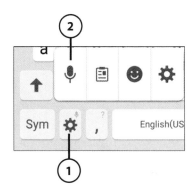

1. Touch and hold the Settings icon.

2. Tap the Microphone icon.

3. Wait until you see the green Microphone icon and start speaking what you want to be typed. You can speak the punctuation, for example "new line," "question mark," "exclamation mark," or "period."

4. Words that your S7 is not 100% sure of are underlined. If you see an underlined word that is not correct, tap it to change it.

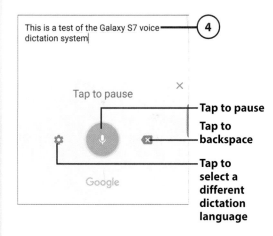

Edit Text

After you enter text, you can edit it by cutting, copying, or pasting the text. This task describes how to select and cut text so you can paste over a word with the cut text.

1. While you are typing, touch and hold a word you want to copy.

2. Slide the blue end markers until you have selected all of the text you want to copy.

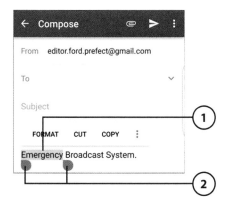

3. Tap Copy.

Cutting Text

Cutting text places it in the Clipboard, just like a Copy action would do.

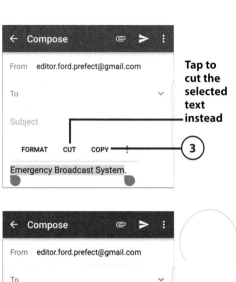

Tap to cut the selected text instead

4. Touch and hold the word you want to paste over.

5. Tap the Menu icon.

6. Tap Paste to paste what you copied over the word you have selected.

Placing a Cursor

You can also simply place a cursor on the screen and move it around to do manual text editing, such as backspacing to delete letters or manually inserting a new word. To do this, tap the screen in the text area. A single blue marker displays; drag that marker to the point in the text where you want to make changes. Start typing or tap Backspace, and the action occurs at the cursor position.

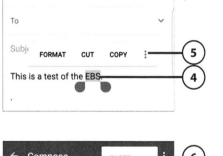

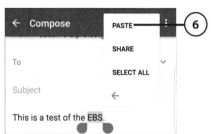

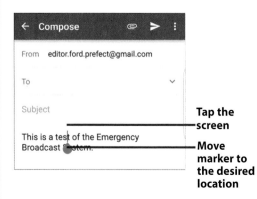

Tap the screen

Move marker to the desired location

Keyboard Tricks

You can write instead of typing, use emoticons (smiley faces), and enable a one-handed keyboard.

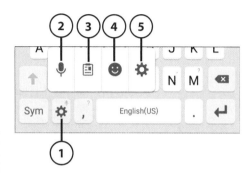

1. Touch and hold the settings key (to the right of the Sym key).

2. Tap to use dictation.

3. Tap to see everything you have previously copied to the Clipboard. If there is text, you can touch it to paste it at the cursor position.

4. Tap to type emoticons (smiley faces).

5. Tap to change keyboard settings, including choosing a new keyboard.

>>>Go Further

ONE-HANDED TYPING

If you would prefer to have the ability to type with one hand, you can choose the one-handed keyboard mode. This mode squashes the keyboard so that you can type with one thumb. To enable one-handed mode, open Settings, tap Advanced Features, and tap One-Handed Operation. Tap the on/off switch to the right of One-Handed Input to enable the one-handed input method (which includes the one-handed keyboard). While this is enabled, a shrunken keyboard appears on the bottom-right of the screen, which enables you to type with one thumb. Tap the arrow to switch the location between the bottom-right and bottom-left of the screen.

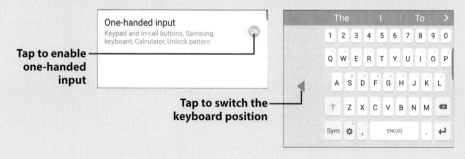

Menus

Your Galaxy S7 has two types of menus: app menus and context menus. All applications use an app menu. To see the app menu, tap the Menu icon, which is normally on the top-right of the screen. As an alternative (but slower) method, you can touch and hold the Back button to see the app menu.

A context menu applies to an item on the screen. If you touch and hold something on the screen (in this example, a button that links to a new page), a context menu appears. The items on the context menu are based on the type of object you touched.

Tap to see the app menu

http://www.samsung.com/us/explore/galaxy-s7-features-and-specs/#promo

Open in new tab

Open in incognito tab

Copy link address

Copy link text

Save link

Touch and hold a link or button to reveal the link context menu

>>>Go Further

OLDER APPS AND THE MENU BUTTON

Some older Android apps that have not been updated to handle newer model Samsung devices may not display the regular Menu icon (three vertical dots) because they think that the Samsung phone has a physical Menu button. Because newer Samsung phones (including your Galaxy S7) no longer have a physical Menu button, if you suspect that the app you are using should have a Menu icon, touch and hold the Back button to trigger the app menu.

Touch and hold for the app menu

Switch Between Apps

You can switch between running apps and close apps using the multi-tasking feature.

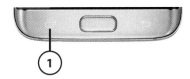

1. Tap the Recent Apps button (to the left of the Home button).

2. Scroll up and down the list of running apps.

3. Tap an app to switch to it.

4. Touch and hold an app icon to see memory and processor usage for each active app.

5. Tap to open the app in split-screen mode. This opens the app so that it only takes up the top half of the screen (not all apps support split-screen mode). See more about running multiple apps at the same time in the next section.

6. Swipe an app left or right off the screen to close it or tap the X on the top right of the app.

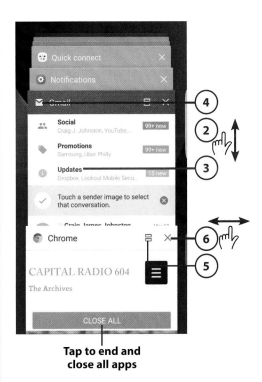

Tap to end and close all apps

Run Multiple Apps on the Screen at the Same Time

Your Galaxy S7 has a feature called Multi Window that allows certain apps to run on the same screen at the same time. They can either run in a split-screen configuration, in multiple separate small windows, or a combination of both.

Two Apps Together on a Split-Screen

This section explains how to run two apps at the same time in a split-screen configuration.

1. Touch and hold the Recent Apps button while on the Home screen to see apps that support Multi Window.

2. Tap an app you want to run. The app launches in the top half of the screen.

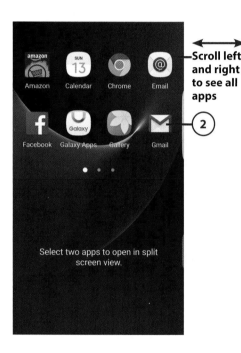

Scroll left and right to see all apps

Select two apps to open in split screen view.

It's Not All Good

Not All Apps Support Multi Window

Apps must be specially written to take advantage of Samsung's Multi Window mode because Multi Window mode is not part of the Android operating system. This means that you might not see the apps you are looking for until the developer updates the app to support Samsung's Multi Window mode.

3. Tap a second app icon to launch it in the bottom half of the screen.

4. Drag the circle up or down to give more or less room to each app.

5. Tap the circle to reveal extra Multi Window features.

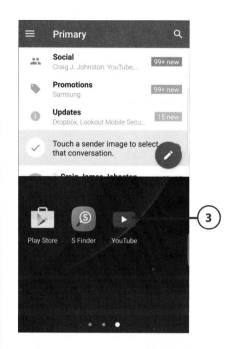

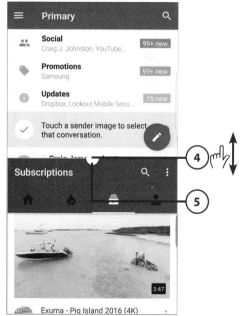

6. Tap to swap the position of the apps on the screen.

7. Tap to enable dragging content (such as text or an image) between windows.

8. Tap to minimize the selected app to a small draggable circle on the screen. A blue box indicates which is the selected app.

9. Tap to maximize the selected app to full screen. A blue box indicates which is the selected app.

10. Tap to close the app in the selected window. The selected app has a blue box around its perimeter.

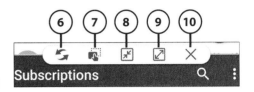

>>>Go Further
MINIMIZED APPS

When you choose to minimize an app as shown in step 8, the app shrinks to a small circle on the screen. You can drag the minimized app anywhere on the screen. If you touch and hold the app, a trash can icon appears; drag the app to the trash can to close the app. If you tap the minimized app, it enlarges to a pop-up window instead of maximizing back to its original window in the split screen. You can then continue working on the app in its small window. When an app is in a pop-up window, you can resize it by dragging the blue border around the app. Minimized and pop-up apps continue to be shown no matter what screen you are on and what app you are running.

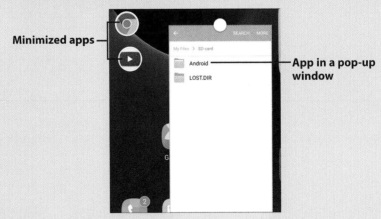

Minimized apps

App in a pop-up window

Quicker Way of Running Multi Window

If you only want to use apps that are already running in Multi Window, you can do this more quickly. Tap the Recent Apps button. Tap the Multi Window icon on any running app. That app switches to Multi Window mode and displays in the top half of the screen. Next, tap a second app to run in the bottom half of the screen. Remember that not all apps support Multi Window so some apps may not have the Multi Window icon.

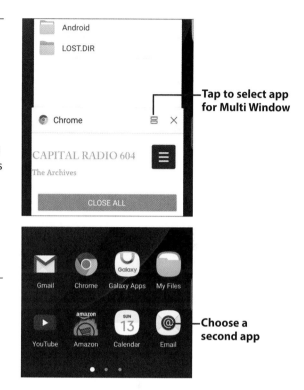

Tap to select app for Multi Window

Choose a second app

Installing Synchronization Software

Because your Galaxy S7 is tightly integrated with Google and its services, all media that you purchase from the Google Play Store on your phone is stored in the Google cloud and accessible anywhere, anytime. However, you might have a lot of music on your computer and need to copy that to your Google cloud. To do that, you need to install the Google Music Manager software or the Android File Transfer app for your Mac to copy any files back and forth.

Install Android File Transfer (Apple Mac OS X)

You only need the Android File Transfer app when using a Samsung Android phone (such as your Galaxy S7) on an Apple Mac running OS X.

1. From your Mac, browse to http://www.android.com/filetransfer/ and download the Android File Transfer app.

2. Click the Downloads icon.

3. Double-click the app in your Safari Downloads.

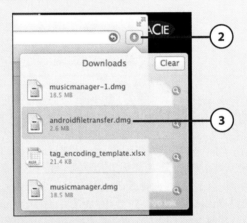

4. Drag the green Android to the Applications shortcut to install the app.

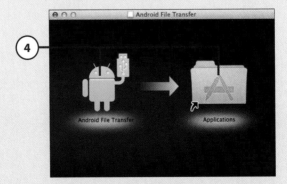

Install Google Music Manager (Apple Mac)

Don't install Google Music Manager unless you plan to upload files from your computer to the Google cloud.

1. Visit https://music.google.com/music/listen#manager_pl from your desktop web browser and log in to your Google account if you're prompted.

2. Click to download Music Manager.

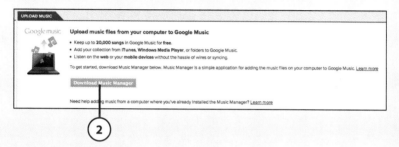

3. Click the Downloads icon.

4. Double-click the app in your Safari Downloads.

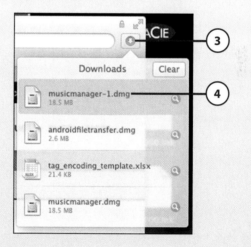

5. Drag the Music Manager icon to the Applications shortcut to install the app.

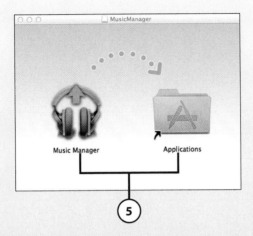

6. Double-click the Music Manager icon in the Applications folder.

7. Skip to the "Configure Music Manager" section to complete the installation.

Install Google Music Manager (Windows)

Don't install Google Music Manager unless you plan to upload files from your computer to the Google cloud.

1. Visit https://music.google.com/music/listen#manager_pl from your desktop web browser and log in to your Google account if you're prompted.

2. Click to download Music Manager.

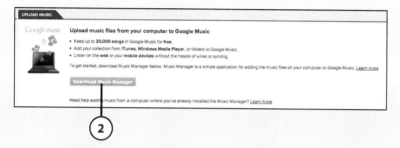

3. Double-click the app in your Downloads folder.

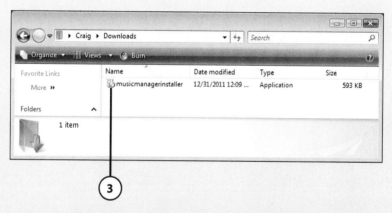

4. Skip to the "Configure Music Manager" section to complete the installation.

Configure Music Manager (Windows and Apple Mac)

   1. Click Continue.

   2. Enter your Google (Gmail) email address.

   3. Enter your Google (Gmail) password.

   4. Click Continue.

5. Choose where you keep your music.

6. Click Continue.

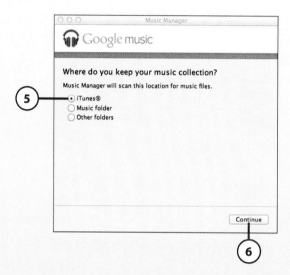

7. Choose whether to upload all of your music or just some of your playlists. Remember that you can only upload 20,000 songs for free. Skip to step 12 if you chose to upload all music.

8. Check if you also want to upload podcasts.

9. Click Continue.

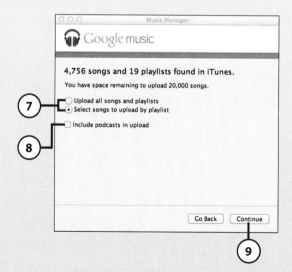

10.   Select one or more playlists of music.

11.   Click Continue.

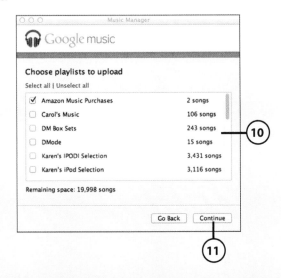

12.   Choose whether you want to automatically upload any new music that is added to your computer.

13.   Click Continue.

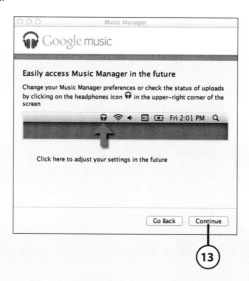

14.   Click Close.

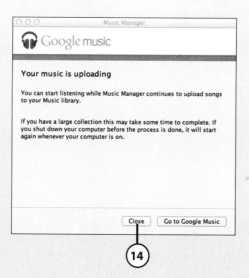

Tap to choose a
new wallpaper

Tap to choose where
to use the wallpaper

In this chapter, you find out how to customize your Galaxy S7 to suit your needs and lifestyle. Topics include the following:

→ Using wallpapers and live wallpapers
→ Replacing the keyboard
→ Adding widgets
→ Adjusting accessibility settings
→ Adjusting sound and display settings
→ Customizing S7 edge settings
→ Managing privacy and security features

Making the S7 Your Own

Your Galaxy S7 arrives preconfigured to appeal to most buyers; however, you might want to change the way some of the features work, or even personalize it to fit your mood or lifestyle. Luckily, your Galaxy S7 is customizable.

Changing Your Wallpaper

Your Galaxy S7 comes preloaded with a cool wallpaper. You can install other wallpapers, use live wallpapers that animate, and even use pictures in the Gallery application as your wallpaper.

1. Touch and hold in an open area on one of the Home screen panes.

2. Tap Wallpapers.

3. Tap to select where you want to change the wallpaper. You can choose a new wallpaper for the Home screen only or the Lock screen only, or you can use the same new wallpaper for both the Home and Lock screens.

4. Tap the slider to turn on the Wallpaper Motion Effect. The Wallpaper Motion Effect creates an illusion that the icons on your Home screen panes are floating above the wallpaper.

Conserving Battery

Although the Wallpaper Motion Effect looks very cool, it does use up a bit of battery power.

---

5. Use the steps in one of the following three sections to choose the type of wallpaper to use as well as to select your new wallpaper.

Set Up Wallpaper from Gallery Pictures

You can use any picture in your Gallery as a wallpaper.

1. Swipe from left to right over the wallpaper thumbnails until you see one labeled From Gallery.

2. Tap From Gallery.

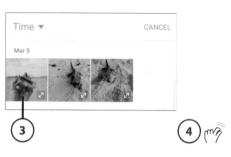

3. Navigate your photo albums and tap a photo you want to use for your wallpaper.

4. Zoom in and out of the picture using the pinch gesture. Sometimes if the photo you have chosen is very large, you will not be able to zoom in or out.

5. Move the photo by dragging it so that the part of it you want to use is visible.

6. Tap Set as Wallpaper.

Set Up Live Wallpaper

Live wallpaper is wallpaper with some intelligence behind it. It can be a cool animation or even an animation that keys off things such as the music you are playing on your Galaxy S7, or it can be something simple such as the time. There are some very cool live wallpapers in the Google Play Store that you can install and use.

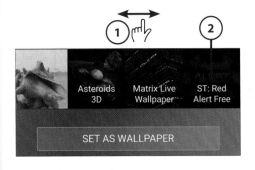

1. Swipe from left to right over the wallpaper thumbnails until you see the thumbnails with titles. Live wallpapers are kept on the right side of the wallpaper thumbnails.

2. Tap the live wallpaper you want to use.

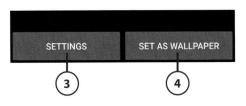

3. Tap Settings to change the way the live wallpaper works (not all live wallpapers have settings that you can adjust).

4. Tap Set as Wallpaper to use the live wallpaper.

Finding More Wallpaper

You can find wallpaper or live wallpaper in the Google Play Store. Tap the Play Store icon to open the Google Play Store app and search for "wallpaper" or "live wallpaper." Read more on how to use the Google Play Store in Chapter 12, "Working with Android Applications."

Set Up Wallpaper

Choose a static wallpaper that is preloaded and sized correctly for your screen.

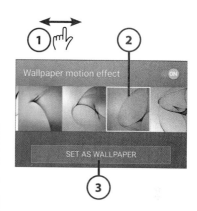

1. Swipe left and right over the wallpaper thumbnails to see static wallpaper options. Static wallpapers are in between the From Gallery option and the live wallpapers.

2. Tap a wallpaper to preview it.

3. Tap Set as Wallpaper to use the wallpaper.

Changing Your Keyboard

If you find it hard to type on the standard Galaxy S7 keyboard, or you just want to make it look better, you can install replacement keyboards. You can download free or purchase replacement keyboards from the Google Play Store. Most, if not all, keyboards come with their own installation wizard that walks you through adding and activating a keyboard, but if the one you installed does not have a wizard, or you want to manually switch keyboards in the future, these steps will be useful.

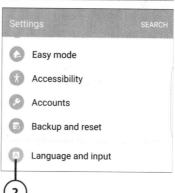

1. Pull down the Notification bar and tap the Settings icon.

2. Tap Language and Input.

3. Tap Default Keyboard.

4. Tap Set Up Input Methods.

5. Tap the On/Off switch to the right of the keyboard you want to enable. In this example the keyboard is called SwiftKey Keyboard.

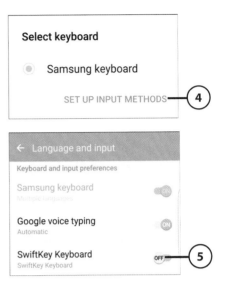

Doing Your Research

When you choose a different keyboard in step 5, the Galaxy S7 gives you a warning telling you that nonstandard keyboards have the potential for capturing everything you type. Do your research on any keyboards before you download and install them.

6. Tap OK to confirm that you want to enable and use this keyboard.

What Can You Do with Your New Keyboard?

Keyboards you buy in the Google Play Store can do many things. They can change the key layout, change the color and style of the keys, offer different methods of text input, and even enable you to use an old T9 predictive input keyboard that you might have become used to when using an old "dumb phone" that had only a numeric keypad.

7. Tap the back icon to return to the previous screen.

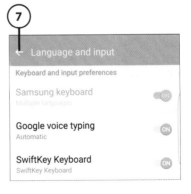

8. Tap Default Keyboard one more time.

9. Tap the keyboard you enabled in step 5. In this example it is the SwiftKey Keyboard.

Adding Widgets to Your Home Screens

Some applications that you install come with widgets that you can place on your Home screen panes. These widgets normally display real-time information, such as stocks, weather, time, and Facebook feeds. Your Galaxy S7 also comes preinstalled with some widgets.

Add a Widget

Your Galaxy S7 should come preinstalled with some widgets, but you might also have others that have been added when you installed applications.

1. Touch and hold an open area on the Home screen.

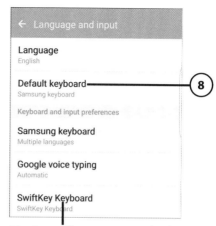

Tap to configure your new keyboard

2. Tap Widgets.

3. Touch and hold a widget to move it to a Home screen pane. Keep holding the widget as you move to step 4.

4. Position the widget where you want it on the Home screen pane.

5. Drag the widget to different Home screen panes if you want to place it on a different pane, or drag it to the right-most pane to create a new Home screen pane and place the widget on the new pane.

6. Release your finger to place the widget (not shown). Some widgets may prompt you with a few setup questions after they are positioned.

How Many Widgets Can I Fit?

By default, each Home screen pane is divided into a grid of four blocks across and four blocks down (4x4). In the figure for step 3, the widgets show their size in blocks across and down (such as 2x1). From that, you can judge whether a widget is going to fit on the Home screen pane you want it to be on, but it also helps you position it in step 4. You can increase the number of blocks available in the grid pattern by touching and holding an open area on the Home screen and tapping Screen Grid. On the Screen Grid screen, choose between a screen grid of 4x4, 4x5, or 5x5. Notice that app shortcuts and widgets shift closer together when you've chosen more grid rows and columns. Tap Apply when you are satisfied with your new Screen Grid choice.

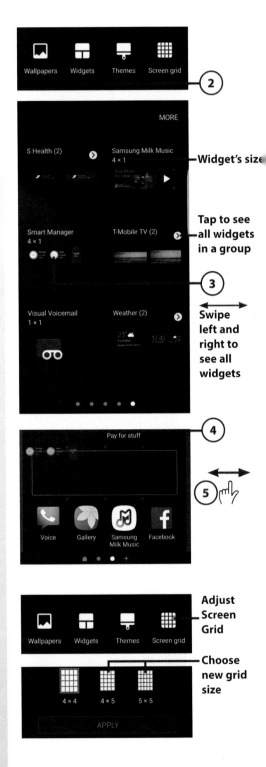

2

Widget's size

Tap to see all widgets in a group

3

Swipe left and right to see all widgets

4

5

Adjust Screen Grid

Choose new grid size

Resizing Widgets

Some (not all) widgets can be resized. To resize a widget, touch and hold the widget until you see an outline and then release it. If the widget can be resized, you see the resizing borders. Drag them to resize the widget. Tap anywhere on the screen to stop resizing.

Drag to resize

Remove and Move a Widget

Sometimes you want to remove a widget or move it around.

1. Touch and hold the widget until the widget zooms out, but continue to hold it.

2. Drag the widget to the word Remove to remove it.

3. Drag the widget around the screen or drag it to one of the Home screen panes to reposition it.

4. Release the widget (not shown).

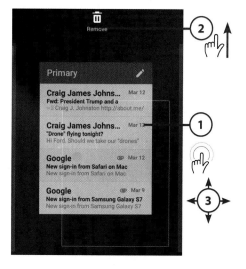

Setting the Language

If you move to another country or want to change the language used by your Galaxy S7, you can do so with a few taps.

1. Pull down the Notification bar and tap the Settings icon.

2. Tap Language and Input.

3. Tap Language.

4. Tap the language you want to switch to. The language is changed, and you are returned to the previous screen automatically. The choice of available languages is based on your wireless carrier and where in the world you purchased your Galaxy S7 or S7 edge.

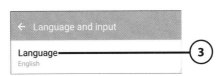

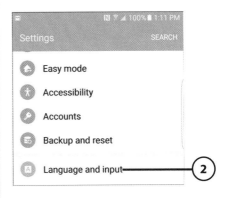

What Obeys the Language Setting?

When you switch your Galaxy S7 to use a different language, you immediately notice that all standard applications and the Galaxy S7 menus switch to the new language. Even some third-party applications honor the language switch. However, many third-party applications ignore the language setting on the Galaxy S7. Therefore, you might open a third-party application and find that all its menus are still in English.

Changing Accessibility Settings

Your Galaxy S7 includes built-in settings to assist people who might otherwise have difficulty using some features of the device. The Galaxy S7 has the ability to provide alternative feedback, such as vibration and sound. It can even read menu items aloud to you.

1. Pull down the Notification bar and tap the Settings icon.

2. Tap Accessibility.

3. Tap one of the categories on the Accessibility screen and use the following sections to change the settings in the different categories.

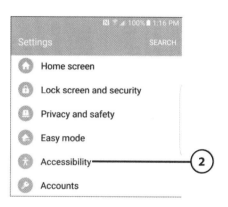

Voice

1. Tap to enable or disable Voice Assistant and change the Voice Assistant settings. When enabled, Voice Assistant speaks everything, including menus, but it also has other features, such as requiring that you double-tap something to select it instead of single tapping. When Voice Assistant is turned on, the options in steps 2–4 become available.

2. Tap to enable the Dark Screen feature. After this feature is enabled, you double-press the Power key to enable and disable the Dark Screen functionality. When you have it enabled, your screen remains off for privacy.

3. Tap to enable the Rapid Key Input feature. When enabled, it overrides the TalkBack requirement of having to double-tap each key while typing.

4. Tap to enable Speak passwords. When this feature is enabled, Voice Assistant speaks each character of your password as you type it.

5. Tap to change the settings for the text-to-speech engine provided by Samsung or to switch to the Google text-to-speech engine.

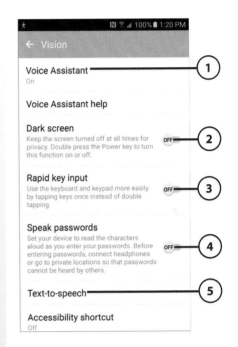

More About Text-to-Speech

By default, your Galaxy S7 uses the Samsung Text-to-Speech service with an option to use the Samsung service to speak any text you need to read. You can install other text-to-speech software by searching for it in the Google Play Store. After you've installed the software, you'll have multiple choices.

6. Tap to enable or disable the Accessibility Shortcut feature. When it's enabled, you can access accessibility features by performing certain gestures.

7. Swipe up for more settings.

8. Tap to record voice labels and write them to Near Field Communication (NFC) tags.

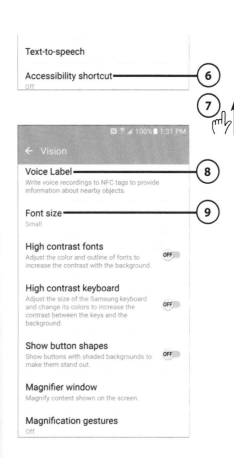

What Is a Voice Label?

Imagine if you could hold your S7 or S7 edge near an NFC tag that was close to an object in the room, and you heard a recording that tells you about the object. Voice Labels allow you to do just that. When you tap Voice Label in step 8, you can record your voice saying the name of the object, or something relevant about the object (for example, a refrigerator). After you have recorded what you want to say, you are prompted to hold a new NFC tag against the back of your S7 or S7 edge and your recording is written to the NFC tag. You can then stick the NFC tag near the object. When your S7 or S7 edge comes close to the NFC tag in the future, what you recorded is automatically played back.

9. Tap to set the font size used on your Galaxy S7. You can choose sizes ranging from tiny to huge.

10. Tap to enable or disable High contrast fonts. Once enabled the text on-screen will be easier to read if you suffer from certain vision impairments.

11. Tap to enable or disable the high contrast keyboard. Once enabled the keys on the on-screen Samsung keyboard will be easier to see if you suffer from certain vision impairments.

Only for Samsung Keyboards

Please note that the High Contrast Keyboard feature works only when you are using the standard Samsung keyboard and have not installed a third-party keyboard.

12. Tap to enable or disable button shapes. Once enabled any on-screen buttons will be easier to see if you suffer from certain vision impairments.

13. Tap to enable or disable a magnifier window that can magnify whatever is under it. You can change the size of the magnify window and how much magnification is applied.

14. Tap to enable or disable magnification gestures, which include the ability to magnify any screen by triple-tapping it. When a screen is magnified, you can pan around it.

15. Swipe up for more settings.

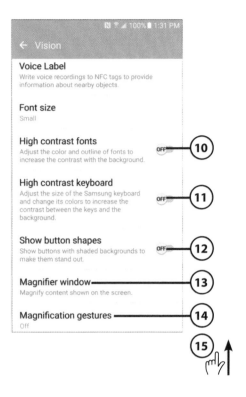

16. Tap to enable or disable the Grayscale feature, which makes everything on the screen grayscale instead of full color.

17. Tap to enable or disable the Negative Colors feature, which makes all colors displayed on your Galaxy S7 reversed. (For example, black text on a white background instead appears as white text on a black background.)

18. Tap to enable the Color Adjustment Wizard, which helps you adjust the screen colors if you have difficulty reading the screen with the default colors.

19. Tap to save your changes and return to the previous screen.

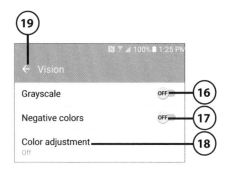

Hearing

1. Tap to enable or disable an option that makes your S7 vibrate when it detects a baby crying or a doorbell ringing.

2. Tap to enable or disable making your S7 light up the camera flash when you have a new notification.

3. Tap to turn off all sounds.

4. Tap to enable or disable improving the sound quality if you use a hearing aid.

5. Tap to enable video subtitles provided by Samsung and adjust how the subtitles appear on the screen.

6. Tap to enable or disable video subtitles provided by Google and adjust how the subtitles appear on the screen.

7. Swipe up for more settings.

8. Tap to adjust the balance of audio played when wearing earphones.

9. Tap to use mono audio when wearing one earphone.

10. Tap to save your changes and return to the previous screen.

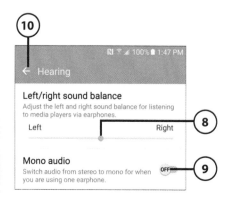

Dexterity and Interaction

1. Tap to manage using universal switches to control your Galaxy S7. Switches can include tapping on the screen; detecting movement of your head, eyes, or mouth; and pressing buttons on an externally connected accessory.

2. Tap to enable or disable the Assistant menu. When it is enabled, you can set your dominant hand, reorder the menu items, and adjust the level of zoom. The Assistant menu appears as a small gray box on your screen at all times. When you tap it, it provides quick access to common device functions.

3. Tap to enable or disable the Gesture Wake Up feature. When this feature is enabled, you can wake up your phone by waving your hand over the front of the device while it lies on a flat surface.

4. Tap to adjust the press and hold delay (also known as touch and hold).

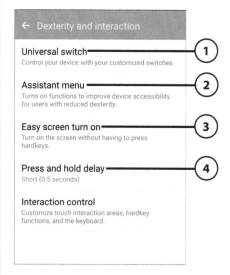

5. Tap to enable or disable interaction control, which includes blocking areas of the screen so they do not respond to taps.

6. Tap to save your changes and return to the previous screen.

Direction Lock

1. Tap to enable Direction Lock. When you enable it, you are asked to draw a series of directions on the screen (consisting of up, down, left, and right) that can be used as an unlock pattern.

2. Tap to change the screen security from Direction Lock to something else.

3. Tap to receive vibration feedback each time you successfully draw a direction on the screen.

4. Tap to hear a sound played each time you successfully draw a direction on the screen.

5. Tap to see an arrow showing the direction you just drew on the screen.

6. Tap to hear a voice speaking the direction you just drew on the screen.

7. Tap to save your changes and return to the previous screen.

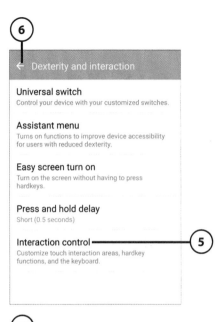

Direct Access

1. Tap to enable or disable direct access to certain accessibility settings. When this feature is enabled, press the Home button three times in quick succession to see the Direct Access menu.

2. Choose which accessibility settings you want direct access to.

3. Tap to save your changes and return to the previous screen.

Notification Reminder

1. Tap to enable or disable extra notifications for certain apps.

2. Choose whether your S7 vibrates when one of your chosen apps sends a notification.

3. Choose the reminder interval if you have not responded to the notification.

4. Turn this switch on if you want to receive extra notifications from all apps. Turn this switch off to allow you to choose which apps you will receive this extra notification from.

5. Choose which apps should give you this extra notification, if you have turned the switch in step 4 off.

6. Tap to save your changes and return to the previous screen.

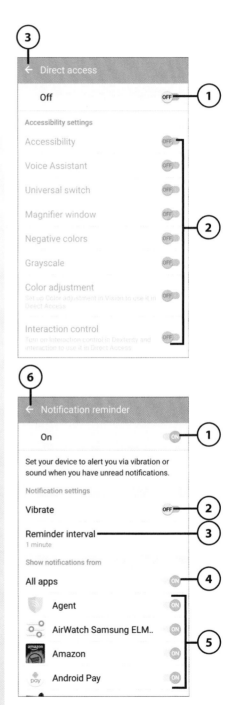

Answering/Ending Calls

1. Tap to enable or disable answering a call by pressing the Home button.

2. Tap to enable or disable using voice commands to answer or reject calls. When enabled, just say "Answer" or "Reject."

3. Tap to enable or disable ending a call by pressing the Power button.

4. Tap to save your changes and return to the previous screen.

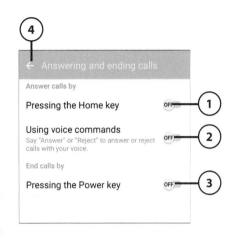

Manage Accessibility

1. Tap to import accessibility settings that someone has shared with you or to export your settings.

2. Tap to share your accessibility settings with friends. You must first export your settings as mentioned in step 1.

3. Tap to return to the previous screen.

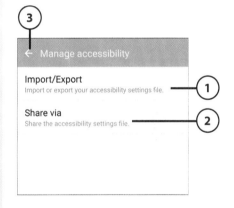

Adjusting Sound, Vibration, and Notification Settings

You can change the volume for games, ringtones, and alarms, change the default ringtone and notification sound, plus control what system sounds are used.

Adjust Sound and Vibration Settings

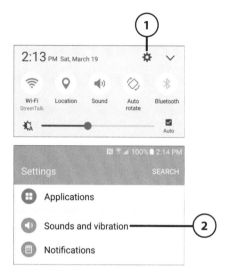

1. Pull down the Notification bar and tap the Settings icon.

2. Tap Sounds and Vibration.

3. Tap to change the sound mode between Sound (play all sounds), Vibrate (vibrate instead of playing sounds), or Mute (silence all sounds and vibrations).

4. Tap to choose whether you want your Galaxy S7 to also vibrate when receiving an incoming call.

5. Tap to change the volume for ringtones, music, video games, and other media, notifications, and system alerts.

6. Tap to choose the vibration intensity for incoming calls, notifications, and vibration (or haptic) feedback.

7. Tap to change the ringtone that plays when there is an incoming call. You can choose from the ringtones that came with your Galaxy S7, or choose from any audio that you have on your S7, including songs and tunes you may have downloaded.

8. Tap to select a vibration pattern that is triggered when there is an incoming call.

9. Tap to change the sounds for notifications from Messages, Calendar, and Email, as well as adjust system sounds.

10. Tap to choose whether you want to enable Do Not Disturb, and choose any exceptions.

11. Swipe up for more settings.

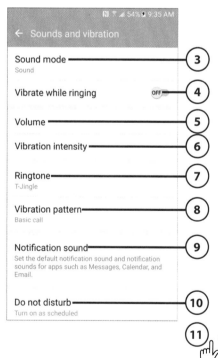

12. Tap to enable or disable playing a sound when you interact with the touchscreen, such as when you tap a menu item.

13. Tap to enable or disable playing a sound when you lock or unlock your Galaxy S7.

14. Tap to enable or disable playing a sound when you plug your Galaxy S7 in to charge, or place it on a wireless charging pad.

15. Tap to choose whether you want vibration (haptic) feedback when you tap the Recent Apps and Back buttons, and for performing a touch and hold gesture.

16. Tap to enable or disable playing touch tone sounds when typing a phone number on the dialpad.

17. Tap to enable or disable playing a sound for each key that you tap on the Samsung on-screen keyboard.

18. Swipe up for more settings.

19. Tap to choose whether you want to feel a vibration as you type on the Samsung on-screen keyboard.

20. Tap to choose whether you want to go through a wizard so that your S7 can adapt its audio output to your ears, and choose whether you want to enable SoundAlive and its audio enhancing features. See the "Sound Quality and Effects" task later in this chapter for more information.

21. Tap to save your changes and return to the previous screen.

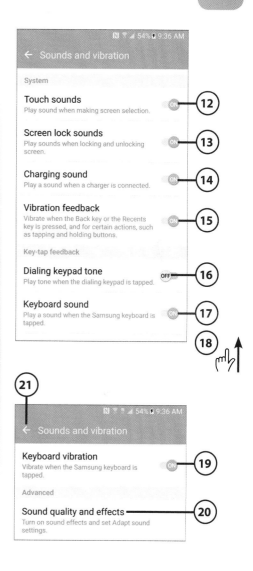

Adjust Notification Settings

Choose which apps can send you notifications, choose which apps are considered a priority, and decide how the notifications look and behave.

1. Pull down the Notification bar and tap the Settings icon.

2. Tap Notifications.

3. Tap the on/off switch next to each app to choose whether you want to receive notifications from that app.

4. Tap Advanced to decide how notifications from each app behave, and whether an app's notification should be considered a priority. See more about this feature in the next section, "Advanced Notification Settings."

5. Tap to save your changes and return to the previous screen.

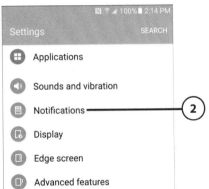

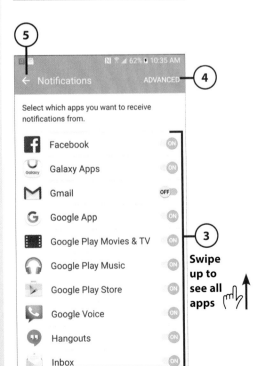

Swipe up to see all apps

Advanced Notification Settings

This task picks up after you have tapped Advanced in step 4 of the "Adjust Notification Settings" task.

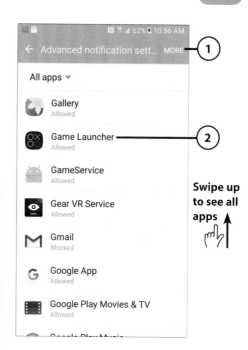

1. Tap More to choose whether you want to see built-in system apps in this app list and whether you want to reset all of the notifications settings back to their default settings.

2. Tap an app to modify its advanced notification settings.

3. Tap to choose whether you want notifications from this app to be considered as priority notifications. Priority notifications always appear at the top of a list of notifications. When you activate the Do Not Disturb mode, you can allow priority notifications to be exceptions.

4. Tap to choose whether you want the notifications from this app to appear in a pop-up window at the top of the screen.

5. Tap to choose whether you want to hide notifications from this app on your Galaxy S7's Lock screen. You may choose to do this if you consider notifications from this app as containing personal or sensitive information.

6. Tap to choose whether you want to hide the content of notifications from this app on your Galaxy S7's Lock screen. You may choose to do this if you consider notifications from this app as containing personal or sensitive information. When this option is turned on, the notification appears on the Lock screen, but none of its content is visible.

7. Tap to save your changes and return to the previous screen.

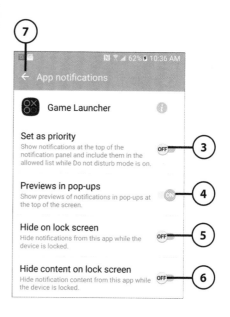

Sound Quality and Effects

This task picks up after you have tapped Sound Quality and Effects in step 20 of the "Adjust Sound and Vibration Settings" task.

1. Tap Equalizer to choose between preset equalizer audio adjustments including Pop, Classic, Jazz, Rock, and Custom.

2. Drag the blue selector to manually adjust the audio to either favor bass or treble. Any adjustments you make to this selector are saved in the Custom equalizer preset.

3. Drag the blue selector to manually adjust the audio to either favor instruments or vocals. Any adjustments you make to this selector are saved in the Custom equalizer preset.

4. Tap Advanced to make more precise adjustments to the audio using a graphic equalizer. Any changes you make using the graphic equalizer are saved in the Custom equalizer preset.

5. Tap UHQ Upscaler if you want your Galaxy S7 to enhance audio by simulating a higher sample frequency. This option is only available when you're using a headset (Bluetooth or connected via a cable).

6. Tap Surround to let your Galaxy S7 simulate full surround sound. This option is only available when you're using a headset (Bluetooth or connected via a cable).

7. Tap to enable or disable the Tube Amp Pro feature that simulates a tube amplifier. You can only enable this feature if you have a wired or Bluetooth headset connected.

8. Swipe up for more settings.

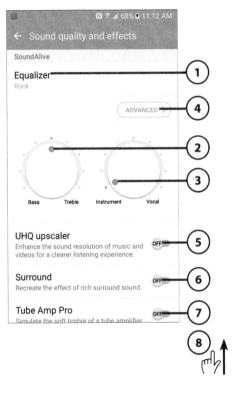

9. Tap to enable or disable the Concert Hall feature that simulates the reverberation of a concert hall. You can only enable this feature if you have a wired or Bluetooth headset connected.

10. Tap to run through an audio test to determine your exact auditory range. After the test, your S7 customizes the sound to best suit your hearing abilities when you are wearing a headset.

11. Tap to save your changes and return to the previous screen.

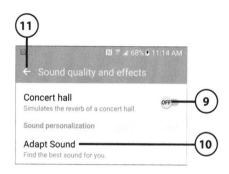

Do Not Disturb

This task picks up after you have tapped Do Not Disturb in step 10 of the "Adjust Sound and Vibration Settings" task.

1. Tap to enable or disable Do Not Disturb manually. When enabled, you will receive no notifications unless you specify exceptions.

2. Tap to set a schedule when Do Not Disturb is automatically enabled and disabled. For example you may want to set it to be enabled when you go to sleep and disabled when you wake up.

3. Set the Do Not Disturb schedule.

4. Tap to allow exceptions to the Do Not Disturb rule. For example, you probably want to allow the alarm to still wake you up in the morning and maybe allow incoming calls from certain people.

5. Tap to allow alarms as an exception to Do Not Disturb.

6. Tap to allow calls from people who contact you more than once during a 15-minute period.

7. Tap to choose to allow calls from specific people.

8. Tap to allow messages from all people, only people in your Contacts app, or only people who you have marked as a favorite in the Contacts app.

9. Tap to allow alerts from tasks and events on your calendar.

10. Tap to allow reminders.

11. Tap to allow notifications from apps that you have set to have priority notifications.

12. Tap to save your changes and return to the previous screen.

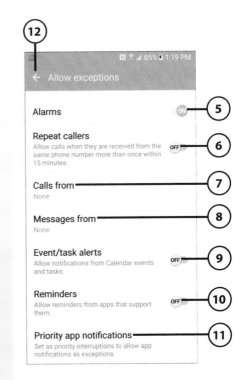

Modifying Display Settings

You can change many display settings, the screen mode, the wait time before your Galaxy S7 goes to sleep, the size of the font used, and the pulse notification light settings.

1. Pull down the Notification bar and tap the Settings icon.

2. Tap Display.

3. Tap to change the screen brightness manually or set it to automatic. When on automatic, your Galaxy S7 uses the built-in light sensor to adjust the brightness based on the light level where you are.

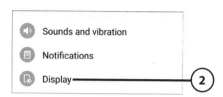

4. Tap to change the system font and how large the font style is. The system font is used for all menus, notifications, alerts, and warnings on your Galaxy S7.

5. Tap to choose whether a shaded background should be added to icons so that they stand out on the screen, or whether they should appear in their original form. Adding a shaded background to icons may help you see them better.

6. Tap to choose how many minutes of inactivity must pass before your Galaxy S7 puts the screen to sleep.

7. Tap to enable Smart Stay. When this feature is enabled, your Galaxy S7 uses the front-facing camera to look for your eyes. It keeps the screen on as long as it detects that you are looking at the screen.

8. Tap to choose whether you want to use the Always On Display. When enabled, instead of your S7 turning off its screen when it goes to sleep, it keeps displaying a little bit of useful information. The information could be the time, your calendar, or a choice of three static images. The Always On Display also shows battery percentage and number of missed calls.

9. Tap to enable or disable the Night Clock on the Galaxy S7 edge. When enabled, the Night Clock displays the time on the curved part of the screen. The Night Clock is useful as a bedside clock.

10. Swipe up for more settings.

11. Tap to choose the Screen mode, which is how the screen represents colors. You can manually choose AMOLED Cinema, AMOLED Photo, and Basic, or leave it set to Adaptive Display, which means your Galaxy S7 chooses the best settings based on usage.

12. Tap to choose whether you want the Light Emitting Diode (LED) indicator to illuminate when you are charging, using the Voice Recorder, or when you receive a notification.

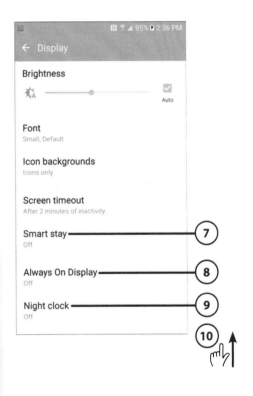

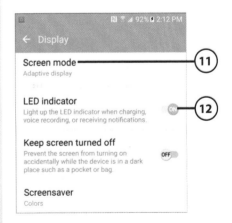

13. Tap to choose whether you want your S7 to keeps its screen off when it detects that it is in a dark place, such as in your pocket or in a bag. Having this enabled may save your battery life a bit.

14. Tap to enable or disable the Screensaver, decide what must be displayed when the Screensaver is triggered, and when the Screensaver must activate.

15. Tap to save your changes and return to the previous screen.

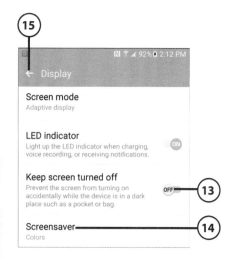

Is Adaptive Display Mode Good?

If you leave your screen mode set to Adaptive Display, you should know that your Galaxy S7 adjusts the color range, saturation, and sharpness of the screen for the Gallery, Camera, Internet Web Browser, Samsung Video, Samsung Smart Remote, and Google Play Books apps only. All other system apps and apps that you install are not optimized. With this in mind, you might prefer to manually select an appropriate screen mode in step 11.

Aren't Screensavers Obsolete?

In step 14 you can enable and manage the Screensaver feature. For many years now, screensavers have not been needed because we no longer use Cathode Ray Tube (CRT) monitors and screens. In the days when we used CRTs, if an image remained in one spot for a long time, it would be burned into the front of the screen. Having a screensaver on a CRT monitor made sense because the images were moving and changing constantly. Screensavers continued to be used because people liked seeing the patterns and images in the screensavers. Once the screensaver is activated, it can display your photos or cool color patterns after a period of inactivity, when you plug your Galaxy S7 into a dock, or when it is charging.

Adjusting the S7 Edge Settings

If you own a Galaxy S7 edge, there are some additional features that make use of the curved edges of the screen. The steps below do not work on a regular S7; they're only for the S7 edge.

1. Pull down the Notification bar and tap the Settings icon.

2. Tap Edge Screen.

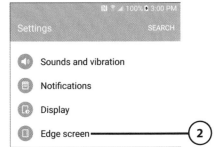

3. Use the following sections to manage your S7 edge features.

Set Up Edge Panels

Edge Panels, when enabled, allows you quick access to apps, shortcuts, contacts, and additional information such as news and weather.

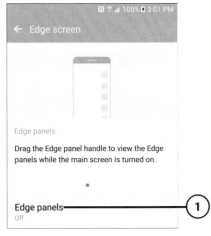

1. Tap Edge Panels.

2. Tap to enable or disable Edge Panels.

3. Tap to enable or disable a particular Edge Panel.

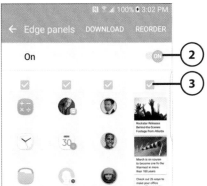

4. Tap to configure a specific Edge Panel.

5. Swipe left and right to see all Edge Panels.

6. Tap reorder the Edge Panels.

7. Tap to download more Edge Panels from the Samsung App Store.

8. Tap to choose whether the Edge Panel handle appears on the right edge or left edge of the display, and select how transparent it appears.

9. Tap to save your changes and return to the previous screen.

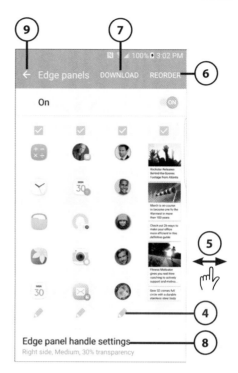

>>>Go Further

HOW DO EDGE PANELS WORK?

Edge Panels provide convenient access to apps that you use regularly, tasks that you perform regularly (for example, a task may be to take a panoramic picture, which effectively launches the camera app and switches to the panoramic picture mode for you), people whom you contact often, and information like weather, news, and sports.

Edge Panels are normally hidden. To access them, look for a thin, partially transparent white bar on the curved edge of your screen. This is called the Edge Panel Handle. Swipe the Edge Panel Handle toward the middle of the screen to reveal the Edge Panels. Once the Edge Panels appear, you can swipe left and right to move between the Edge Panels themselves.

You can change the order of the Edge Panels as described in step 6 of the "Set Up Edge Panels" task. You change the exact content of each Edge Panel as described in step 4 or by tapping the Configure icon (which looks like a gear). To hide the Edge Panels, simply tap in an open area of the screen.

Swipe toward the middle of the screen to reveal the Edge Panels

There are three Edge Panels enabled by default: Apps Edge, which provides quick access to apps; Tasks Edge, which provides quick access to tasks (such as taking a selfie) within an app; and People Edge, which provides quick access to people whom you call, text, or email often. You can add additional Edge Panels including

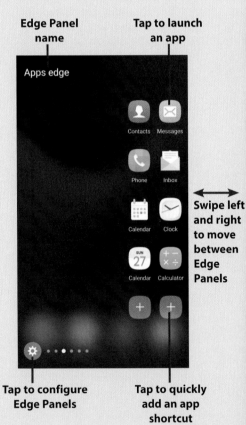

Edge Panel name

Tap to launch an app

- **Quick Tools**—Provides a compass, access to the flashlight, and a ruler that appears on the curved edge of your S7

- **Data Usage Manager**—Keeps track of your cellular data usage

- **Weather**—Provides the local weather forecast

- **My Places**—Provides quick access to tasks and apps based on where you are

- **Yahoo! Finance**—Tracks stocks

- **Internet**—Provides quick access to websites using the Samsung Internet web browser

- **Yahoo! Sports**—Helps you follow your favorite teams.

Swipe left and right to move between Edge Panels

You can download many more Edge Panels from the Samsung App Store. Some Edge Panels are free, but others cost you about $1.50 per panel.

Tap to configure Edge Panels

Tap to quickly add an app shortcut

Edge Feeds

When Edge Feeds is enabled, you can use a swiping gesture along the curved edge of your screen to see information feeds such as weather, notifications, sports scores, financial information, and more. The Edge Feeds gesture is a little tricky to master. To see the Edge Feeds, while your phone's screen is off, swipe your finger across the curved edge of the screen in one direction, and in the same motion, swipe it back.

1. Tap Edge Feeds.

2. Tap to enable or disable Edge Feeds.

3. Check the boxes on top of each feed to manage which ones you want to see in the Edge Feed.

4. Tap to edit a feed to modify the information it displays.

5. Tap to choose the number of seconds the Edge Feed remains visible.

6. Swipe left and right to see all feeds.

7. Tap to change the order in which feeds appear when you are looking at Edge Feeds.

8. Tap to download more feeds from the Samsung App Store.

9. Tap to save your changes and return to the previous screen.

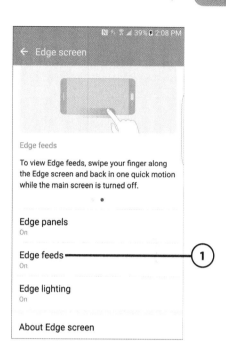

Edge feeds

To view Edge feeds, swipe your finger along the Edge screen and back in one quick motion while the main screen is turned off.

Edge panels
On

Edge feeds
On

Edge lighting
On

About Edge screen

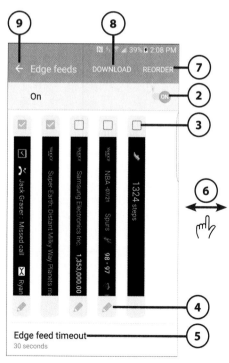

Edge Lighting

Edge Lighting, when enabled, lights up the curved edge of the screen when you receive an incoming call, and your Galaxy S7 edge is lying upside down on its screen. If you also have People Edge enabled (see the next section), the color of the light used matches the color you have chosen for the caller.

1. Tap Edge Lighting.

2. Tap to enable or disable Edge Lighting.

3. Tap to enable or disable the ability to send a quick reply to the caller and manage the text of the message.

How Does Quick Reply Work?

To start, make sure that you have Edge Lighting enabled, you have enabled Quick Reply, and have set a Quick Reply message. Then make a habit of placing your Galaxy S7 edge upside down on its screen when you are not using it. When someone calls, emails, or sends you a text message, you see the curved edge of the screen start pulsating with white light. If you have added contacts to the People Edge, the color of the pulsating light indicates who is calling or sending a message. If it is an incoming call and you would like to send the caller a Quick Reply message, place your finger over the heart rate sensor for two seconds. Your Galaxy S7 edge sends the Quick Reply message to the caller as an SMS (text message).

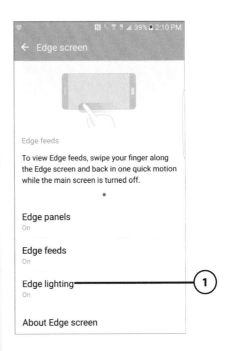

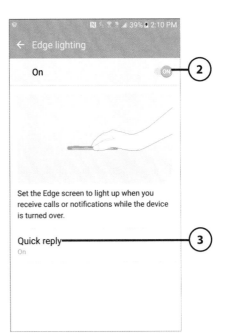

4. Tap to enable or disable Quick Reply.

5. Tap to change the Quick Reply message that is sent.

People Edge

People Edge works in conjunction with the Edge Lighting feature to enable you to assign a color to up to five contacts. This then allows you to identify who is calling by the color of the edge light. People Edge also allows you to quickly call, text, or email up to five contacts.

1. Swipe the Edge Panel Handle toward the middle of the screen to reveal the Edge Panels.

2. Swipe left or right until you see the People Edge panel.

3. Tap to add a contact to one of the five positions in the People Edge panel.

4. Tap to access the OnCircle feature, which enables you to send scribbles, quick messages, images, or stickers to other people who are using a Samsung Galaxy S6 edge or Galaxy S7 edge.

5. Tap one of the five people in your People Edge panel to call them, or send email or text messages to them. If that contact also uses OnCircle, you can send them scribbles, images, and stickers.

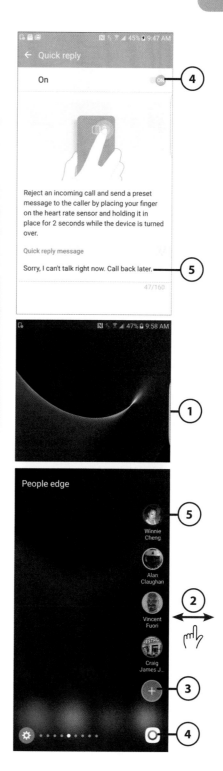

>>>Go Further
HOW DOES PEOPLE EDGE WORK?

To start, make sure that you have Edge Lighting enabled. Then make a habit of placing your Galaxy S7 edge upside down on its screen when you are not using it. When someone calls, emails, or sends you a text message, you see the curved edge of the screen start pulsating with light. The color of the pulsating light indicates who is calling, texting, or emailing. If the pulsating light is white, it means that the caller or sender is not one of the five people you have chosen. If it is an incoming call and you would like to send the caller a Quick Reply message, place your finger over the heart rate sensor for two seconds. Your Galaxy S7 edge sends the Quick Reply message to the caller as an SMS (text message). If you recognize who is calling because of the color of the light, pick up your Galaxy S7 edge and answer the call as you normally would. If you miss the call, when you later look at your phone, you see a block of color on the curved edge of your screen indicating that one of your People Edge contacts called. Swipe the block of color inward and choose a method of contacting them. You can call them, send them an SMS (text message), or send them an email.

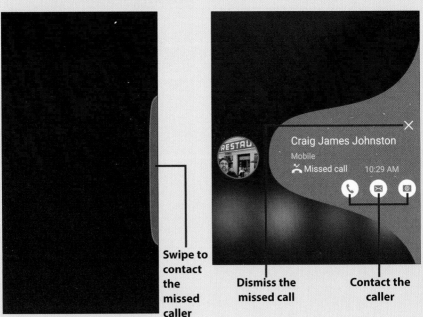

Craig James Johnston
Mobile
Missed call 10:29 AM

Swipe to contact the missed caller

Dismiss the missed call

Contact the caller

>>>Go Further

USING ONCIRCLE

OnCircle is a feature that allows you to send scribbles, stickers, and images to your friends who are also using OnCircle and who have a Samsung Galaxy S6 edge or a Samsung Galaxy S7 edge. Tap the person's contact picture to send taps and scribbles. Tap the smiley face icon to send stickers. Stickers are little animations. Tap the camera icon to either take a picture or use one already saved on your phone. You draw on the picture and then send it. Instead of a picture, you can create an animated GIF and send that. If your friends send you items using OnCircle, you can see them all in one place by tapping the OnCircle icon at the bottom of the People Edge panel.

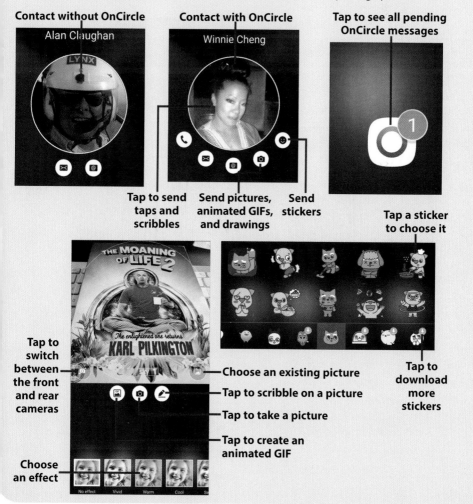

Contact without OnCircle

Alan Claughan

Contact with OnCircle

Winnie Cheng

Tap to see all pending OnCircle messages

Tap to send taps and scribbles

Send pictures, animated GIFs, and drawings

Send stickers

Tap a sticker to choose it

Tap to switch between the front and rear cameras

Choose an existing picture

Tap to scribble on a picture

Tap to take a picture

Tap to create an animated GIF

Tap to download more stickers

Choose an effect

Using Easy Home Screen Mode

Home Screen mode changes which widgets are placed on your Home screen and how many widgets you have on the Home screen. When Easy mode is enabled, a lot of widgets that have shortcuts to many apps are placed on the Home screen, and their icons are larger.

1. Tap Easy mode in Settings.

2. Tap to enable Easy mode.

3. Swipe up to select which apps you want to have shortcuts to on your Home screen.

4. Tap Done to save your changes. You return to the Easy Mode Home screen.

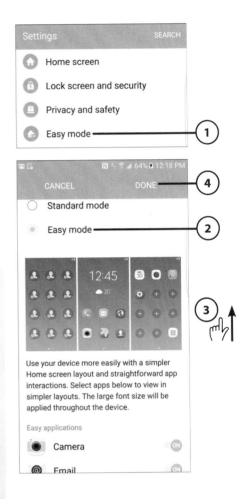

Setting Privacy and Safety Options

Privacy and Safety enables you to set whether you want to allow your geographic location to be available to Google and apps running on your phone, manage Private mode, and set up a feature that allows your phone to send information to people when you are in an emergency situation.

1. Tap Privacy and Safety in Settings.

2. Tap to manage whether Google or apps running on your phone have access to your geographic location.

3. Tap to manage which apps have permission to access and modify information on your S7. For example, you could allow the Contacts app to access the Camera or the Facebook app to access the microphone.

4. Tap to manage Private mode.

5. Tap to enable or disable allowing your phone to report diagnostic information to Google.

6. Tap to manage how SOS messages are handled.

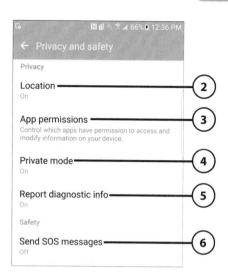

Private Mode

Private mode is a bit confusing at first, but while it is enabled, you can move content from certain apps to a secret area on your Galaxy S7 or S7 edge. When Private mode is disabled, the content is invisible unless you come back into Settings and enable it again.

1. After performing step 4 of the "Setting Privacy and Safety Options" section, tap to enable or disable Private mode.

2. Choose a method for securing Private mode. The method you use here is in addition to the method you already use for unlocking your Galaxy S7 or S7 edge. You only need to do this the first time you want to enable Private mode.

3. Tap to change the method for securing Private mode.

4. Tap to return to the previous screen.

5. Tap to enable or disable automatically disabling Private mode when the screen turns off. This is recommended.

6. Tap to save your changes and return to the previous screen.

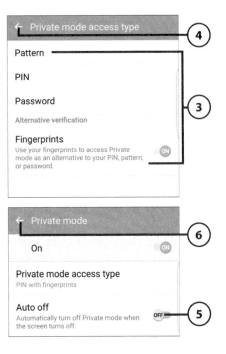

>>>Go Further
USING PRIVATE MODE

Private mode is a confusing feature. Essentially when Private mode is enabled, you can move content from certain apps to a secret, hidden area on your Galaxy S7 or S7 edge. You are also able to see content that you previously moved to this secret area. When you disable Private mode, anything in the secret area becomes unavailable and invisible. To re-enable Private mode, you have to use a password, PIN, pattern, or your fingerprint. Private mode only works with the following apps (that Samsung has heavily modified): Gallery, Video, Music, Voice Recorder, My Files, and Internet (not the Chrome browser). When Private mode is enabled, you can tap the Menu icon to reveal a new menu item called Move to Private.

Move selected items to the Private area

Send SOS Messages

When you have this feature enabled, if you find yourself in an emergency situation where you need help, you can press the Power button on your Galaxy S7 or S7 edge three times in quick succession, and your phone starts taking note of your geographic location, recording audio, taking pictures, and sending it all to one or more contacts that you have previously set up.

1. Tap to enable the Send SOS Messages feature. The first time you enable it, you are asked to choose at least one person from your contacts or to enter a new mobile phone number to be used by the feature.

2. Tap to manage which contacts will be sent your location, audio, and pictures when you trigger this feature. You can use more than one contact.

3. Tap to enable or disable including pictures with the SOS messages.

4. Tap to enable or disable including audio recordings with the SOS messages.

5. Tap to save your changes and return to the previous screen.

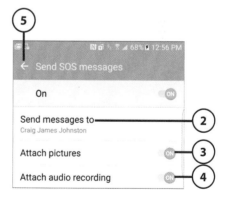

>>>Go Further
USING THE SEND SOS MESSAGES FEATURE

If you find yourself in an emergency situation, press the Power button on your Galaxy S7 or S7 edge three times in quick succession. Your phone immediately starts sending SOS text messages to the people you have set up to receive them. If you have turned on the Attach Pictures feature, your phone starts taking pictures and sending them to the designated contact. Finally, if you have turned on the Attach Audio Recording feature, your phone starts recording audio and sending it to your chosen contacts. The SOS behavior continues until you stop it. To stop sending SOS messages, press the Power button on your phone three times in quick succession.

Changing Themes

Themes are packaged settings that change the look and feel of your Galaxy S7 and S7 edge. Themes affect the system sounds, wallpaper, icons, fonts used, and colors used in phone menus, including the Notification screen. The themes can also modify the look and feel of some core Samsung apps such as the Phone app.

1. Pull down the Notification bar and tap the Settings icon.

2. Tap Themes.

3. Tap a theme to download it. Some themes are free whereas others have a small fee.

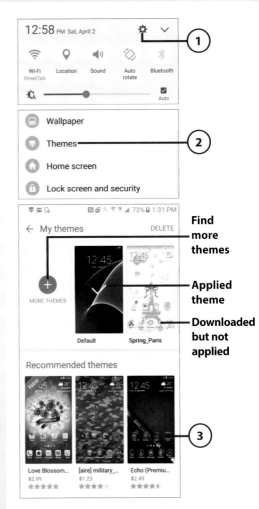

4. Tap Download to download and install the theme. If the theme was previously downloaded and installed, skip to step 5.

5. Tap Apply.

6. Tap Apply to acknowledge that you understand that any unsaved work in your open apps will be lost when you apply the theme.

Scroll left and right to see all screenshots of the theme

Tap to delete the theme

Configuring Lock Screen and Security

With the settings screens in the Lock Screen and Security section you can control what is shown on the Lock screen, how your device is unlocked, whether you want non-Google Play apps to be installed, and many other security-related options.

1. Pull down the Notification bar and tap the Settings icon.

2. Tap Lock Screen and Security.

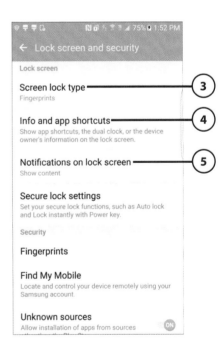

3. Tap to change what you must do to unlock your phone's screen. You can choose to do nothing, require a swipe across the screen, or use a security method (a numeric PIN, a pattern, a password, or your fingerprint).

4. Tap to choose what information is shown on the Lock screen and what app shortcuts you want to see. You can choose to show a Dual Time Zone clock and your name. You can also change the standard Phone and Camera app shortcuts that appear on the bottom-left and bottom-right of the Lock screen. You can also turn one or both of the app shortcuts off.

5. Tap to choose whether you want to see content from notifications on the Lock screen, and which apps you want to be able to send notifications to the Lock screen.

6. Tap to choose whether you want your S7 to lock automatically after a certain number of minutes, decide whether you want your S7 to lock when you press the Power button, require that your phone wipes itself back to the factory default if the Lock screen password is entered incorrectly 15 times, and choose whether you want to use Smart Lock, which keeps your S7 unlocked if you're in a specific location, you're near a trusted device (like a smartwatch or Bluetooth headset), your phone hears your voice, or if it detects that it is on your body.

7. Tap to manage your fingerprints. This includes adding or removing fingerprints, choosing when to use your fingerprint, and changing the backup password that you use when your fingerprint cannot be detected.

8. Tap to enable and manage Samsung's Find My Mobile service. After it's enabled, you can log in to the Find My Mobile website to track your stolen phone and send a remote wipe command to it. Read more about Find My Mobile in the sidebar at the end of this chapter.

9. Swipe up for more settings.

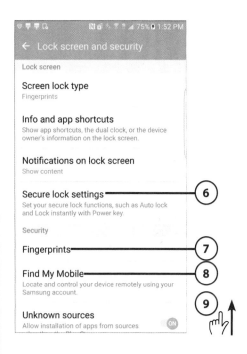

10. Tap to have the ability to install Android apps that are not found in the Google Play Store. This is not recommended because apps not found in the official app store may contain viruses and malware; proceed with caution if you choose to enable this option. If you have enrolled your device in your company's Mobile Device Management (MDM) system, you may be required to enable this option.

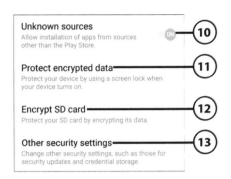

11. Tap to require a PIN to be entered when you first power on your S7, before Android loads. This adds an additional layer of protection before the data on your phone is decrypted.

12. Tap to encrypt your SD card. If you have an SD card inserted into your S7, you can choose to encrypt it. Be aware that once your SD card is encrypted, it can only ever be read by your phone. If you buy a new phone next year, the encrypted SD card will not work in it unless you first decrypt it before removing it from your current phone.

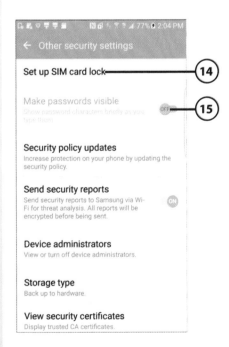

13. Tap to see other security settings.

14. Tap to set and manage a PIN to unlock your SIM card. If you use a PIN to lock your SIM card, you need to enter it in addition to entering any security measures you set for your phone.

15. Tap to enable or disable briefly showing each character of a password as you type it.

16. Tap to manage how your phone gets security policy updates from Samsung. You can choose to have them automatically downloaded and installed, and you can choose to only have them download over Wi-Fi. Think of Samsung's security policy updates like virus definition updates on a Windows computer.

17. Tap to enable or disable automatically sending security reports to Samsung.

18. Tap to manage Device Administrators.

More About Device Administrators

Device Administrators are apps that you have given permission to administer your phone. One of the Device Administrators is the Android Device Manager. This enables you to log in to www.google.com/android/ devicemanager on a desktop computer and reset your device password or erase all your device's data if it has been stolen. If you enroll your phone in your company Enterprise Mobile Management (EMM) system, like those made by AirWatch or MobileIron, those systems also add a Device Administrator.

19. Tap to view storage type information. Here you can see whether your phone supports storing your private encryption keys in the hardware (hardware-backed) or whether it is stored only in software.

20. Swipe up for more settings.

21. Tap to view and select or deselect trusted certificates that the Android system uses and certificates you may be using.

22. Tap to view and select or deselect user certificates that the Android system uses and certificates you may be using.

23. Tap to install certificates from your phone's storage. You can use this feature only if you have previously saved the certificate to storage.

24. Tap to remove all trusted user certificates (if you are using any).

25. Swipe up for more settings.

26. Tap to manage the Trust Agents. Today there is only one Trust Agent. Read more about Trust Agents in the margin note "More About Smart Lock and Trust Agents."

27. Tap to enable or disable Screen Pinning, which allows you to "pin" an app so that the person using it cannot exit the app.

28. Tap to manage which apps running on your phone are allowed to collect app usage information about all apps you have installed. This usage information includes how often each app is run, how long it sits in the foreground (active on your screen), and how long it sits in the background (still running but not visible).

29. Tap to manage which apps have access to notifications that appear on your phone. Typically if you use an Android Wear smartwatch, the Android Wear app is listed in this screen.

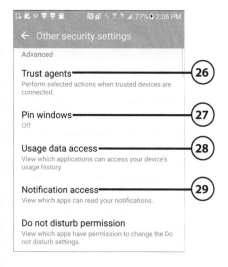

30. Tap to view which apps have permission to change the Do Not Disturb setting.

31. Tap to save your changes and return to the previous screen.

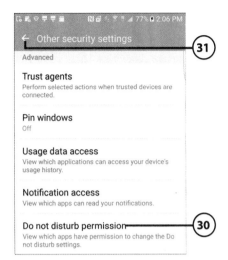

More About Smart Lock and Trust Agents

Trust Agents are services that you and your phone trust are safe, and therefore you allow them to perform functions that override regular Android functionality. Today there is only one Trust Agent: Smart Lock. Smart Lock overrides your phone's ability to lock the screen as long as it detects that your have a Bluetooth or NFC device close (for example, it detects your SmartWatch, you are sitting in your car, or you place your phone on an NFC tag), you are in a specific geographic location, or it is able to recognize your face using the front-facing camera when you pick it up. To set up Smart Lock, from the Settings screen, tap Lock Screen and Security, Secure Lock Settings, Smart Lock and then follow the steps to configure either a trusted Bluetooth or NFC device, a trusted geographic location, a trusted face, or a combination of these things to keep your phone unlocked.

>>>Go Further

MORE ABOUT PINNING AN APP

When you enable Screen Pinning in step 27, you are enabling a feature that allows you to "pin" an app to the screen. When an app is pinned to the screen, you cannot exit the app, go back to the Home screen, pull down the Notification or Quick Settings bars, or do anything other than interact with the app. You can pin only the last app you ran. To pin an app to the screen, first run the app so that it is the most recently used app. Tap the Recent Apps button, slide the app up so that you can see the pin icon. Tap the pin icon to pin the app to the screen. To exit pinned mode, touch and hold the Back and Recent Apps buttons at the same time. Pinning an app to the screen is a quick way to allow someone to use your phone without letting them access anything else other than the app they should be using.

Tap to pin an app —

>>>Go Further
MORE ABOUT FINGERPRINTS

You can store one or more thumb- or fingerprints on your Galaxy S7 or S7 edge. You can choose to use the prints to unlock your phone, but you can also use them to sign in to websites and verify your Samsung account. To manage your fingerprints, tap Settings, Lock Screen and Security, Fingerprints. As you add a new fingerprint, your phone walks you through the process of capturing your fingerprint via the fingerprint sensor in the Home button. You can also choose or change your backup password. Your backup password can be used if the fingerprint sensor cannot detect your fingerprint.

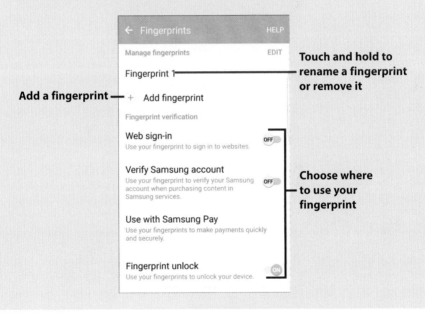

>>>Go Further

MORE ABOUT FIND MY MOBILE

If you have a Samsung account, and you have enabled Find My Mobile in step 8 of the "Configuring Lock Screen and Security" task, you can locate and remotely wipe your phone if it ever gets lost. To do this, open a web browser on a computer, browse to https://findmymobile.samsung.com, and log in with your Samsung account. When you're logged in, click Registered Device to select the device you want to work with (if you have more than one device registered). You can then locate your device, make the device play a ringtone (if you lost it in the couch and need to find it), enable emergency mode, and enable ultra power saving mode to conserve the battery. You can also remotely lock your device's screen or send a wipe command that will wipe your device and set it back to factory condition. You would use this last option in a situation where your device has been stolen and you want to make sure that the thief doesn't get to your data.

Choose device if you have more than one

>>>Go Further

DO I NEED TO USE SAMSUNG'S FIND MY MOBILE?

Google already provides a feature called Android Device Manager that does the same thing as Samsung's Find My Mobile. If you use a desktop computer to browse to http://www.google.com/android/devicemanager and log in using the same Google account that you used to activate your S7, you can find your S7 on a map, make it play a sound, lock the screen, and erase all data on your S7 if it is lost or stolen.

Turn your current call
into a conference call

In this chapter, you find out how to make and take phone calls (including conference calls) using your Galaxy S7. Topics include the following:

→ Getting to know the Phone app
→ Receiving phone calls
→ Making phone calls
→ Configuring the Phone app

Making and Receiving Calls

As a cellular phone, your Galaxy S7 includes powerful features that enable you to make phone calls swiftly and easily.

Getting to Know the Phone App

With the Phone app, you can quickly make and receive calls across the cellular network. This section introduces you to some of the features you might frequently use.

Open and Navigate the Phone App

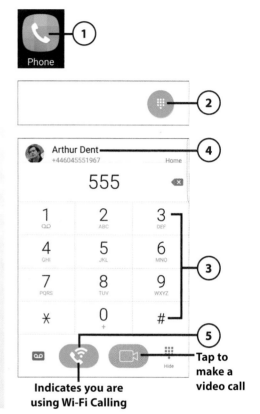

The Phone app contains three tabs that enable you to make calls in various ways and to track the calls you receive.

1. On the Home screen, tap Phone.

2. Tap the dialpad icon to display the dialpad. The dialpad icon is always visible on the bottom right of the screen while you are in the Phone app.

3. Tap the keys to dial a number.

4. If the Phone app displays a suggested contact with a matching number, you can tap the contact if it is the one you want.

5. Tap the green phone icon to place the call.

Indicates you are using Wi-Fi Calling

Tap to make a video call

What Is Wi-Fi Calling?

The technical name for Wi-Fi Calling is Universal Media Access (UMA). This technology is provided by some carriers around the world and enables your Galaxy S7 to roam between the cellular network and Wi-Fi networks. Typically when you are connected to a Wi-Fi network, any calls you make are free and of higher audio quality because of the faster speeds. As you move out of Wi-Fi coverage, your S7 hands the call off to the cellular network—and vice versa—allowing your call to continue without interruption. The Phone app indicates when you are using Wi-Fi Calling by placing a Wi-Fi symbol next to the phone icon. If you want to read more about UMA or Wi-Fi Calling, read this online article: http://crackberry.com/saving-call-charges-recession-your-blackberry. The article is on a BlackBerry blog, but the descriptions of the technology still apply.

What Is Video Calling?

Your Galaxy S7 allows you to make video calls to friends that also own a Samsung device that supports video calling. Not all Samsung devices support video calling. Your cellular provider must also allow the video calling feature for this to work.

Call Log

The Log tab shows all activity in the Phone app, including incoming calls, missed calls, and placed calls.

1. Tap Log to see a list of the calls you have missed, placed, and received.

2. Tap a log entry to see more information about the caller.

3. Tap the phone icon to place a call to the caller.

4. Tap the video camera icon to place a video call to the caller.

5. Tap the envelope icon to send an SMS (text message) to the caller.

6. Tap Edit to delete one or more call log entries for this caller.

7. Tap More to view the full contact record for this caller, or add the caller to your Auto Reject List.

Favorites

The Favorites tab shows contacts whom you have marked as favorite and contacts whom you call often.

1. Tap Favorites to see your favorite and frequently called contacts.

2. Tap the contact to place a call to them.

3. Tap the information icon to the right of a favorite contact's name to see all of the information about the contact.

4. Tap Add to add additional favorite contacts from your Contacts list.

5. Tap More to remove favorite contacts, or to reorder their positions on the Favorites tab.

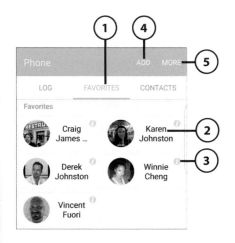

Contacts

The Contacts tab shows all of the contacts that you have added to the Contacts app.

1. Tap Contacts to see all of your contacts.

2. Tap a contact to see all information about that contact.

3. Tap to search for a contact.

4. Tap Create to add a new contact.

5. Tap More to remove contacts or see your Speed Dial screen.

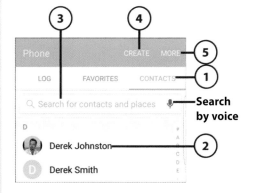

>>>Go Further

SPEED DIAL

Speed dialing is a bit of a holdover from the 1980s and '90s when phones weren't as sophisticated as they are today. However, you might still find it useful to touch and hold one key to call a number. To add or edit your Speed Dial numbers, tap the Menu icon and tap Speed Dial. (Voicemail is already assigned to speed dial 1.) Tap the plus symbol for a numbered entry to add a contact for that Speed Dial number. To use Speed Dial, while the keypad is visible, touch and hold a number associated with a Speed Dial contact. That number will be dialed.

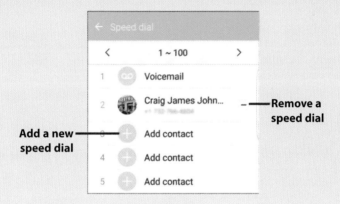

Add a new speed dial

Remove a speed dial

Receiving a Call

When someone phones your Galaxy S7, you can accept the call, reject it, or reject it and send a text message.

Accept a Call

1. When the phone rings, look at the contact name (if it is available) or the phone number (if the contact name is not available) and decide whether to take the call.

2. Swipe the green phone icon to the right to accept the call.

3. Tap to switch the call audio to the speaker.

4. Tap to switch the call audio to a Bluetooth device you have previously paired, such as a headset, your smartwatch, or your vehicle's built-in Bluetooth.

5. Tap to mute the call. Tap again to turn off muting.

6. Tap to show the keypad if you need to type extra numbers after the call is connected.

7. Tap to boost the call volume if the caller speaks softly.

8. Tap to put the call on hold.

9. Tap to create a conference call. See the "Make Conference Calls" task later in this chapter for more information.

10. Swipe to the right to see more options, such as the ability to write a memo that is associated with the caller.

Recent interactions with the caller

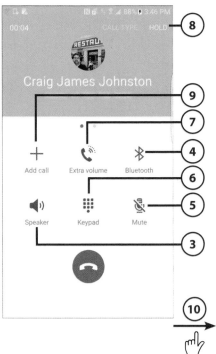

11. Tap to write a memo that is associated with the caller while you're on the call.

12. Tap to open the Calendar app, view the calendar, and create a new appointment if needed.

13. Tap to open the Internet browser and use it while on the call.

14. Tap to send an SMS (text message) to the caller.

15. Tap to send an email to the caller.

16. Tap to show the caller's information in the Contacts app.

17. Swipe to the left to return to the main call screen.

18. Tap to end the call.

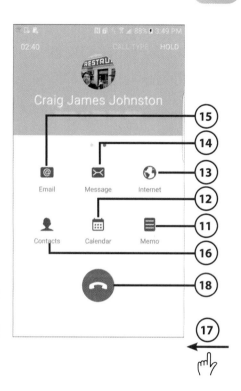

Reject a Call

If you do not want to accept the call, you can reject it so that it goes to your voicemail.

1. When the phone rings, swipe the red phone icon to the left to reject the call.

   The call goes to voicemail, and your Galaxy S7 displays the screen you were using before the call came in.

Reject a Call and Send a Text Message

Instead of simply declining a call and sending it to your voicemail, you can send an SMS (text message) straight back to the caller. Your Galaxy S7 provides a selection of canned messages for general needs. You can also create your own messages or type custom messages for particular calls.

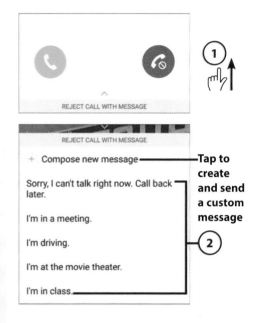

1. When the phone rings, swipe up to display the Reject Call with Message shade.

2. Tap to send one of the canned messages.

Creating Your Own Reject Messages

To create and save your own reject messages, open the Phone app and tap More. On the More menu, tap Settings, Call Blocking, Call-Reject Messages. On the Call-Reject Messages screen, type a new rejection message and tap the plus symbol to create a new rejection message, or tap an existing message to open it for editing. Tap the red minus symbol to delete a rejection message.

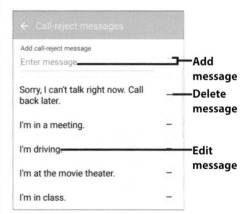

Handle Missed Calls

If you miss a phone call, you can quickly locate it in the Phone app's logs so that you can return it, but you can also take actions on missed calls from the Lock screen or any other screen.

1. Tap to see the missed call from the Lock screen. If you use a Lock screen password or other method of locking your S7, you are required to use that method to unlock your S7 before you can continue.

2. Swipe from left to right across the missed call log entry to call the number back.

3. Swipe from right to left across the missed call log entry to send an SMS (text message) to the caller.

4. Tap the missed call log entry to see its details.

5. Tap to call the person back.

6. Tap to place a video call to the person.

7. Tap to send an SMS (text message) to the caller.

8. Tap to delete one or more call log entries from this caller.

9. Tap to view the caller's full contact information (if you already have the person in your Contacts), or add the number to your Auto Reject list. When someone's number is on the Auto Reject list, your S7 automatically rejects calls from that number.

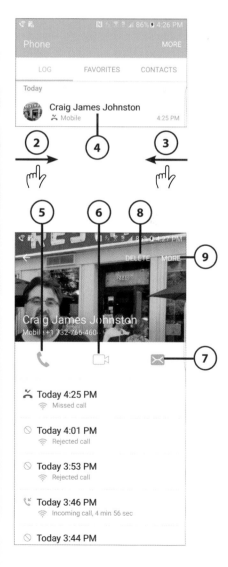

Making Calls

Aside from making a call the traditional way—by using the dialpad to punch in the numbers—you can voice dial a call on your Galaxy S7, or you can make a conference call.

Starting a Call from the Contacts App

Instead of launching the Phone app and then tapping the Contacts tab to go to the Contacts app, you can start a call directly from the Contacts app. Tap Contacts on the Home screen or the Apps screen to launch the Contacts app, tap the contact to display his or her details, and then tap the green phone icon to the right of the number you want to call.

Dial Using Your Voice

Using Google Now, your Galaxy S7 enables you to dial calls using your voice.

1. Say "OK Google." A white box appears on the screen indicating that Google Now is listening for a command.

2. Say "Call," followed by the contact's name; if the contact has multiple phone numbers, say the type of number as well. For example, say "Call Dana Smith mobile" or "Call Craig at Home."

3 Wait while your S7 dials the number. The Dialing screen appears.

Using S Voice Instead of Google Now

By default, Google Now acts as your voice assistance on your Galaxy S7. You wake up Google Now by saying "OK Google." If you would prefer to use Samsung's S Voice, open the S Voice app. It walks you through creating your S Voice Wake Up command. It can be anything, for example "Hi Galaxy." After you have set up S Voice, you can say "Hi Galaxy" and a command.

Using Other Apps During a Call

During a call, you can use most other apps freely, but you cannot play music or video. You can take photos with the Camera app, but you cannot shoot videos. To switch to another app, either use the Recent Apps list or press the Home button and use the Apps screen as usual. While you are using another app, your Galaxy S7 displays a green bar at the top of the screen to remind you that you are in a call. Pull down the Notification panel to control the call or return to it or take actions such as switch to speakerphone, mute, and hang up.

Green bar indicates call is in progress.

Tap to return to your call.

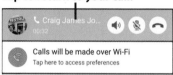

Make Conference Calls

You can quickly turn your current call into a conference call by adding other participants.

1. With a call in progress, tap Add Call on the call screen.

2. Dial the call in the most convenient way. For example, either type out the phone number or dial from the call log, Favorites, or Contacts.

3. Tap to swap between the original call and the one you just added, if you need to.

4. Tap Merge to merge the calls and complete the conference call setup.

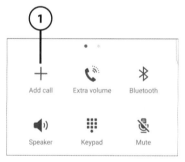

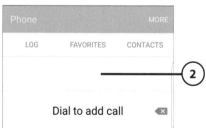

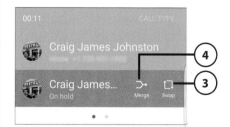

5. Repeat steps 1–4 to add additional callers. The exact number of callers you can have on a conference call is governed by your wireless carrier.

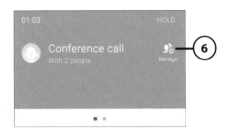

6. Tap Manage if you need to hang up on only one of the conference call parties, or if you need to split one of the parties off the conference call while still keeping them connected and on hold. On some versions of the Galaxy S7, the Manage menu is missing, preventing you from performing steps 6, 7, and 8.

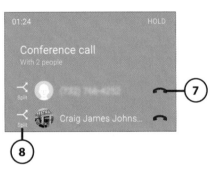

7. Tap the red phone icon to the right of a conference party you want to hang up on and remove from the conference call.

8. Tap Split if you want to remove the party from the conference call, but need to keep them connected to your phone and on hold.

Configuring the Phone App

To make the Phone app work your way, you can configure its settings.

1. Tap More.

2. Tap Settings.

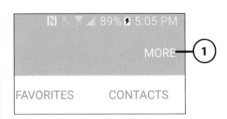

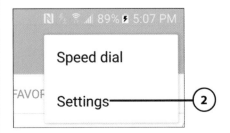

3. Tap to enable or disable the feature that allows you to swipe over a call log entry to either place a call to that number or send a text message to it.

4. Tap to enable or disable the feature that makes the Phone app show only contacts who have phone numbers, and hide contacts that have no phone numbers.

5. Tap to choose certain numbers for which calls will be automatically rejected. Tapping here also lets you edit your canned call rejection messages.

What Does Call Rejection Do?

Your Galaxy S7's call rejection feature allows you to specify certain numbers to automatically reject, or to reject incoming calls that have no number or show as Unknown. Automatically rejecting specific numbers enables you to avoid calls from people you do not want to talk to.

---

6. Tap to choose whether you want to use Voice over LTE (VoLTE) when it is available.

What Is VoLTE?

LTE (or Long-Term Evolution) is the fourth generation of cellular data technology (not to be confused with the slightly faster version of 3G technology that has been incorrectly called 4G for years). VoLTE stands for Voice over LTE. Effectively, your voice call is sent as regular data over the LTE data channel as opposed to over the cellular voice channel. Voice quality is much better due to the higher rate at which the data is transmitted and received, and if the person you are calling also uses VoLTE, you can speak at the same time. Most wireless carriers treat VoLTE as regular voice minutes and don't let it count against your data plan. However, you should verify the situation with your local wireless carrier; otherwise, your data plan might take an unexpected hit.

7. Tap to choose how you want to answer and end calls. You can choose to allow pressing the Home or Power buttons to answer an incoming call. You can also automatically answer an incoming call if you have your S7 connected to a Bluetooth device or your vehicle's built-in Bluetooth.

8. Tap to choose options for vibrations, cell status tones, and alerts during calls. You can choose whether your Galaxy S7 vibrates or plays a tone when someone answers your call and when they hang up. You can also choose to receive or suppress notifications during calls.

9. Tap to choose the ringtone that plays when you receive an incoming call. You can also choose whether you want your phone to vibrate when you receive an incoming call, and what vibration pattern to use.

10. Swipe up for more settings.

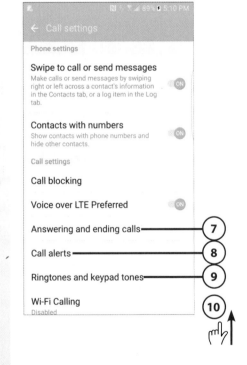

11. Tap to enable or disable Wi-Fi Calling, and choose how you want your S7 to utilize Wi-Fi Calling. You can choose to have your S7 prefer Wi-Fi but use cellular if Wi-Fi is unstable; prefer the cellular network, and only use Wi-Fi if cellular service is unavailable; or only use Wi-Fi for all calls.

12. Tap to see additional settings, including how to handle Caller ID, call forwarding, call waiting, and Fixed Dialing Numbers (FDN). When you tap, the settings are loaded over the wireless network, so you might need to wait a few seconds before they appear.

13. Tap to choose which voicemail service to use (if you have more than one option). If you use Google Voice, it is common to use the Google Voice voicemail system as opposed to the one provided by your wireless carrier.

14. Tap to adjust voicemail settings (if options are available).

15. Tap to choose your ringtone for announcing voicemail.

16. Tap to choose to also vibrate when you are notified of a new voicemail.

17. Tap to save your changes and return to the main phone screen.

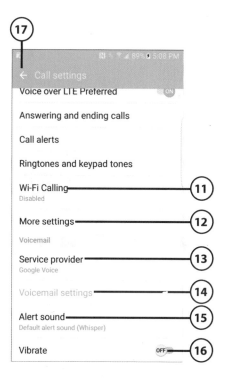

Store, manage, and use all your contacts

Search for contacts on your Galaxy S7

In this chapter, you find out how to add and search contacts and calendar events. Topics in this chapter include the following:

→ Setting up contacts accounts
→ Managing contacts
→ Searching for contacts
→ Linking contacts to social network website accounts
→ Using contacts

Managing Contacts

Your Galaxy S7 is highly capable of helping you organize your busy life. The preinstalled Contacts app helps you improve your daily efficiency by enabling you to manage personal contacts. This chapter takes a close look at what you can do with the Contacts app.

Managing Contacts

The Contacts app enables you to manage all the important information you receive from colleagues, friends, and prospective business associates. Think of your Galaxy S7 as a virtual filing cabinet or Rolodex where you can store contact information such as names, addresses, emails, and notes. If you collect contacts with other social networking services, you can also configure Contacts to sync information between accounts.

Set Up Contacts Accounts

The Galaxy S7 can synchronize its contacts information with multiple accounts, such as Google, Corporate Exchange, other email providers, and sites such as Facebook and Google+. Information on your Galaxy S7 is updated when you make changes to information in your accounts.

1. Tap the Apps icon on the Home screen.

2. Tap the Settings icon.

Where's the Settings Icon?

The default location for the Settings icon is on the second page of the Apps screen, but if you reorganize your app icons, it might eventually end up in a different location. The first time you're looking for it, though, swipe from left to right to find it on the second page.

3. Swipe from right to left in the Settings screen until you open the Personal tab in the menu bar.

4. Tap Accounts.

5. Tap Add Account.

6. Tap an account that you would like to set up. This example uses a Google account.

7. Follow the prompts to set up each account that you would like to add. The accounts you add appear in the Accounts area within the Settings list.

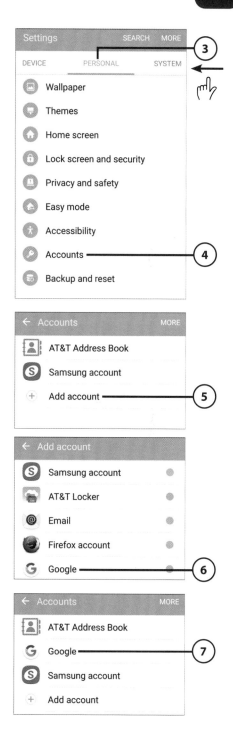

Add Contacts

Using the Contacts app, you can store contact information for family, friends, and colleagues for quick access and to send messages.

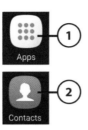

Apps

Contacts

1. Tap the Apps icon on the Home screen.

2. Tap Contacts.

Why Do I See a Data Backup Setup Screen?

After you tap the Contacts icon, you might see a screen asking you if you want to back up your contacts and other phone data to your data carrier's online file storage service. You can choose to set up your backup service or skip setup to continue with step 3 in these instructions.

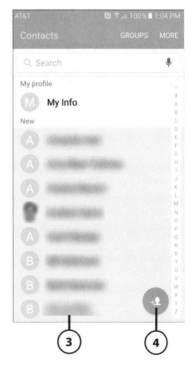

3. You see a list of all contacts.

4. Tap the Add icon to open the Save Contact To window.

Why Can't I Sync Contacts I Add to the Galaxy S7?

The Galaxy S7 can't sync contacts you add to the device itself to any other device to which you connect the Galaxy S7. If you want to sync to other devices, you can add the contact to your online contact database stored in your Samsung, Google, or Microsoft Exchange ActiveSync account.

5. Tap Device to choose whether to save the contact on your phone SIM card, on another account, or to Device so you save the contact on your Galaxy S7. Device is the default storage location.

6. Tap the camera icon to add a contact photo by either selecting a photo stored on your Galaxy S7 or taking a photo with the Galaxy S7 camera. After you select or take the photo, the photo appears to the left of the contact name.

7. Type the first and last name in the Name field.

8. If you want to add the first and last name in different fields, tap the arrow icon located to the right of the Name field to add a Name Prefix, First Name, Middle Name, Last Name, and Name Suffix to the contact. There is no need to use the Shift key on the keyboard to capitalize the name because the Galaxy S7 does this automatically.

9. Tap the plus icon to the right of the Phone section text to add a phone number.

10. Type the phone number in the Phone field starting with the area code.

Don't Worry About Formatting

You don't need to type parentheses or dashes for the phone numbers you enter. The Galaxy S7 formats the number for you.

11. Specify the type of phone number you entered, such as the contact's home phone number, by tapping Mobile to the right of the phone number.

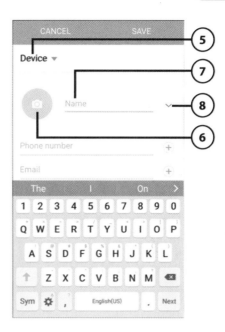

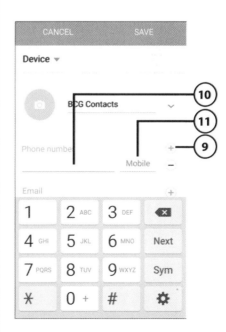

12. Tap the phone number type in the Select Phone Number Type window. After you tap the phone number type, the new type appears to the right of the phone number in the contact screen.

13. Return to the contact screen without making any changes by tapping the Back icon in the menu bar.

14. Tap the plus icon to the right of the Phone header text to add an additional field, or tap the minus icon to remove a field.

15. Close the keyboard by tapping the Back touch button.

16. Tap the plus icon to the right of the Email section text to add an email address.

17. Type the email address in the Email field.

18. Specify the type of email address you entered, such as the contact's work email address, by tapping Home to the right of the email address.

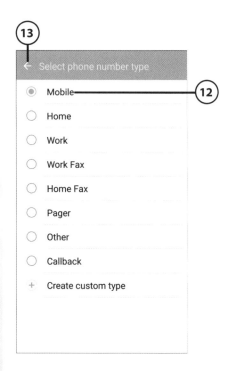

19. Tap the email address type on the Select Email Address Type screen. After you tap the email address type, the new type appears to the right of the email address in the contact screen.

20. Return to the contact screen without making any changes by tapping the Back icon in the menu bar.

21. Tap the plus icon to the right of the Email header text to add an additional field, or tap the minus icon to remove a field.

22. Close the keyboard by tapping the Back touch button.

23. Tap Groups to select a group in the Select Group screen.

24. Tap one or more checkboxes for the groups to which you want to assign a contact. You can select as many as eight groups: ICE-Emergency Contacts, Favorites, Business, Co-Workers, Family, Friends, My Contacts, or Starred in Android.

25. If you select one or more groups and then change your mind, you can undo assignment to one or more groups by tapping the Not Assigned checkbox.

26. Return to the contact screen by tapping the Back icon in the menu bar.

27. Tap More to add more contact information.

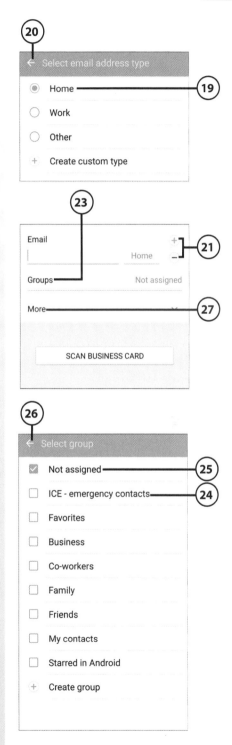

28. Swipe up on the screen to view the first 10 options you can add or change.

29. Tap Ringtone to specify a unique ringtone that sounds when this contact calls you.

30. Swipe up in the screen to view the last two options you can change as well as the Scan Business Card button.

31. Tap Message Tone to specify a unique ringtone that sounds when this contact sends you a text message.

32. Tap Vibration Pattern to specify a unique vibration pattern that you feel when this contact either calls you or sends you a text message.

33. Tap Scan Business Card to open the Galaxy Apps app so you can download and install the SnapBizCard app. SnapBizCard scans the text of a printed business card and then places the scanned text in a new contact record within the Contacts app.

34. For this example, add an event by swiping up on the screen until you see the Event field on the screen.

35. Tap the Add button to the right of the Event field.

36. Tap the Birthday label to choose the type of event you want to add, such as a birthday or anniversary.

37. Select the date by tapping Date and then selecting the date in the Date window.

38. Tap Save to complete the new contact.

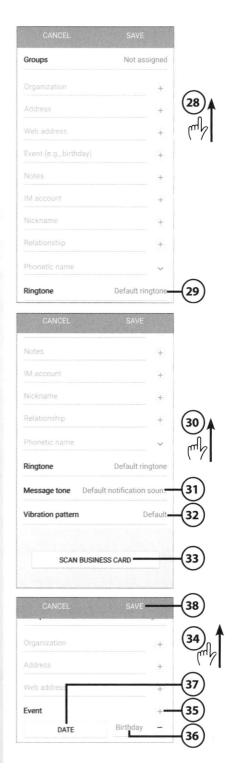

>>>Go Further

UPDATING A CONTACT AND DISPLAYING CONTACTS

You can update a contact by first tapping an existing contact in the Contacts list and then tapping the Edit button located at the upper right of the screen. The contact screen opens so that you can edit or add information.

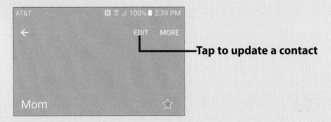

Tap to update a contact

You can control how your contacts are listed by setting sorting and display preferences. After you launch the Contacts app, you can tap the More button located at the upper-right corner of the screen, tap Settings, and then tap Sort By. The Display Contacts By menu enables you to list by First Name (which is the default setting) or by Last Name.

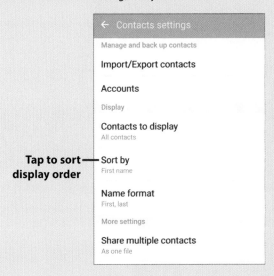

Tap to sort display order

Search for Contacts

Your list of contacts is sure to grow
the longer you have your Galaxy S7.
So how do you search your large list
of contacts for a specific contact?

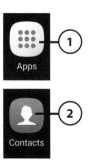

1. Tap the Apps icon on the Home
   screen.

2. Tap Contacts in the Apps screen.

3. Tap the Search field and use the
   keyboard to type the name of
   the contact you are looking for.
   As soon as you begin to type, the
   screen displays the contact that
   most closely reflects what you've
   typed into the field. Continue typing until you have narrowed the
   search.

4. View the contact in its entirety by
   tapping the contact in the list.

Link Contacts

When you synchronize the contacts on
your Galaxy S7 with multiple accounts,
such as the contact information you
have on your Google account, you can
have varying numbers and address
information for a single contact. You can
combine all the contacts' numbers and
addresses in a single contact entry by
linking contacts.

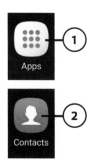

1. Tap the Apps icon on the Home
   screen.

2. Tap Contacts in the Apps screen.
   Your contact information appears
   on the screen.

3. Scroll down the contact list if necessary until you find the contact to which you want to join another contact. Tap the contact name in the list.

4. Tap the More option.

5. Tap Link Contacts in the menu.

6. Swipe down the list if necessary until you see the name of the contact you want to link to the contact you selected in step 3.

7. Tap the name in the list; an orange checkbox with a white checkmark appears to the left of the contact name.

8. Tap Link.

How Many Contacts Can I Link?

You can link as many as nine contacts at one time. As you tap each name in the list, you see the number of contacts you've linked out of the maximum nine you selected in the orange menu bar at the top of the screen. For example, if you see 3/9 in the menu bar, you know you've selected three of the maximum nine contacts you can link.

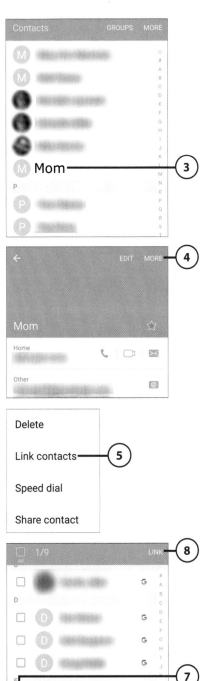

9. The contacts are now linked and the information for both entries in each account has merged.

10. Add another contact by tapping More and then repeating steps 5 through 8.

11. Close the Contact window by tapping the Back icon in the menu bar.

How Do I Unlink Contacts?

Unlink contacts by tapping the linked contact name in the contact list. Next, tap More in the upper-right corner of the screen and then tap Unlink Contacts in the menu. In the Linked Contact window, tap the red minus icon to the right of the contact name you want to unlink. The contact name you unlinked no longer appears in the Linked Contact window. Tap the Back touch button to view the newly unlinked contact's information screen.

Use Contacts

After you have entered a contact in your Galaxy S7, you can utilize a few functions and displays directly from the Contacts page. Start by opening a contact's record.

1. Tap the star icon to the right of the contact name to set that contact as a favorite. The star color changes from gray to gold, which signifies the contact is a favorite.

2. Return to the contact list by tapping the Back icon in the menu bar.

3. Tap the Groups button to view the list of contacts you have assigned to a group.

4. Press and hold your finger on a contact's name in the contact list. After a second, an orange checkbox with a white checkmark appears to the left of the contact name.

5. Tap the Share button to open the Share Namecard With/Via window.

6. Select how you want to share the contact in the Share Contact As window. Tap vCard file (VCF) or Text.

7. Select how to share the contact information. Choices are Android Beam, your carrier mail service if you have one, Bluetooth, Google Drive, in an email message sent using the Email or Gmail apps, Facebook, or Hangouts. You can also copy the information to the Clipboard to paste into another app.

8. Tap the page icon to view more sharing options on the second page within the window.

9. Paste the contact information into the Memo app, share the information in an email message using the Messages app, or share the information directly with another device using Wi-Fi Direct.

10. Close the window without sharing your selected contact by tapping the Back touch button.

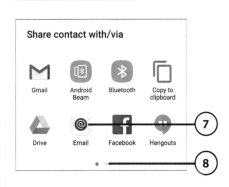

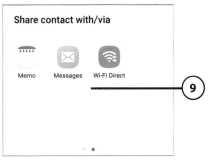

Track your
appointments
and events

Add events and
tasks to your
calendar

In this chapter, you find out how to organize your daily schedule and add calendar events within the preinstalled Calendar app. Topics in this chapter include the following:

→ Creating calendar events
→ Using calendar views
→ Adding and managing tasks

Using the Calendar

The preinstalled Calendar app on the Galaxy S7 helps you improve your daily efficiency by enabling you to schedule and stay apprised of important appointments. This chapter takes a close look at how you can use the Calendar app to help keep your daily life on track.

Managing Your Busy Schedule

The Calendar app enables you to manage all your appointments and events from one convenient location. Calendar enables you to view a busy schedule in multiple views such as Day, Week, Month, Year, and Agenda. You can also instruct Calendar to send you a reminder, in the form of an alert, before an event to help ensure that you never miss a meeting and are always on time.

Create Calendar Events

Your Galaxy S7 was designed for you
to be mobile while still enabling you
to manage the important stuff, such as
doctor appointments, business meetings, and anniversaries. The Calendar
app enables you to add important event
dates to calendars to help ensure that
you do not overlook them.

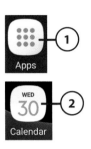

1. Tap the Apps icon on the Home
   screen.

2. Tap Calendar.

3. By default, the calendar opens
   to the Month and Agenda view.
   The current date is indicated by
   a green circle around the date.
   Dates in the month that have
   events associated with them have
   a green dot below the date.

4. Tap the date for which you want
   to add an event. A green circle
   appears around the date.

5. If the date has one or more events
   associated with it, such as the day's
   weather forecast, the information
   appears in the Agenda window
   below the date. Close the window
   by tapping and holding on the
   separator bar and then swiping
   down to the bottom of the screen.

6. Tap the + button in the lower-
   right corner of the screen to open
   the Appointment screen.

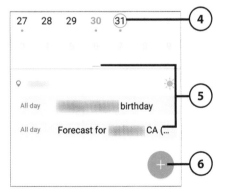

How Do I Open the Agenda Window Again?

If you closed the Agenda window, you
can open it again by tapping and holding
on the bottom of the screen and then
swiping up until you see the entire window in the bottom third of the screen.

7. The Title field is selected by default. Type a title for the event in the field.

8. Tap the palette icon to select an event color in the Select Event Color window.

9. Slide the All Day slider from left (Off) to right (On) if the event will happen all day.

10. Tap the date and time in the Start box to enter the start date and time of the event. You can also use the controls in the Set Date and Time window to designate an event for a future date and not just the date you specified in step 4. When you tap the date and time in the Start field, the Calendar window appears so you can select a future date and time.

11. The current month appears in the calendar, and the date you set for the event in step 4 is highlighted in the calendar. Change the event date by swiping left and right within the calendar to view months and dates and then tap the date for the event within the calendar.

12. Swipe up and down within the hour and minute tiles to enter the start time for the event.

13. Tap the time of day tile to change the time between AM and PM.

14. Tap Done.

15. Tap the date and time in the End box to bring up the controls and set the date and time for the event as you did when you set the date in the Start field.

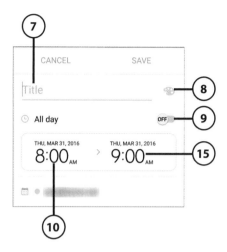

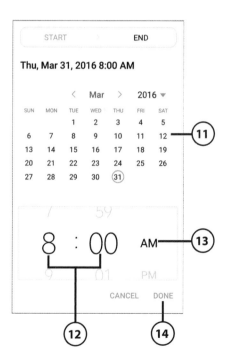

Can I Set the Start and End Times Within the Calendar Window?

When you set the start or end times for an appointment, the Start or End buttons are highlighted in green at the top of the Calendar window depending on the time you're editing. If you want to change the start or end time without exiting the window, tap the white Start or End button at the top of the window to change the start or end time, respectively.

16. Tap the email address to change the account that contains the calendar to which you want to add the event.

17. Tap the account in the Calendar window. Since this is an event, you can choose from one of the three options in the Save as Event section: My Calendars, which is the calendar stored on the Galaxy S7, Samsung Calendar, or another calendar, such as the one stored in your Google account.

18. Tap the Reminder button to choose an alarm time for the event.

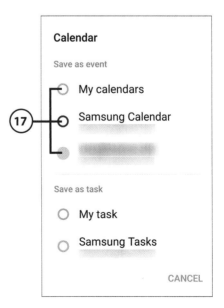

19. Tap Notification to have the event reminder appear as a notification, or you can send the notification to your email account.

20. Tap the time you want the alarm to appear. You can select from five options from On Time (the time the event starts) to one day before the start time. You can also customize the alarm time by tapping Customize and then setting the time in the Reminder window.

21. Remove the alarm by tapping the red minus icon.

22. Tap the green plus icon at the right of the Reminder field to add another notification that will appear at a different time and/or be delivered in a different manner.

23. Tap the Location field to add a location for the event.

24. If you want to find the location in the Maps app, tap Map to the right of the field. You find out more about using the Maps app in Chapter 7, "Google Now and Navigation Using Google Maps."

25. Tap Repeat if you need to set a repeating cycle for the event.

26. Tap Invitees to add names from your contacts.

27. Tap Notes to type a description for the event.

28. Make the event private (that is, viewable only by you) by tapping Privacy. Otherwise, the event is public, so anyone who sees your calendar can view the event.

29. Tap Time Zone to change the time zone for the event.

30. Tap Save to complete the event and save it to your calendar.

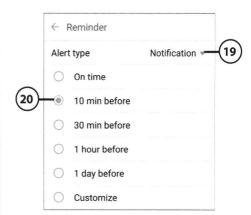

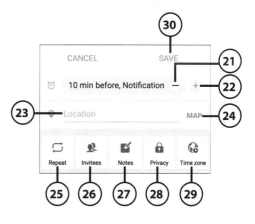

How Do I View the Reminder in the Status Bar?

When you receive a reminder, you get an audio reminder and also see a reminder icon at the left side of the Status bar. Tap and hold your finger on the top edge of the screen and swipe down to open the Quick Settings and Notification screen. The reminder displays at the bottom of the Notification area.

Use Calendar Views

The four views in which you can see the contents of your calendar are Year, Month and Agenda, Week, and Day. This section examines each view.

Year View

The Year view shows the entire calendar year. Open the Year view by tapping the calendar view, such as the month, at the left side of the menu bar and then tapping Year in the list.

The current year appears above the calendar. Swipe from left to right to view the calendar for the previous year, or swipe from right to left to view a calendar for the following year. When you change the year, your selected year appears at the left side of the menu bar. Tap Today in the menu bar to highlight the current date in the calendar.

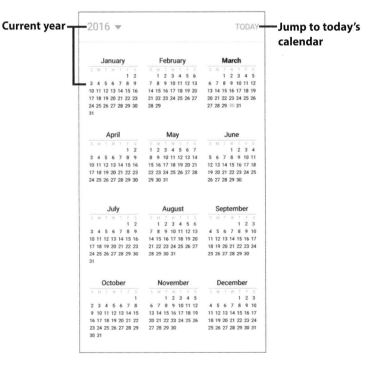

Current year 2016 ▼   TODAY **Jump to today's calendar**

Day View

The Day view is composed of a list of events over the current day. These events are blocked for the amount of time you specified when you set up the event. Open the Day view by tapping the calendar view, such as the year or the current month, at the left side of the menu bar. Then tap Day in the menu.

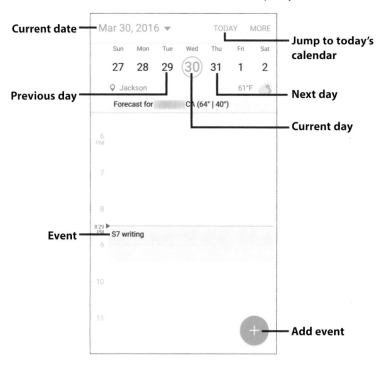

You can press your finger to the list and flick up or down to scroll through the list of events. All events scheduled with a duration of All Day are located at the very top of the list.

Tap Today in the menu bar to open the calendar for the current date. The timeline located just under the menu bar enables you to tap specific days three days before and three days after the current day. Swipe to the left or right within the timeline to move to the previous or following week, respectively. Tap Today in the menu bar to return to the current day's schedule no matter where you are in the calendar.

You can tap an event in the window to view notes, edit the entry, delete the event, or share it as a VCS or text file using your phone carrier's mail service (if any), Android Beam, Bluetooth, OneNote, in a memo, on the clipboard, the Google Drive online file storage service, the Email or Gmail apps, Facebook or Google+, the Memo app, the Messages or Hangouts instant messaging apps, Samsung Quick Connect, or Wi-Fi.

Week View

The Week view is arranged into seven-day parts. Open the Week view by tapping the calendar view, such as the year or the current day, at the left side of the menu bar. Then tap Week in the menu.

Within the current week row, swipe right and left to view the previous and following week, respectively. Tap Today in the menu bar to highlight the current date.

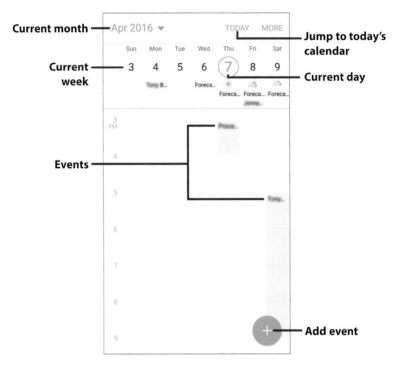

Each event for that week is found in its respective scheduled day block. You can tap an event title within the day block to view notes, edit the entry, delete the event, or share it as a VCS or text file using your carrier's mail service (if any), Android Beam, Bluetooth, on the clipboard, the Google Drive online file storage service, the Email or Gmail apps, Facebook, the Memo app, the Messages or Hangouts instant messaging apps, or Wi-Fi Direct.

Month and Agenda View

The Month and Agenda view provides a broad view of events for a given month. Month and Agenda view contains a monthly calendar with an agenda of events and tasks listed within each calendar date box. Open the Month and Agenda view by tapping the calendar view, such as the year or the current week, at the left side of the menu bar. Then tap Month and Agenda View in the menu.

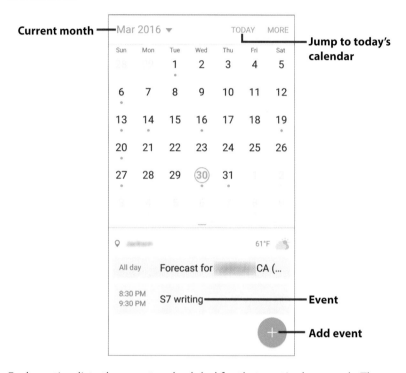

Current month ——— Mar 2016

Jump to today's calendar

Event

Add event

Each section lists the events scheduled for that particular month. The current day block you are viewing is highlighted within the calendar section. Any event designated as an All Day Event is highlighted in the day block of the Calendar view.

Tap Today in the menu bar to highlight the current date in the calendar. The current month appears above the calendar. Swipe from left to right to view the calendar for the previous month, or swipe from right to left to view a calendar for the following month. When you change the year, your selected month appears in the upper-left corner of the screen.

Tap the date to view the agenda for the day in the Agenda window. You can close the window by tapping and holding on the separator bar and then swiping down to the bottom of the screen.

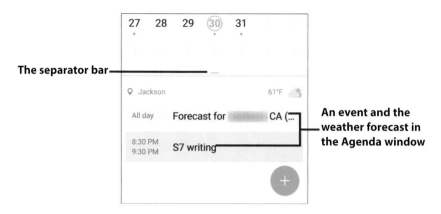

The separator bar

An event and the weather forecast in the Agenda window

You can tap an event in the window to view notes, edit the entry, delete the event, or share it as a VCS or text file using your phone carrier's mail service (if any), Android Beam, Bluetooth, OneNote, in a memo, on the clipboard, the Google Drive online file storage service, the Email or Gmail apps, Facebook or Google+, the Memo app, the Messages or Hangouts instant messaging apps, Samsung Quick Connect, or Wi-Fi.

View More Event Options

Within the Month and Agenda, Week, and Day views you can access more options for finding events and tasks, managing your calendars, and changing settings.

1. Tap More in the menu bar.

2. Tap Search to open the Search screen and search for one or more events.

3. Tap Manage Calendars to open the Manage Calendars screen so you can add an account with a calendar to create a combined calendar view across all accounts. You can also determine what information appears in your agenda for each day, such as the day's weather forecast.

4. Tap Settings to change app setting information including showing or hiding declined event information.

Add a Task to Your Calendar

It's easy to add a task to your calendar so you can be reminded about deadlines for getting something important done.

1. Tap the current view information, such as the year or the current month, at the left side of the menu bar.

2. Tap Tasks in the menu to open the Tasks screen.

3. In the window, tap in the Enter New Task field.

4. Type a title for the task in the Enter New Task field. When you start typing you see buttons and options appear around the field.

5. Tap Today to set the current day as the due date.

Do I Have to Retype a Recurring Task Title Every Time I Add a New Task?

If you entered a task title previously, when you start typing you'll see a list of previously entered task titles underneath the Today and Tomorrow icons. You can tap the title in the list to save yourself time and effort.

6. Tap Tomorrow to set the next day as the due date.

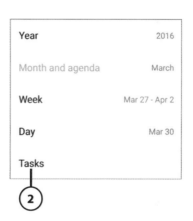

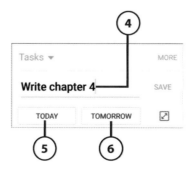

Setting a Different Due Date

See steps 8–12 for information about setting a due date other than the current or next day's date.

7. Save the task by tapping Save. If you don't specify a due date, you'll see the task in the task list under the No New Date section. The last two sections in this chapter explain more about the task list.

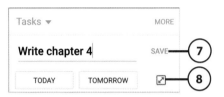

8. Tap the Expand icon to view and change all details within the task.

9. Tap Set Date to enter the due date for the task.

10. Tap the left or right arrows on either side of the current month to move to the previous month or following month, respectively. You can also swipe to the left and right in the calendar to move to the following or previous month, respectively.

11. If you want to set the due date in a different year, tap the year. You can swipe up and down in the pop-up menu to view past and future years as well as the current year. When you find the year, tap it in the menu.

12. When you see the calendar for the month in which you want to set the due date, tap the due date in the calendar. The date is high-lighted with a green circle.

13. Tap Done.

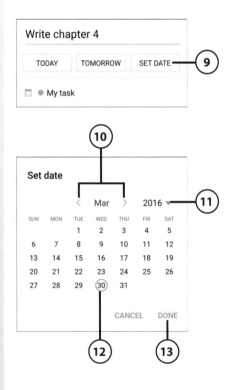

14. Tap My Task to open the Task window and determine where you want to store the task. By default, you store tasks on your Galaxy S7, but you can store tasks in another account such as your Samsung account.

15. Tap Reminder to open the Reminder window and set a reminder type. You can set a reminder on the due date or set a customized reminder, which is on a date of your choosing.

16. Tap Notes to type a description for the task.

17. Tap Priority and then tap High in the Priority tile that appears. In the menu, you can change the priority level to High, Medium, or Low. The default priority is High.

18. Tap Save to complete the task and save it to your calendar.

View the Task List and Remove Tasks

After you save the task, the task appears on the date within the calendar. Tasks are categorized by due date, and the task list is sorted from newest to oldest. That is, tasks with the closest due date appear at the top of the list, and future tasks appear further down the list.

View the task details in the Task screen by tapping the task in the list. When you complete the task or you decide to remove it from the list, tap the checkbox to the left of the task name. After you tap the checkbox, tap the Delete All button below the Enter New Task field.

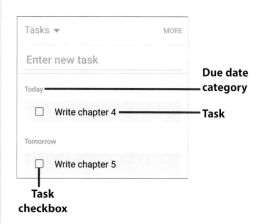

Due date category

Task

Task checkbox

How Can I Keep the Task After I Tap the Checkbox?

If you tapped the checkbox next to a task and decide that you don't want to delete it, just tap the checkbox again. The check-mark in the checkbox and the Delete All button disappear.

View More Task Options

As with the Month and Agenda, Week, and Day views, you can access more options in the Tasks view so you can search for events and tasks, manage your calendars, and change settings. You can also delete one or more tasks from the list as well as share your tasks using a variety of methods.

1. Tap More in the menu bar.

2. Tap Delete to open the Delete screen and then select one or more tasks you want to delete. After you select one or more tasks, tap Delete in the menu bar that appears at the top of the Delete screen.

3. Tap Share to open the Select Tasks screen and select one, several, or all your tasks to share. You can share the task using your phone carrier's mail service (if any), Android Beam, Bluetooth, OneNote, the Google Drive online file storage service, the Email or Gmail apps, the Messages app, Samsung Quick Connect, or Wi-Fi.

4. Tap Search to open the Search screen and search for one or more events or tasks.

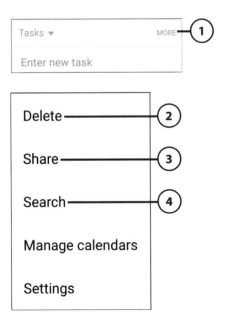

5. Tap Manage Calendars to open the Manage Calendars screen so you can add an account with a calendar to create a combined task view across all accounts. You can also hide tasks on your device or that are stored in other accounts such as your Samsung account.

6. Tap Settings to change app setting information including changing how you are notified of upcoming task due dates including what notification sound plays and/or if you want the Galaxy S7 to vibrate when there's a task coming due.

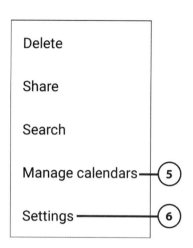

Delete

Share

Search

Manage calendars —⑤

Settings —⑥

>>>Go Further

EDIT A TASK

When you want to edit a task, tap the task name within the Tasks screen. You can also edit a task from within the Month and Agenda, Week, or Day views by tapping the task name below the current date or the week you're viewing, depending on the calendar view.

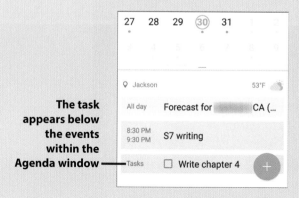

The task appears below the events within the Agenda window

Learn how to browse the Web and view websites using the built-in Internet app

The Galaxy S7 comes with two built-in browsers: Google Chrome and Samsung's Internet app. In this chapter, you see how to browse the Web using the Samsung Internet app, which is designed specifically so you can get the most from the Web on your Galaxy S7. This chapter covers the following topics:

→ Browsing to a URL
→ Searching the Web
→ Viewing web pages
→ Bookmarking websites
→ Returning to previously visited websites
→ Filling in web forms
→ Copying text and images from web pages

Browsing the Web

The Galaxy S7 is a great tool for viewing web pages, whether you're at home or you're on the go. No matter which Galaxy S7 model you use, the screen is much larger than a mobile phone, so you can see more on the Galaxy S7 screen. Because you can touch the screen, you can interact with web content in ways that a computer typically cannot.

Browsing to a URL

It's likely that you already know how to browse to different web pages in your favorite web browser on your computer. The Internet app on the Galaxy S7 works much the same as the browser on your computer, but there are some differences.

1. On the Home screen, tap Internet.

2. Swipe down the screen to view the Address field.

3. Tap the Address field at the top of the screen. The keyboard opens at the bottom of the screen so you can type a Uniform Resource Locator (URL), which can be a website name or a specific page in a website.

4. Start typing a URL, such as samsung.com or play.google.com. You can also tap an icon within the Quick Access site list that appears below the Address field.

5. Tap Go on the keyboard when you finish typing.

Tips for Typing a URL

The Internet app doesn't require you to type the "http://" or the "www." at the beginning of the URL. For example, if you type samsung.com or www.samsung.com, you still go to the Samsung Home web page. However, there might be some instances when you need to type "http://" or even "https://" (for a secure web page) at the beginning of the URL. If you do, the Internet app lets you know so that you can type in the "http://" or "https://" in the Address field.

Searching the Web

The Internet app makes it easy for you to search the Web, so you don't need to know every URL of every web page out there (which is good considering there are literally billions of web pages). As you type, the Internet app suggests search terms you've used in the past as well as search terms you might be looking for.

1. On the Home screen, tap Internet.

2. Tap the Address field at the top of the screen. The keyboard opens at the bottom of the screen so you can type the URL. Start typing your search term. As you type, a list appears underneath the address bar with suggestions. You can stop typing at any time and swipe through the list to find your search term; tap the search term to select it and start the search.

3. If the list doesn't include what you're looking for, open the Google search page by tapping Go in the keyboard.

4. Tap any link on the Google search results page to go to that web page.

>>>Go Further

TIPS FOR SEARCHING THE WEB

You can search deeper within Google itself. For example, if you put a + in front of a search term, you're telling Google that you require the word in the search results. If you put quotes around a search term ("term"), you're telling Google that you want to search for results that contain that term. Scroll to the bottom of the search page and then tap Help to get more information about how you can get the most from your Google searches. You then see the Search Help screen where you can swipe up and down the screen to view help articles in a variety of topics.

If you look at the top of Google's search results page, you see a menu bar so you can search for more than text terms, including Images and Videos. Swipe from right to left within the menu bar so you can search a variety of other areas within Google.

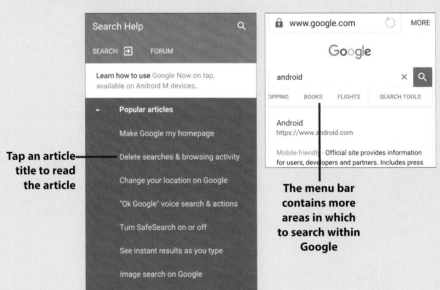

Tap an article title to read the article

The menu bar contains more areas in which to search within Google

Viewing Web Pages

After you open a website, you can control what you view on the web page in several ways. These techniques enable you to access the entire web page and navigate between web pages in the Internet app.

1. Navigate to a web page using one of the two methods described in the previous tasks in this chapter.

2. As you view a page, you can drag up and down the page with your finger. You can also flick with your finger to scroll quickly. After you flick, the screen scrolls, decelerates, and then comes to a stop.

3. Zoom in by pinching out on the screen. Zoom out by pinching in on the screen.

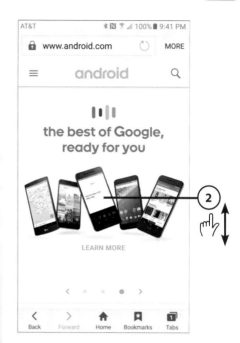

Why Can't I Zoom In and Out on a Web Page?

Many websites have pages that are optimized for reading on a mobile device. What's more, many websites can automatically detect the device you're using to view the website and will load pages that are maximized for best use on your screen. When you're viewing a website page designed for a smartphone like the Galaxy S7, you can't zoom in and out on the page because the page is already sized to the dimensions of your screen.

4. While you're zoomed in, you can touch and drag left, right, up, and down to view different parts of the web page.

5. Move to another web page from a link in the current web page by tapping a link. Links are usually an underlined or colored piece of text, but they can also be pictures or images that look like buttons.

Hunting for Links

Unfortunately, it isn't always easy to figure out which parts of a web page are links and which ones aren't. Back in the early days of the Web, all links were blue and underlined. As web page elements have become more enhanced over time, it's now more common to find links in any color and any text style. What's more, graphics that are links aren't underlined, either.

On a computer's web browser, it's easy to find out which element is a link when you move the mouse pointer over the link because the pointer changes shape. In Android, there is no cursor, so you can't find out if a web page element is a link unless you tap it and see what happens.

Working with Bookmarks

As you browse websites, you might want to save some of the websites in a list of your favorites so you can go back to them later. In browser parlance, this saving process is called "bookmarking." If you find there are websites that you don't visit anymore or that go to obsolete or missing web pages, you can delete a bookmark from the Bookmarks list or from the History list.

Create a Bookmark

1. Navigate to any page in the Internet app.

2. Swipe down the screen to view the Address bar at the top of the screen and the menu bar at the bottom of the screen.

3. Tap Bookmarks to open the Bookmarks screen.

4. Add a bookmark by tapping Add.

5. Edit the title of the bookmark. The official title of the web page is filled in and highlighted for you, but you can change the name by typing the new name using the keyboard. To change the folder in which the bookmark is stored, proceed with step 6. Otherwise, skip to step 11.

6. To change the folder in which the bookmark is stored, tap the folder name, which is Bookmarks in this example.

7. Create a new bookmarks folder by tapping Create.

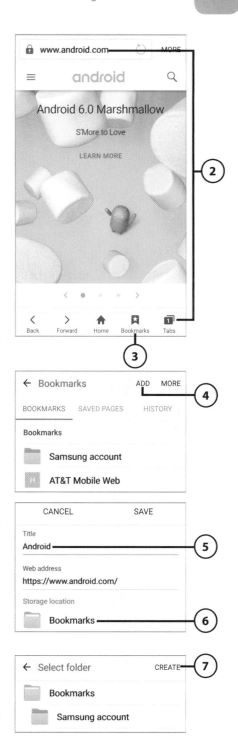

8. Tap the Enter Folder Name field and then type the name of your new folder.

9. Tap Save.

10. Tap the name of the folder into which you want to place the bookmark.

11. Tap Save.

12. Tap the new folder name in the folder list; the new bookmark appears within the folder on the screen.

13. Tap Bookmarks to return to the main Bookmarks folder.

Should I Edit a Bookmark Title?

Because the titles of web pages are usually long and descriptive, it's a good idea to shorten the title to something you can recognize easily in your bookmarks list. Every bookmark also includes a thumbnail picture of what the web page looks like so you can identify the bookmark more easily. If you would rather view your bookmarks by title, tap the Edit button at the bottom of the Bookmark window. In the Bookmark screen, tap the Menu icon at the right side of the menu bar and then tap List View in the menu.

Delete a Bookmark from the Bookmarks List

1. Tap Bookmarks in the menu bar at the bottom of the Internet screen as described in the "Create a Bookmark" task. In the Bookmarks screen, tap the folder (and, if necessary, the subfolder) that contains the bookmark.

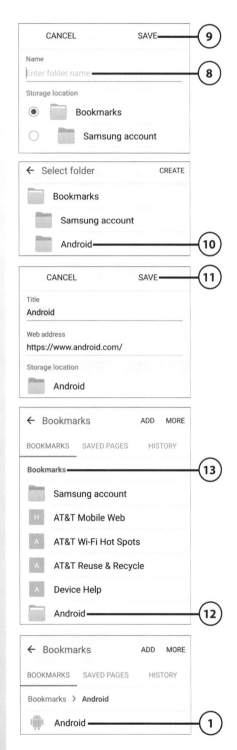

2. Tap and hold your finger on the bookmark you want to delete until a violet checkbox with a white checkmark appears to the left of the bookmark.

3. Delete the bookmark instantly by tapping Delete.

Delete a Bookmark from the History List

1. Tap Bookmarks in the menu bar at the bottom of the Internet screen.

2. In the Bookmarks screen, tap the History tab. This brings up a list of web pages you've viewed recently.

3. Tap and hold your finger on the website entry you want to delete until a violet checkbox with a white checkmark appears to the left of the bookmark.

4. Tap Delete.

5. The website no longer appears in the list of web pages.

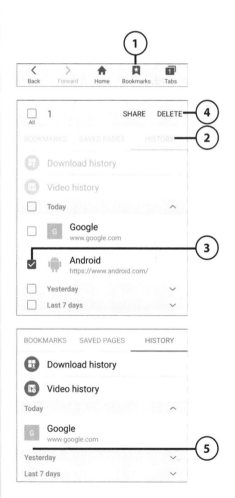

Sync Your Bookmarks

You can sync the bookmarks in your favorite web browser on your desktop or laptop computer with the Internet app so you have maximum control over your bookmarks. You can read more about syncing your Galaxy S7 in Chapter 11, "Sharing and Synchronizing Data."

Returning to Previously Visited Pages

It's easy to return to the last page you visited in the Internet app—just press the Back button. As you keep pressing the Back button, you keep going back to pages you visited. In the History page, the Internet app also keeps a list of all web pages you've visited during your browsing session.

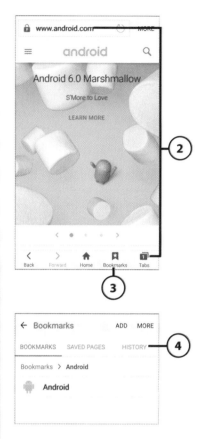

Browsing Forward

Like with any web browser, you can browse more recent pages you've viewed in your current browsing session by tapping the Forward button, which is the right-arrow button immediately to the right of the Back button.

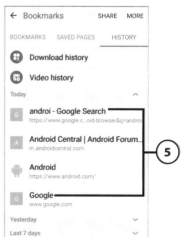

1. Visit several web pages in the Internet app if you haven't done so already.

2. Swipe down the screen to view the Address bar at the top of the screen and the menu bar at the bottom of the screen.

3. Tap Bookmarks.

4. Tap the History tab in the Bookmarks screen.

5. The list of web pages you visited for the current date appears within the Today section.

Tips for Using History

If you want to hide the history for a specific day so you can see history for another day, tap the header for the specific day. For example, if you want to hide all the web pages for today, tap the Today header above the first web page in the Today list. The Today header is still visible, but you won't see the list of web pages. You can view the web pages again by tapping the Today header.

You can also clear the entire history database by tapping More at the right side of the menu bar that appears at the top of the screen. In the menu, tap Clear History.

Filling in Web Forms

On many web pages, you are asked to fill in forms, such as for signing up for a company's email newsletter or to get more information about a product. Filling out web forms on your Galaxy S7 is similar to filling out forms on a computer's web browser, but there are differences.

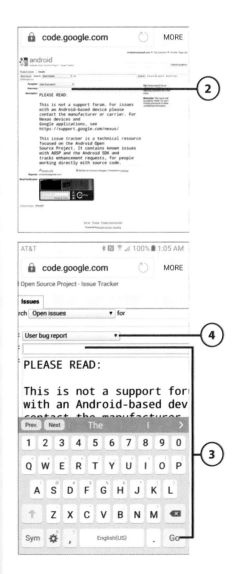

1. Navigate to a page that you know contains a form. (The sample page is at http://code.google.com/p/android/issues/entry.)

2. Tap in a text box.

3. The keyboard appears at the bottom of the screen. Use the keyboard to type text into the box; the screen enlarges so you can see the text box more easily. Tap the Go button when you finish typing.

4. Select an item in a pull-down menu by tapping the box.

5. Tap an item in the menu to select it. If the menu list is long, touch and drag up and down in the menu window to view more selections.

6. The menu closes and the selected item appears in the field.

Special Menus

Some websites use special menus that are built from scratch. In these cases, the menu looks exactly like the one you get when you view the web page on a computer. If the web page is well constructed, it should work fine on the Galaxy S7. However, it might be a little more difficult to make a selection.

Copying Text and Images from Web Pages

The Internet app treats web pages like other documents. That is, you can copy text and images from a web page you view in a browser to another app.

Copy a Block of Text

You can select text from web pages to copy and paste into other documents such as email messages or your own text documents.

1. Navigate to a web page in the Internet app if you haven't done so already.

2. Hold down your finger on the first word in the block of text and then release your finger. The first word is highlighted in blue with "handles" at the beginning and end of the word.

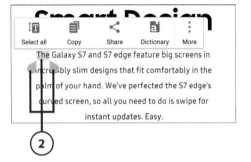

3. Hold down your finger on the bottom handle (the one on the right side of the word) and drag over the text you want to copy. When you are finished, release your finger. The selected text is highlighted in blue.

4. In the pop-up menu that appears above the selected text, tap Copy. Android informs you that the text has been copied to the clipboard. You can now go to another application, such as Gmail (or an email form on another web page), and paste the text into a text area. For example, in Gmail you tap and hold on the cursor in the message for a second or two and then tap Paste in the pop-up menu that appears above the cursor.

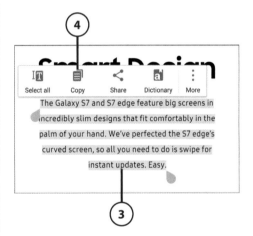

Copy an Image

In addition to being able to copy and paste text from the Internet app, you can also copy images from a web page and save them to an email message or a photo collection.

1. Go to a web page that includes an image on the page.

2. Tap and hold your finger on that image for a couple of seconds and then release your finger. The image menu window appears on the screen.

3. Tap Save Image. This saves your image to the Galaxy S7 so you can view and use it in any app where you select images from your photo albums. Note that the menu options may differ depending on the image you select.

Why Do I See Save Instead of Save Image?

You see the Save Image option for an image after you select an image that has a web page link included. If there is no link included with an image, then you see a smaller image menu window with three options: Save, Copy, and View. Tap Save to save the image to your Galaxy S7.

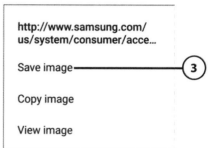

4. As the file downloads, the download icon appears in the Status bar.

5. Hold your finger on the Status bar and swipe down to open the Quick Settings and Notification screen.

6. Swipe through the notification area if necessary and then tap the image filename to open the file in the Gallery or Photos app.

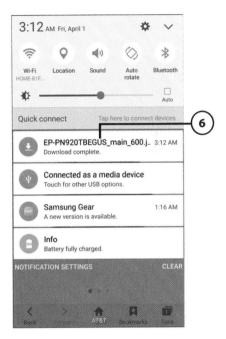

Gmail and other
personal email

Personal and
company email

Text
messages

In this chapter, you discover your Galaxy S7's email applications for Gmail and other accounts, such as POP3, IMAP, and even Microsoft Exchange. In addition, you discover how to use the Messages app for text messaging. Topics include the following:

→ Sending and receiving email
→ Working with attachments
→ Sending and receiving text messages
→ Sending and receiving multimedia messages

Email and Text Messages

Your Galaxy S7 has two email programs: the Gmail app—which works with Gmail, POP3, and IMAP email accounts—and the Email app that works with POP3, IMAP, and Microsoft Exchange (corporate email) accounts. In addition, you can use the Messages app to send and receive text messages

Gmail

When you first set up your Galaxy S7, you set up a Gmail account. The Gmail application enables you to have multiple Gmail accounts, which is useful if you have a business account and a personal account. If you don't want to add a second Gmail account, you can skip this section.

Add a Google Account

When you first set up your Galaxy S7, you added your first Google (Gmail) account, but you might have other Gmail accounts that you'd also like to access through your Galaxy S7. The following steps describe how to add a second account.

1. Pull down the Notification bar and tap the Settings icon.

2. Tap Accounts.

3. Tap Add Account.

4. Tap Google.

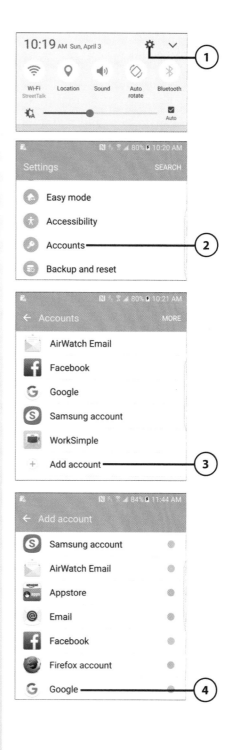

5. Enter your existing Google account name. This is your Gmail address.

6. Tap Next.

What If I Don't Have a Second Google Account?

If you don't already have a second Google account but want to set one up, in step 5, tap Create a New Account. Your Galaxy S7 walks you through the steps of creating a new Google account.

7. Enter your existing Google password.

8. Tap Next.

9. Tap Accept.

10. Select No Thanks and tap Continue to bypass setting up payment information for Google Wallet for this Google account. Right now you just want to set up the email account.

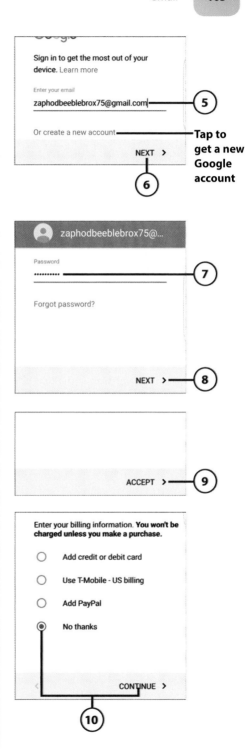

Sign in to get the most out of your device. Learn more

Enter your email
zaphodbeeblebrox75@gmail.com —— 5

Or create a new account —— **Tap to get a new Google account**

NEXT >

6

zaphodbeeblebrox75@...

Password
·········· —— 7

Forgot password?

NEXT > —— 8

ACCEPT > —— 9

Enter your billing information. **You won't be charged unless you make a purchase.**

○ Add credit or debit card

○ Use T-Mobile - US billing

○ Add PayPal

◉ No thanks

CONTINUE >

10

Change What Synchronizes to Your S7

When you finish setting up your new Google account, the choices of what to synchronize to your S7 are made for you. If you want to make changes later, tap Settings, Accounts, Google, the Google account that you want to change, and tap the on/off switch next to each item to enable or disable synchronizing that item.

Why Multiple Google Accounts?

You are probably wondering why you would want multiple Google accounts. Isn't one good enough? Actually, it is not that uncommon to have multiple Google accounts. It can be a way to compartmentalize your life between work and play. You might run a small business using one account, but email only friends with another. Your Galaxy S7 supports multiple accounts, but still enables you to interact with them in one place.

Add a POP3/IMAP Account

Unlike previous versions of the Gmail app, the latest version supports the non-Gmail account types of POP3 and IMAP. If you don't want to add a POP3 or IMAP account to the Gmail app, you can skip this section.

1. Pull down the Notification bar and tap the Settings icon.

2. Tap Accounts.

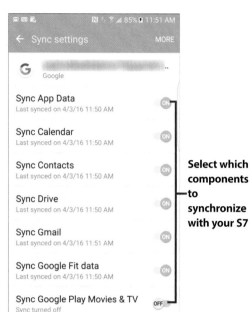

Select which components to synchronize with your S7

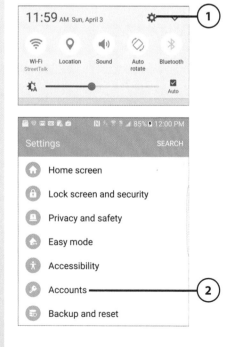

3. Tap Add Account.

4. Tap Personal (IMAP) or Personal (POP3). This example uses an IMAP account type. However, the steps are the same for a POP3 account type.

5. Enter your IMAP account's email address.

6. Tap Next.

What Is Manual Setup?

If you are using an email service provider that is not well known, or you are using email from your personal domain, the Gmail app may not be able to automatically work out the server settings. In that situation you might want to tap Manual Setup, which enables you to enter all information manually.

7. Enter the password for the email account you are adding.

8. Tap Next.

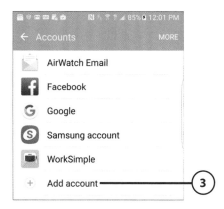

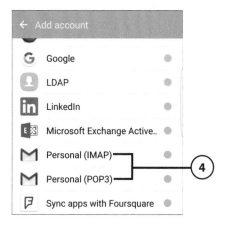

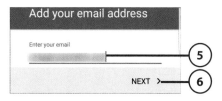

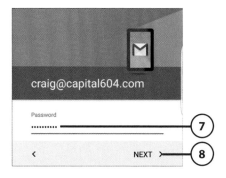

9. Verify the incoming server name and change if needed.

10. Verify the port number and change if needed.

11. Verify the security type and change if needed.

12. Tap Next.

13. Verify the outgoing server name and change if needed.

14. Verify the port number and change if needed.

15. Verify the security type and change if needed.

16. Check the box if your email provider requires that you use your username and password when sending email. This is almost always the case.

17. Tap Next.

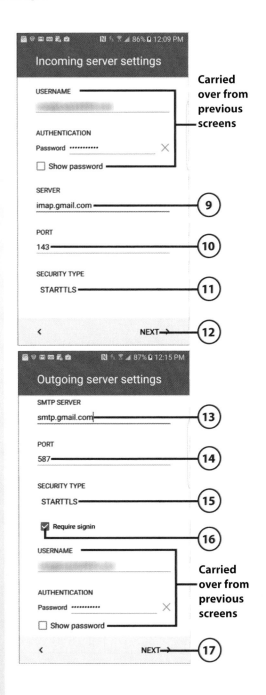

18. Tap to choose how often the Gmail app automatically looks for and downloads new email in this account. You can also set it to Never, which means that email from this account is only downloaded when you open the Gmail app.

19. Check the box to be notified when new email arrives in this account.

20. Check the box if you want to synchronize mail from this account. Unchecking this box means that you don't want email to synchronize (not common).

21. Check the box if you want the Gmail app to automatically download email attachments when it detects that your Galaxy S7 is connected to a Wi-Fi network.

22. Tap Next.

23. Enter a friendly name for this account.

24. Enter the name you want to use when sending email from this account.

25. Tap Next to complete the setup of the email account.

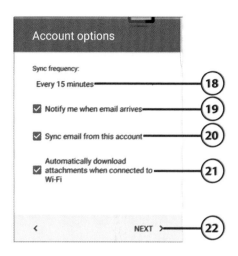

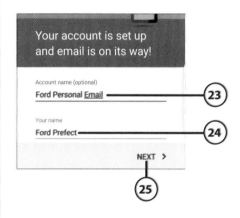

Be Secure If You Can

If your mail provider supports email security such as SSL or TLS, you should strongly consider using it. If you don't, emails you send and receive go over the Internet in plain readable text. Using SSL or TLS encrypts the emails as they travel across the Internet so that nobody can read them. Set this under the Advanced settings for the Incoming and Outgoing Servers.

Navigate the Gmail App

Let's take a quick look at the Gmail app and find out how to navigate the main screen.

1. Tap the Gmail icon to launch the app. Your initial view will be of the Inbox of your primary Google (Gmail) account, which is the account you used when setting up your S7.

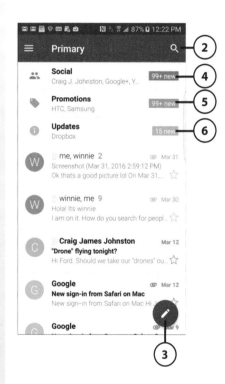

2. Tap to search the current folder for an email.

3. Tap to compose a new email.

4. Tap to see only new messages received from your social networking sites, such as Facebook and Google+. When you have tapped it once, the Social option disappears until new social media emails arrive.

5. Tap to see any new emails that are promotions for products. When you have tapped it once, the Promotions option disappears until more promotional emails arrive.

6. Tap to see any new updates. Updates include messages about updating an app but can also include update email relating to things you have purchased, bills you need to pay, and even updates to meeting invites. After you have tapped Updates once, this option disappears until there are more new updates.

7. Swipe in from the left to reveal the menu.

8. Tap to switch between your email accounts, if you have more than one.

9. Tap to view Social, Promotions, and Updates. These are only visible when viewing Google (Gmail) accounts.

10. Tap to view messages in any forums you are participating in. This is only visible when viewing Google (Gmail) accounts.

11. Tap to switch between your different folders (or *labels,* as the Gmail app calls them).

12. Swipe up to see all of your labels.

13. Swipe the vertical action bar to the left to close the menu.

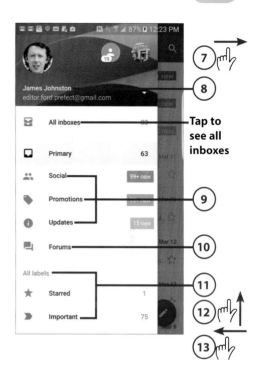

Tap to see all inboxes

>>>Go Further

STARS, LABELS, AND INBOXES

In the Gmail app, you use stars and labels to help organize your email. In most email clients you can create folders in your mailbox to help you organize your emails. For example, you might create a folder called "emails from the boss" and move any emails you receive from your boss to that folder. The Gmail app doesn't use the term *folders;* it uses the term *labels* instead. You can create labels in Gmail and choose an email to label. When you label the email, it is actually moved to a folder with that label. Any email that you mark with a star is actually just getting a label called "starred." However, when viewing your Gmail, you see the yellow star next to the email. People normally add a star to an email as a reminder of something important. The Gmail app allows you to switch between accounts, as shown in step 8; however, if you tap All Inboxes, Gmail shows messages from the Inboxes of all accounts you have added to the Gmail app in one All Inboxes view. This enables you to work with messages no matter which Inbox they are in, and what account that Inbox is from.

Compose an Email

1. Tap the compose icon.

2. Tap to change the email account from which the message is being sent (if you have multiple accounts).

3. Type names in the To field. If the name matches someone in your Contacts, a list of choices is displayed and you can tap a name to select it. If you only know the email address, type it here.

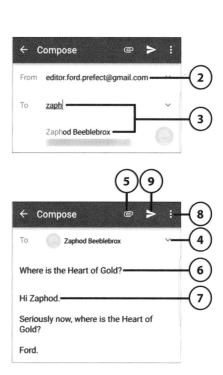

Gmail Not Doing Name Lookups

If you see that the Gmail app is not doing name lookups as you type in the To field, it could be that the Gmail app does not have permissions to do the lookup from the Contacts app. To give Gmail permission to do lookups in the Contacts app, tap Settings, Privacy and Safety, App Permissions. Tap Contacts. Scroll down until you see Gmail, and make sure that the on/off switch is in the on position.

4. Tap to add Carbon Copy (CC) or Blind Carbon Copy (BCC) recipients.

5. Tap the paper clip icon to add one or more attachments or insert links to one or more Google Drive files.

6. Type a subject for your email.

7. Type the body of the email.

8. Tap to save the email as a draft or discard it.

9. Tap to send the email.

Add Attachments or Insert Drive Links

Before sending an email, you can add one or more attachments or insert links to files you have in your Google Drive account. The Gmail app can attach files that you've saved on your phone and in your Google Drive account. Here is how to add attachments and link Drive documents.

1. After filling in the fields as described in the "Compose an Email" task, tap the paper clip icon.

2. Tap either Attach File or Insert from Drive. This example uses the Attach File option.

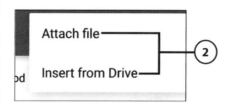

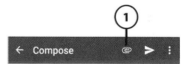

What Is the Difference Between Attaching and Inserting?

When you choose to attach a file to an email, you can choose a file located on your phone, in the Photos app, or in your Google Drive account. The file is then copied from that location and attached to the email. If you choose to insert a file from Google Drive, the file you choose is not actually copied out of Google Drive and attached to the email. Instead, a link to that file is placed in the body of the email. The link enables the recipients to tap the link and open the document right in your Google Drive account.

---

3. Choose where you want to search for the file. This can include your recent downloads, your Google Drive account, the Downloads folder, internal phone storage, or the Photos app.

4. Tap the file to attach it. In this example, the attachment is a document in my Google Drive account.

5. Tap Send.

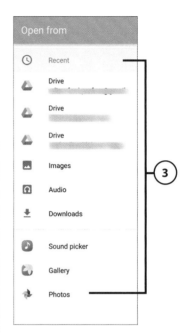

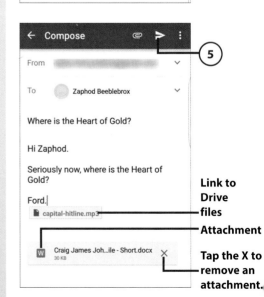

Link to Drive files

Attachment

Tap the X to remove an attachment.

Read an Email

1. Tap an email to open it. Unread emails are in bold, and emails that you have already read are not bold.

2. Tap to mark the email as unread and return to the email list view.

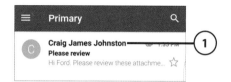

Rich Text Formatting

A Rich Text Formatting (RTF) message is a message formatted with anything that is not plain text. RTF includes bulleted lists, different fonts, font colors, font sizes, and styles such as bold, italic, and underline. Although you cannot type an email on your S7 with the standard keyboard using RTF, when you receive an RTF email, your S7 preserves the formatting and displays it correctly.

3. Tap to reply to the sender of the email. This does not reply to anyone in the CC field.

4. Tap the Menu icon to reply to the sender of the email and any recipients in the To and CC fields (Reply All). You can also choose to forward the email or print it. See steps 11 and 12 for an alternative method for replying to and forwarding messages.

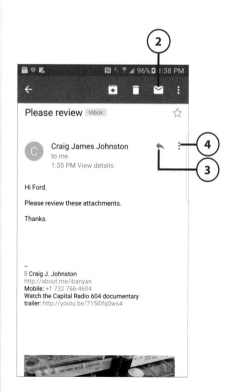

What Are Conversations?

Conversations are Gmail's version of email threads. When you look at the main view of the Gmail app, you are seeing a list of email conversations. The conversation might have only one email in it, but to Gmail that's a conversation. As you and others reply to that original email, Gmail groups those messages in a thread, or conversation.

5. Tap to expand the email header to see all recipients and all other email header information.

6. Tap to "star" the message, or move it to the Starred label.

7. Tap the sender's contact picture to see more contact information about the person.

8. Tap to move the email to the Trash label.

9. Tap the Menu icon and then tap Move To to move the email to a different label.

10. Swipe up to see the rest of the email and extra actions you can take.

11. Tap to reply to the email and all recipients (Reply All).

12. Tap to forward the email.

13. Tap an attachment to open and preview it.

14. Tap to download the attachment to your S7.

15. Tap to save the attachment in your Google Drive.

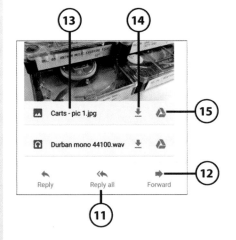

>>>Go Further

GMAILS HAVE EXTRA OPTIONS

If you are receiving email in your Gmail Inbox, you see a few extra options that are specific to Gmail. You can archive an email as well as send it to Trash. You can also mark an email as important, mute the email conversation, report an email as spam, and report an email as a phishing scam. When you mute a conversation, you will no longer see any emails in that conversation (or email thread). For more information on printing emails, and an explanation on what an important email is, see the Go Further sidebars later in the chapter.

Archive email  **Tap for more options**

>>>Go Further

HOW DO I PRINT EMAILS?

When you choose to print an email, the print dialog enables you to choose to print the email to a PDF, which turns the email into a Portable Document Format (PDF) file, or to print the email to any printers you have previously connected to Google Cloud Print using your desktop Chrome web browser. To learn more about how to connect your printers to your Google Cloud Print account, see the instructions at https://support.google.com/chrome/answer/1069693?hl=en.

>>>Go Further

WHAT IS IMPORTANT?

Gmail tries to automatically figure out which of the emails you receive are important. As it learns, it might sometimes be wrong. If an email is marked as important but it is not important, you can manually change the status to "not important." Important emails have a yellow arrow whereas emails that are not important have a clear arrow. All emails marked as "important" are also given the Priority Inbox label. (See the "What Is the Priority Inbox?" note later in this chapter for more information about the Priority Inbox.)

What Happens to Your Spam or Phishing Emails?

When you mark an email in Gmail as spam or as a phishing scam, two things happen. First, it gets a label called Spam. Second, a copy of that email is sent to Gmail's spam servers so that they are now aware of a possible new spam email that is circulating around the Internet. Based on what the servers see for all Gmail users, they block the emails that have been marked as spam and phishing emails from reaching other Gmail users. So the bottom line is that you should always mark spam emails because it helps all of us.

Customize Gmail App Settings

You can customize the way the Gmail app works, and you can also customize how each independent email account functions.

1. Swipe in from the left of the screen.

2. Tap Settings.

3. Tap General Settings.

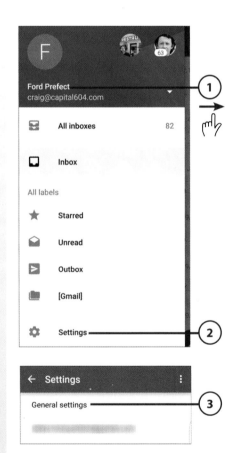

4. Check the box to enable grouping emails in the same conversation (those with the same subject line) together.

5. Check the box to enable the ability to swipe an email left or right to archive it.

6. Check the box to enable showing the email sender's contact image in the conversation list.

7. Check the box to enable making Reply All the default reply action.

8. Tap to enable automatically shrinking the emails to fit on the screen.

9. Tap to choose what happens when you archive or delete a message. Your choices are to show newer messages, older messages, or the conversation list.

10. Swipe up for more settings.

11. Choose which actions you want to show a confirmation screen for.

12. Tap to save your changes and return to the main Settings screen.

13. Tap one of your accounts to change settings specific to that account, and then follow the steps in the following sections.

Additional Options in General Settings
While in the General Settings screen, if you tap the Menu icon, you can clear your email search history or your picture approvals. When you clear picture approvals, you are clearing your previous decisions on which emails you wanted to automatically load the images for.

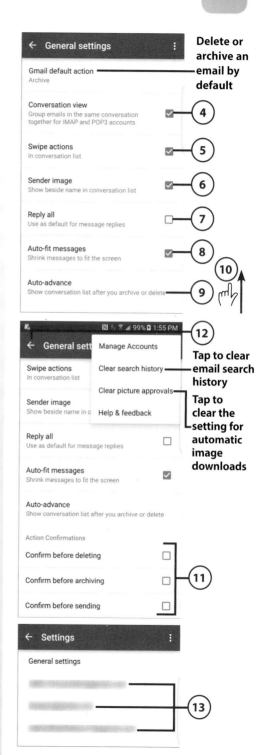

Delete or archive an email by default

Tap to clear email search history

Tap to clear the setting for automatic image downloads

Customize Google Account Settings

1. Tap to choose whether you want to see your Priority Inbox instead of your regular Inbox (Default Inbox) when opening the Gmail app.

2. Tap to choose what Inbox categories are shown. As shown earlier in the chapter, by default the Social and Promotions categories are displayed. You can also show Updates and Forums.

3. Tap to enable or disable notifications when new email arrives for this Gmail account.

4. Tap to select how to get notified when new email arrives for this account. You can choose a different notification for each label and also decide which labels in addition to the Primary label you will be notified for.

5. Tap to enter a signature to be included at the end of all emails composed using this account.

6. Tap to set your Vacation Responder. This is a message that is automatically sent to people when you are on vacation.

7. Swipe up for more settings.

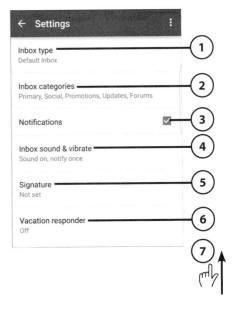

What Is the Priority Inbox?

Google introduced the Priority Inbox as a way to automatically figure out which emails are important to you and place them in a folder called Priority Inbox. It does this by analyzing which emails you open and reply to. If it makes a mistake, you can mark a message as less important or more important. Over time, Google's handle on which emails are important to you gets more accurate. Because the Priority Inbox probably has the most-important emails, you might want to open it first and then go to the regular Inbox later to handle less-important emails. Read more about the Priority Inbox at https://support.google.com/mail/answer/186531?hl=en.

Email Signature

An *email signature* is a bit of text that is automatically added to the bottom of any email you send from your Android phone. It is added when you compose a new email, reply to an email, or forward an email. A typical use for a signature is to automatically add your name and some contact information at the end of your emails. Email signatures are sometimes referred to as email footers.

8. Tap to choose whether to synchronize Gmail to your Galaxy S7. Turning this off stops Gmail from arriving on your phone.

9. Tap to choose how many days' worth of email to synchronize to your phone.

10. Touch to manage labels. Labels are like folders. You can choose which labels synchronize to your phone, how much email synchronizes, and what ringtone to play when new email arrives in that label.

11. Check the box to automatically download attachments to recently received emails while connected to a Wi-Fi network.

12. Tap to choose how images embedded in emails are handled. They can be automatically downloaded, or you can be prompted before they are downloaded for each email.

13. Tap to save your changes and return to the main Settings screen.

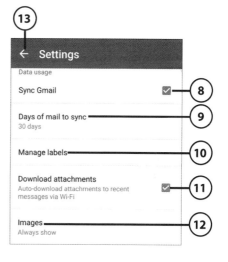

Customize POP/IMAP Account Settings

1. Tap to change the name of your account. This is the friendly name you may have typed when you originally set it up on your phone.

2. Tap to change the full name you want people to see when you reply to emails using this account.

3. Tap to enter a signature to be included at the end of all emails composed using this account.

4. Tap to choose how embedded images in emails are handled. You can set it to always load images or ask before loading images.

5. Tap to change the frequency with which your S7 checks for new email for this account. You can set it to Never, which means that your phone only checks for email when you open the Gmail app, or you can set it to automatically check between every 15 minutes to every hour.

6. Check the box to automatically download attachments to recently received emails while connected to a Wi-Fi network.

7. Swipe up for more settings.

8. Tap to enable or disable notifications when new email arrives for this email account.

9. Tap to select the ringtone to play when you are notified of new email for this account.

10. Check the box if you also want to feel a vibration when new email arrives for this account.

11. Tap to change the incoming email server settings for this account.

12. Tap to change the outgoing email server settings for this account.

13. Tap to save your changes and return to the main Settings screen.

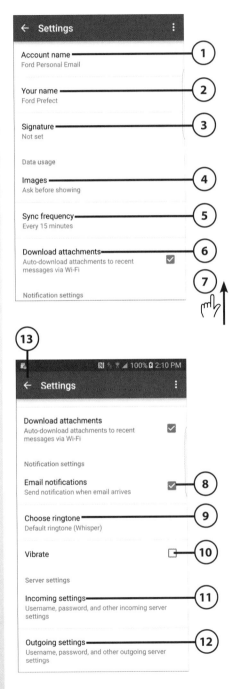

Email Application

The Email application supports all email accounts with the exception of Gmail. This includes any corporate email accounts that use Microsoft Exchange or corporate email systems, such as Lotus Domino/Notes, that have an ActiveSync gateway. In addition to corporate email accounts, the Email application also supports POP3 and IMAP accounts. POP3 and IMAP accounts are also supported by the Gmail app, so this is a duplication of functionality.

Add a Work Email Account

Your Galaxy S7 can synchronize your contacts from your work email account as long as your company uses Microsoft Exchange or an email gateway that supports Microsoft ActiveSync (such as Lotus Traveler for Lotus Domino/Notes email systems). It might be useful to be able to keep your work and personal contacts on one mobile device instead of carrying two phones around all day.

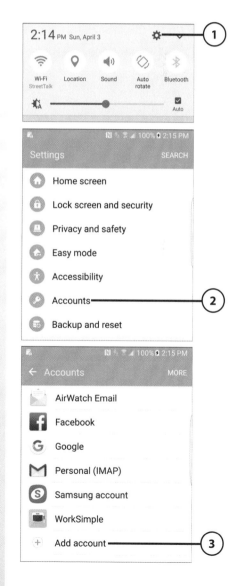

1. From the Home screen, pull down the Notification bar and tap the Settings icon.

2. Tap Accounts.

3. Tap Add Account.

4. Tap Microsoft Exchange ActiveSync.

5. Enter your full corporate email address.

6. Enter your corporate network password.

7. Tap Sign In.

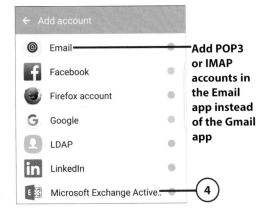

Add POP3 or IMAP accounts in the Email app instead of the Gmail app

Error Adding Account? Guess the Server.

Your Galaxy S7 tries to work out some information about your company's ActiveSync setup. If it can't, you are prompted to enter the ActiveSync server name manually. If you don't know what it is, you can try guessing it. If, for example, your email address is dsimons@allhitradio.com, the ActiveSync server is most probably webmail.allhitradio.com or autodiscover.allhitradio.com. If options like these don't work, ask your email administrator.

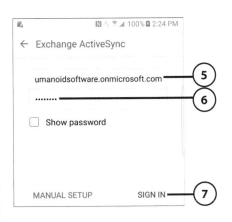

8. Tap to agree that your mail administrator may impose security restrictions on your Galaxy S7 if you proceed.

9. Tap to choose how many days' worth of email to synchronize to your Galaxy S7.

10. Tap to choose how often your corporate email is delivered to your Galaxy S7. Auto means that as it arrives in your Inbox at work, it is delivered to your phone. You can set it to Manual, which means that your work email is only delivered when you open the Email app on your phone. You can also set the delivery frequency from every 5 minutes to every hour.

11. Tap to choose how much of each email is retrieved. You can also set this to have no size limit so that the entire email is downloaded.

12. Tap to choose how many days in the past calendar items are synchronized to your Galaxy S7.

13. Swipe up to see more settings.

14. Tap to enable or disable being notified when new email arrives from your corporate Inbox.

15. Tap to enable or disable synchronizing your corporate contacts to your Galaxy S7.

16. Tap to enable or disable synchronizing your corporate calendar to your Galaxy S7.

17. Tap to enable or disable synchronizing your corporate tasks to your Galaxy S7.

18. Tap to enable or disable synchronizing SMS (text) messages you receive on your Galaxy S7 to your corporate Inbox.

19. Tap Sign In.

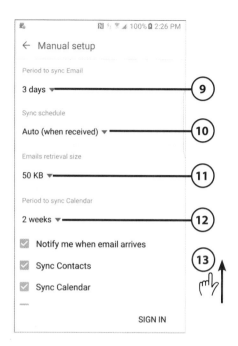

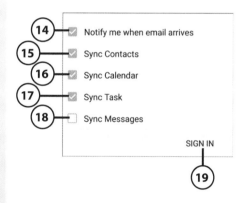

20. Tap Activate to allow your company's mail server to act as a device administrator for your Galaxy S7.

21. Enter a name for this email account. Use something meaningful that describes the purpose of the account, such as Work Email.

22. Tap Done to complete the setup.

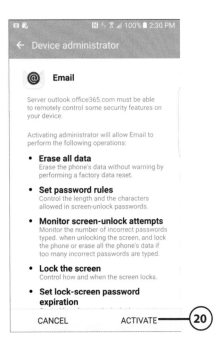

Add a New POP3 or IMAP Account

Remember that the Gmail app also supports POP3 and IMAP accounts, so you may not want to use the Email app for this type of account. It is up to you.

1. Pull down the Notification bar and tap the Settings icon.

2. Tap Accounts.

3. Tap Add Account.

4. Tap Email.

5. Enter your email address.

6. Enter your password.

7. Tap Sign In. If all went well, your account will be added and you will be returned to the accounts screen. If not, perform steps 8–19, which walk through the manual setup of email.

Why Manual Setup?

Your Galaxy S7 tries to figure out the settings to set up your email account. This works most of the time when you are using common email providers such as Yahoo! and Hotmail. It also works with large ISPs such as Comcast, Road Runner, Optimum Online, and so on. It might not work for smaller ISPs, in smaller countries, or if you have created your own website and set up your own email. In these cases, you need to set up your email manually.

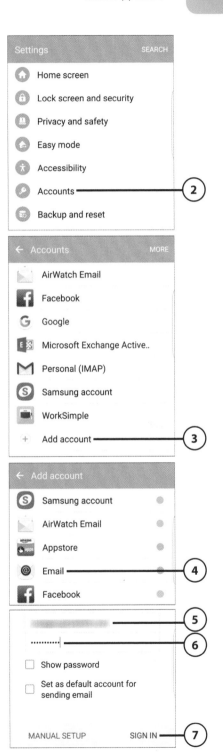

8. Tap POP3 or IMAP. IMAP has more intelligence to it, so select that option when possible.

9. Ensure that the information on the incoming server screen is accurate.

10. Swipe up for more settings.

Where Can I Find This Information?

If you need to manually set up your email account, you must have a few pieces of information. Always check your ISP's (or email service provider's) website, and look for instructions on how to set up your email on a computer or smartphone. This is normally under the Support section of the website.

Username and Password

On the Incoming Server and Outgoing Server screens, your username and password should already be filled out because you typed them in earlier. If not, enter them.

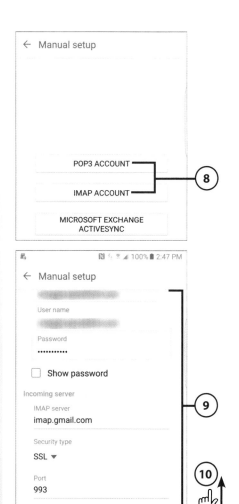

11. Ensure that the information on the outgoing server screen is accurate.

12. Tap Sign In.

13. Tap to change how far back in the past email must synchronize.

14. Tap to change the frequency with which email from this account synchronizes to your Galaxy S7.

15. Tap to check the box if you want to be notified when new email arrives into this account.

16. Tap Sign In.

17. Enter a friendly name for this account, such as Home Email.

18. Enter your full name or the name you want to be displayed when people receive emails sent from this account.

19. Tap Done to save the settings for this account and return to the Add Accounts screen.

Be Secure If You Can

If your mail provider supports email security, such as Secure Sockets Layer (SSL) or Transport Layer Security (TLS), you should strongly consider using it. If you don't, emails you send and receive go over the Internet in plain readable text. Using SSL or TLS encrypts the emails as they travel across the Internet so nobody can read them. Set this under the Advanced settings for the incoming and outgoing servers.

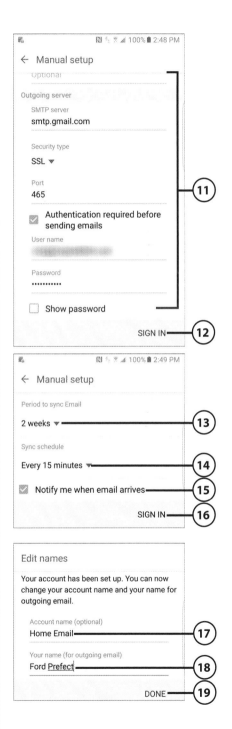

Working with the Email App

Now that you have added two new accounts, you can start using the Email application. Everything you do in the Email application is the same for every email account. The Email app enables you to work with email accounts either separately or in a combined view.

Navigate the Email Application

Before you learn how to compose or read emails, you should become familiar with the Email application.

1. Tap to launch the Email app.

2. Tap to switch between email accounts or select Combined Inbox, which shows all emails from all accounts.

3. Tap the star to mark a personal account (POP3/IMAP) email as flagged.

4. Each color represents a specific email account.

5. Tap to compose a new email.

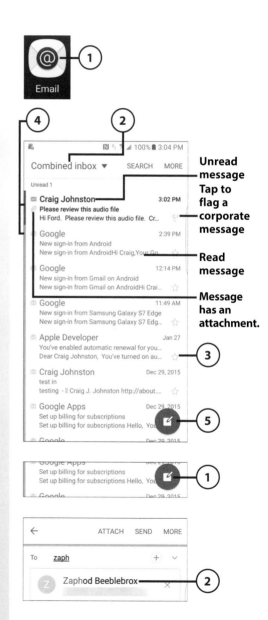

Compose an Email

1. Tap to compose a new email.

2. Enter one or more recipients. As you type, your Galaxy S7 tries to guess whom you want to address the message to. If you see the correct name, tap it to select it. This includes names stored on your Galaxy S7 and in your company's corporate address book.

3. Enter a subject.

4. Type the body of the email.

5. Tap to send the message.

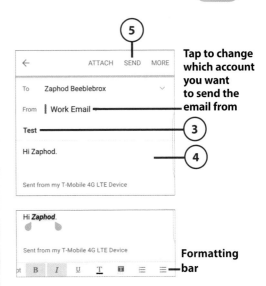

Tap to change which account you want to send the email from

Enable Rich Text

If you want to format your email using different fonts, bold, italic, and embedded images, you can tap More and then tap Turn On Rich Text. A bar with formatting options displays. Swipe left and right over the formatting bar to see all formatting options. To change the formatting of a specific word, touch and hold the word, drag the end markers to select more words if needed, and then change the formatting using the formatting bar.

Formatting bar

Add Attachments to a Message

Before you send your message, you might want to add one or more attachments. You can attach any type of file, including pictures, video, audio, contacts, and location.

1. Tap Attach.

2. Choose one or more pictures from the Gallery app.

Tap to attach any file on your S7, including pictures from the Photos app

Tap to attach any documents on your S7

3. Tap the red minus symbol to the right of an attachment to remove it from the email.

4. Tap to send your email.

Other Options Before Sending

Before you send your email, you can change a few additional options. To see these additional options, tap More. Tap Priority to change the priority of the email to high, normal, or low. Tap Security Options to encrypt the email or digitally sign it. To encrypt or sign an email, you need certificates installed on your Galaxy S7. When you are sending an email using your company's Exchange email system, tap Permissions to set the permissions for what happens to the email after it has been sent, including preventing it from being forwarded or setting an expiration date on the email. The Permissions options are set by your email administrator.

Read Email

Reading messages in the Email application is the same regardless of which account the email has come to.

1. Tap an email to open it.

2. Tap to reply to the sender of the email. This does not reply to anyone in the Cc field.

3. Tap to forward the email.

4. Tap to expand the email header to see all recipients and all other email header information.

5. Tap to mark the message as flagged for followup (Exchange email) or starred (personal email).

6. Tap to preview the attachment. In this example it is an audio file.

7. Tap to save the attachment to your phone.

8. Tap to delete the message.

9. Tap More to see other options.

10. Tap to mark the message as unread.

11. Tap to move the message to a different folder.

12. Tap to save the email as a file on your phone (outside the Email app).

13. Tap to set yourself a reminder to respond to this email.

14. Tap to mark the message as spam or junk mail.

15. Tap to add the sender to the Priority Sender list. Email from people in the Priority Sender list are displayed in the Priority Sender view.

16. Tap to add a new event in your Calendar based on this email.

17. Tap to print the email on a Samsung printer available on the Wi-Fi network, or save the email as a Portable Document Format (PDF) file.

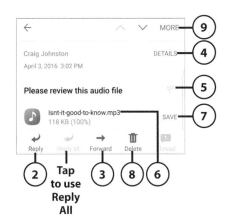

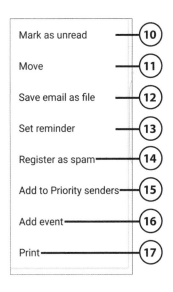

Change Email App Settings

1. Tap More from the main Email screen.

2. Tap Settings.

General Settings

General settings are settings that take effect no matter what type of email account you are working with.

1. Tap More and then tap Set Default Account to choose which account will be used as the default account when composing new email. This is only relevant if you have more than one account added to the Email app.

2. Tap to enable or disable auto fit. When Auto Fit Content is enabled, your Galaxy S7 adjusts emails so they fit on the screen properly when you read them.

3. Tap to manage when you will receive notifications of new emails. You can choose to receive notifications when senders you have placed on the Priority Senders list send you email, and you can choose which email accounts to receive notifications from.

4. Tap to manage your spam address list. This includes manually adding email addresses and removing ones already on the Spam list.

5. Tap to choose whether you want the Email app to show a split screen with folders on the left and messages on the right when you turn your S7 sideways.

6. Tap to choose whether you want to see a confirmation screen when you delete emails.

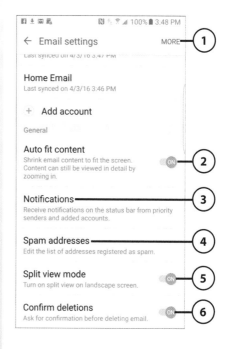

What Is the Priority Sender List?

Emails received from people whom you have listed in the Priority Sender list are shown in the Priority Sender Inbox as well as in the regular Inbox. Opening the Priority Sender Inbox folder shows only emails from these people, which can be a way of filtering email so that you respond to the important people first and then switch to the regular Inbox and respond to everyone else.

Corporate Account Settings

You are able to change your email signature as well as control what components are synchronized and how often they are synchronized.

1. Tap your corporate email account.

2. Tap to choose whether you want this account to synchronize with your Galaxy S7.

3. Tap to change the friendly name for this account.

4. Tap to choose whether to always Bcc or Cc yourself on emails you send.

5. Tap to enable or disable using an email signature, add an email signature, or edit a signature.

6. Tap to enable or disable automatically loading embedded images in emails sent to you on this account.

7. Choose whether you want to email attachments automatically downloaded when your Galaxy S7 is connected to a Wi-Fi network.

8. Swipe up for more settings.

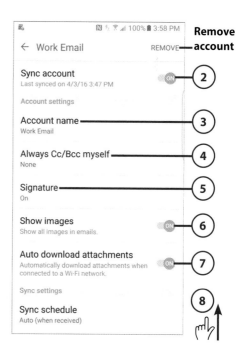

9. Tap to manage the synchronization settings for this account. This includes choosing different synchronization options depending on peak and off-peak times.

10. Tap to choose how far back in the past your email synchronizes.

11. Tap to choose how much of each email is retrieved.

12. Tap to choose how much of each email is retrieved when you are roaming outside your home cellular provider network.

13. Tap to set whether you are out of the office and your out-of-office message. This synchronizes to the out-of-office feature on your corporate mailbox so your out-of-office messages are sent by your mail server.

14. Tap to choose which folders (excluding Inbox and Outbox) you want to synchronize from your office email account and when they synchronize based on the peak and off-peak schedule.

15. Tap to choose how far back in the past your calendar synchronizes.

16. Tap to empty your Trash folder on the email server back in the office.

17. Swipe up for more settings.

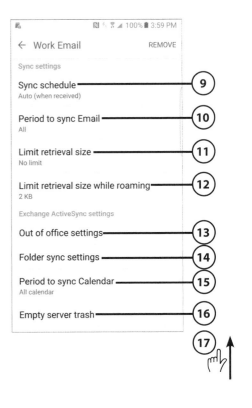

Why Empty the Office Trash Folder?

Step 16 describes how you can choose to empty your Trash folder back in the office. This feature is useful because sometimes your email administrator sets a limit on the size of your mailbox, and when you reach that limit, you are unable to send emails. By emptying your Trash folder back at the office, you might be able to clear a little bit of space in your mailbox so you can send that important email.

18. Tap to change which device wins if there is a conflict between your phone and your email account back at the office.

How Are There Conflicts?

A conflict can occur if you or someone who has delegate access on your email account makes a change in your mailbox using a desktop email client such as Outlook (for example, your delegate moves an email to a folder) and you then make a change on your Galaxy S7 (say, you delete that same email). Now there is a conflict because an email has been both moved and deleted at the same time. If you set the server to have priority, then the conflict is resolved using your rule that the server wins. In this example, the email is not deleted but rather is moved to a folder.

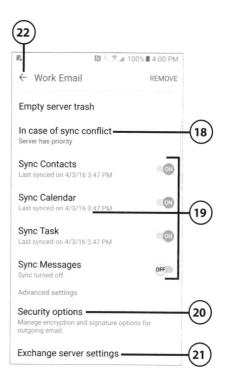

18. Select what to synchronize between your Galaxy S7 and your office email account.

20. Tap to set advanced security options, including whether you want to encrypt your emails, sign emails with an electronic signature, and email certificates to use with S/MIME (if your company supports it).

21. Tap to change the Exchange mail server settings for this account. This includes your account username and password if these have changed.

22. Tap to return to the previous screen.

POP/IMAP Account Settings

1. Tap your POP3 or IMAP email account.

2. Tap to choose whether you want this email account to synchronize with your Galaxy S7.

3. Tap to change the friendly name for this account.

4. Tap to edit the name that is displayed when you send email to others.

5. Tap to choose whether to always Bcc or Cc yourself on emails you send.

6. Tap to enable or disable using an email signature, add an email signature, or edit a signature.

7. Tap to enable or disable automatically loading embedded images in emails sent to you on this account.

8. Tap to enable or disable automatically downloading email attachments when your Galaxy S7 is connected to Wi-Fi.

9. Swipe up for more settings.

10. Tap to manage the synchronization settings for this account. This includes choosing different synchronization options depending on peak and off-peak times.

11. Tap to choose how far back in the past your email synchronizes.

12. Tap to choose how much of each email is retrieved.

13. Tap to choose how much of each email is retrieved when you are roaming outside your home cellular provider network.

14. Tap to change the incoming and outgoing server settings for this account.

15. Tap to return to the Settings main screen.

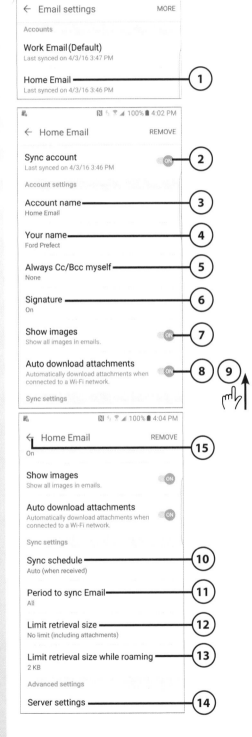

SMS and MMS

Short Message Service (SMS), also known as text messaging, has been around for a long time. Multimedia Message Service (MMS) is a newer form of text messaging that can contain pictures, audio, and video as well as text. Your Galaxy S7 can send and receive both SMS and MMS messages.

Get to Know the Messages App

The Messages app is what you use to send and receive text messages. This app has all the features you need to compose, send, receive, and manage these messages.

1. Tap the Messages icon.

2. Tap to compose a new text message.

3. Tap the picture of someone who has sent you a message to show their contact card. You can then contact the person using email, phone, and other methods.

4. Tap a message thread to open it.

5. Tap More to see other options.

6. Tap to select one or more message threads and delete them or mark them as spam.

7. Tap to open the Locked Messages folder. Locked messages are messages that you have chosen to lock so they are not accidentally deleted. See the "How Do I Lock Messages?" note for more information.

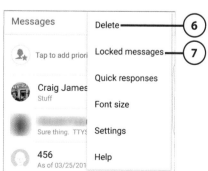

8. Tap to select from a list of Quick Responses to send and manage the current Quick Responses. When you select a Quick Response, a new message opens with that Quick Response added to the text field.

9. Tap to choose to use your Galaxy S7's built-in font size, or select a smaller or larger size while you have the Messages app open.

10. Tap to open the Settings screen. See the next section for more on settings.

How Do I Lock a Message?

You might want to lock a message so that it does not get accidentally deleted when you delete the message thread. To lock a message, touch and hold on the message and choose Lock when the menu pops up. The lock symbol displays just below the locked message. To unlock the message, touch and hold on the message and choose Unlock.

>>>Go Further

SWIPE TO CALL

If you would like to call the sender of an SMS or MMS message, swipe the message from left to right to dial that person's number.

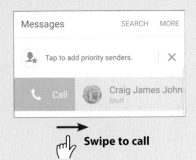

Swipe to call

Manage Settings for the Messages App

You use the settings of the Messages app to manage how the app handles your SMS and MMS messages.

1. Tap More on the main Messages screen.

2. Tap Settings.

3. Tap to manage how the Messages app looks. You can choose what kind of bubble style is used for text message display, and choose which background the app uses for messages.

4. Tap to manage the settings for detecting spam messages. Spam messages are unwanted commercial messages. You can also choose what mobile numbers and text phrases are treated as spam.

5. Tap to manage whether you want to send read receipts, if you want to be warned when you are sending a multimedia message larger than a specific size, whether to automatically download multimedia messages while roaming, the size of images to download, and if you want to show others when you are typing a message.

6. Tap to manage which emergency alerts you want to receive. These alerts are sent out by your government or law enforcement (for example, AMBER alerts).

7. Tap to see more settings.

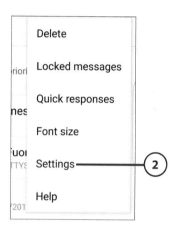

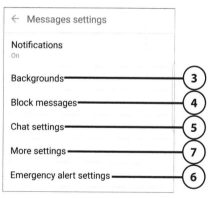

8. Tap to control and manage text messages. This includes choosing to receive a delivery report for text messages you send, choosing the input mode (leaving it set to Automatic is recommended), and managing text messages that may still be on your old SIM card.

9. Tap to control how the Messages app handles multimedia messages. Settings include the ability to request delivery and read reports as well as to control whether to automatically retrieve multimedia messages while roaming outside your wireless carrier's home area.

10. Tap to enable or disable receiving messages "pushed" from the server. Push messages arrive at your Galaxy S7 shortly after they arrive at the server, which is usually faster than waiting until the Galaxy S7 checks for messages. You can also choose how to handle remote requests to load services. Your choices are Always, Prompt, and Never.

11. Tap to enable or disable automatically deleting old text or multimedia messages when the limit you set is reached. When the limit is reached, messages within the thread or conversation are deleted using the FIFO method.

12. Tap to enable or disable splitting the screen when you rotate your S7 into landscape mode. When the screen is split, conversation headings are on the left, and messages in that conversation are on the right.

13. Tap to save your changes and return to the previous screen.

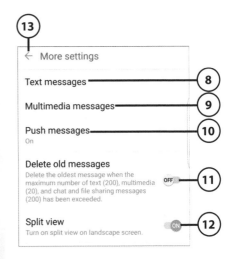

What Does the Manage SIM Card Messages Option Do?

Many old cell phones store text messages on the SIM card and not in the phone's memory. If you have just upgraded from an older phone, you might still have text messages on the SIM card that you would like to retrieve. If you choose the option to manage text messages on your SIM card, as mentioned in step 8, you can then copy the messages to your Galaxy S7's memory and copy the senders to your contacts in the Contacts app.

Don't Auto-Retrieve MMS While Roaming

Disable the automatic retrieval of multimedia messages when you travel to other countries because automatically retrieving these messages when you're roaming can result in a big bill from your provider. International carriers love to charge large amounts of money for people traveling to their countries and using their networks. The only time it is a good idea to leave this enabled is if your carrier offers an international SMS or MMS bundle, where you pay a flat rate up front before leaving. When you have the auto-retrieve feature disabled, you see a Download button next to a multimedia message. You have to tap it to manually download the message.

What's the Difference Between a Delivery Report and a Read Report?

A delivery report indicates that the message has reached the destination device. A read report indicates that the message has been opened for viewing. There is still no guarantee that whoever opened the message has actually read it, let alone understood it.

Compose Messages

When you compose a new message, you do not need to make a conscious decision whether it is an SMS message or an MMS message. As soon as you add a subject line or attach a file to your message, your Galaxy S7 automatically treats the message as an MMS message.

1. Tap the pencil compose icon to compose a new message.

2. Start typing the recipient's name or phone number, or if the person is in your contacts, type the name. If a match is found, tap the mobile number.

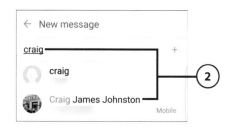

3. Tap and start typing your message.

4. Tap to send your message.

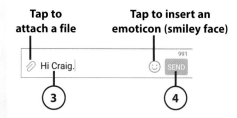

Delay Sending the Message

You might decide that you want a text message to be sent automatically at a later time. To do this, before sending the message, tap More and choose Schedule Message. Choose the date and time you want your message to be sent and tap Done. Then tap the Send button, and your message will send when you set it to.

Attach Files to Messages

If you want to send a picture, audio file, or video along with your text message, all you need to do is attach the file. Be aware that attaching a file turns your SMS text message into an MMS multimedia message and may be subject to additional charges.

1. Tap the paper clip icon to attach a file.

2. Choose a picture that you recently took on your Galaxy S7 from the Gallery app.

3. Tap Other to choose other attachment types, including pictures in the Photos app.

4. Tap Camera to take a picture or record a video and send it.

5. Tap to send your MMS.

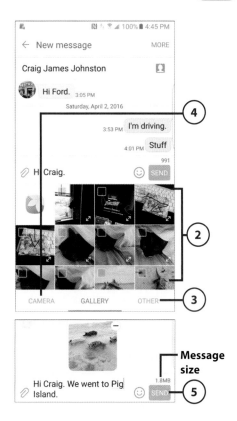

Message size

Receive Messages

When you receive a new SMS or MMS message, you can read it, view its attachments, and even save those attachments to your Galaxy S7.

1. When a new SMS or MMS message arrives, your Galaxy S7 plays a ringtone and displays a notification in the status bar (not shown).

2. Pull down the notification shade to see newly arrived messages.

3. Tap a message alert to display the message and reply to it.

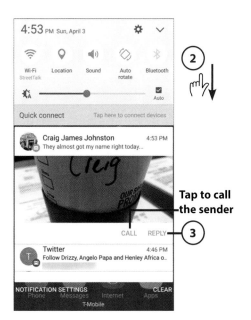

Tap to call the sender

4. Tap an attachment to open it for viewing.

5. Touch and hold a message to display the Message Options dialog. Skip to step 7 for more about the additional options.

6. Tap to write a reply to the message.

7. Tap to delete the message. This deletes just the message and not the entire thread.

8. Tap to copy the message text so you can paste it elsewhere.

9. Tap to forward the message and attachment to someone else.

10. Tap to share the message via social media or other methods.

11. Tap to lock the message against deletion if you later decide to delete the message thread.

12. Tap to save the attachment to your Galaxy S7.

13. Tap to view a slideshow of attached images.

14. Tap to view the message details, such as its size and the date and time it was sent.

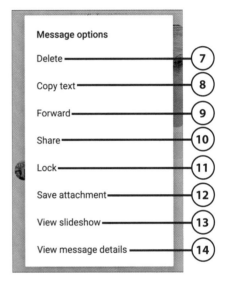

Usable Content

If a text message contains links to websites, phone numbers, or email addresses, tapping those links makes the Galaxy S7 take the appropriate action. For example, when you tap a phone number, your Galaxy S7 calls the number; when you tap a web link, the Galaxy S7 opens the page in Chrome or your other default browser.

>>>Go Further

USING GOOGLE HANGOUTS FOR SMS AND MMS

You may decide that because you already use Google Hangouts to instant message your friends and family, as well as to video chat with them, it makes sense to set the Google Hangouts app to handle text messages (SMS) and multimedia messages (MMS) so that all communications with your friends and family are in one place. To set this, open the Google Hangouts app. Swipe in from the left of the screen and tap Settings. Tap SMS. Under General, tap SMS Disabled and tap Yes when prompted. The way in which you interact with SMS and MMS while using the Hangouts app is very similar to the way it works in the Messages app, so the steps in this chapter should help you. Even the settings for handling SMS and MMS are similar. When one of your contacts has signed up for a Google account and has started using Google Hangouts, you can switch from sending and receiving SMS and MMS messages with them and start using Hangouts messages instead. Doing this saves you from costly SMS and MMS charges and just uses your data plan.

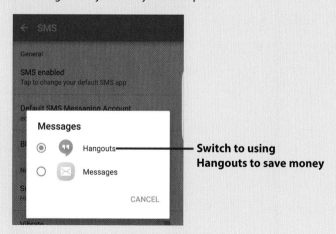

Switch to using Hangouts to save money

See stocks

Search Google

See the
weather

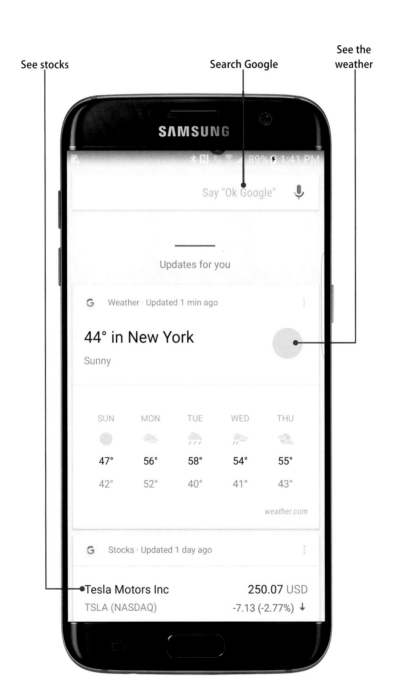

Say "Ok Google"

Updates for you

Weather · Updated 1 min ago

44° in New York

Sunny

SUN	MON	TUE	WED	THU
47°	56°	58°	54°	55°
42°	52°	40°	41°	43°

weather.com

Stocks · Updated 1 day ago

Tesla Motors Inc   250.07 USD
TSLA (NASDAQ)   -7.13 (-2.77%)

In this chapter, you find out how to use Google Maps for step-by-step navigation and Google Now. Topics include the following:

→ Using Google Now
→ Using Google Maps for navigation
→ Taking map data offline

Google Now and Navigation Using Google Maps

You can use your Samsung Galaxy S7 as a GPS navigation device while you walk or drive around. Your phone also includes an app called Google Now that provides all the information you need when you need it.

Google Now

You can access Google Now from any screen that enables you to search the Internet (except the Lock screen). Google Now provides you with information such as how long it takes to drive to work and the scores from your favorite teams.

Access Google Now

You can access Google Now from any app or the Home screen pane by pressing and holding the Home button.

Press and hold

1. Cards automatically appear based on your settings. Examples of these cards are scores for the stocks you track, sports teams you follow, upcoming meetings, weather in the location where you work, and traffic on the way to work.

2. Say "OK Google" to speak a search or to command Google Now to do something. You can also type your search terms.

3. Information relevant to your search appears.

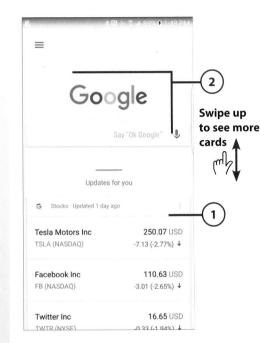

Swipe up to see more cards

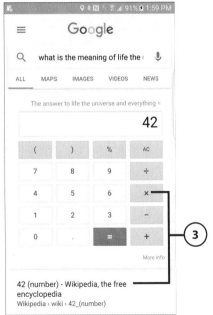

Commanding Google Now

In addition to searching the Internet using Google Now, you can command Google Now to do things for you. For example, you can tell Google Now to set an alarm for you, compose a text message, or even send an email. This is just a small list of the types of things you can have Google Now do for you. To see a comprehensive list of commands, visit http://trendblog.net/list-of-google-now-voice-commands-infographic/.

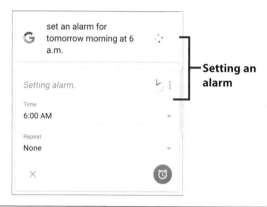

Setting an alarm

Set Up Google Now

For Google Now to work for you, you need to set it up correctly. This also means sharing your location information with Google.

1. Swipe in from the left bezel to reveal the menu.

2. Tap to add and manage reminders.

3. Tap Customize to customize what kinds of Google Now cards are displayed. This includes choosing sports teams, stocks, places, and TV and video.

4. Tap Settings.

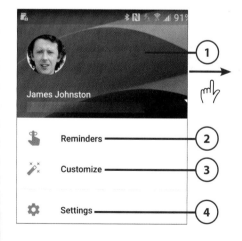

5. Tap to manage what Google Now can search for. This can include apps you have installed, bookmarks and web history in the Chrome web browser, your contacts, Google Play Books, Movies & TV, and Music.

6. Tap Voice to manage how and when Google Now responds to your voice.

7. Tap to choose the languages that Google Now responds to.

8. Tap to choose whether Google Now should be listening for you to say "OK Google."

9. Tap to choose whether Google Now works with a connected headset. You can choose to let Google Now use a paired Bluetooth device, a headset connected by a cable, or both.

10. Tap to choose when Google Now speaks back to you. Your choices are On (which means always), Off (which means never), or only when you are using a hands-free device (such as a Bluetooth headset or your car's built-in Bluetooth connection).

11. Tap to manage whether Google Now speech recognition can work even when there is no Internet connection. This is achieved by downloading one or more languages to your phone.

12. Tap to block offensive words being spoken when search results are returned by voice.

13. Tap to allow Google Now to record your voice using your Bluetooth headset or built-in car Bluetooth.

14. Tap to save your changes and return to the main Google Now settings screen.

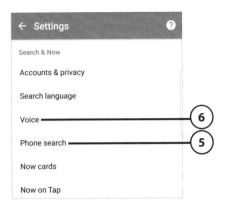

15. Tap Accounts & Privacy.

16. Tap to choose which of your Google accounts (if you have more than one) you want to use for Google Now.

17. Tap to manage any nicknames that you have previously set up (if any).

18. Tap to manage what information Google stores from your S7 to improve its capabilities. You can also see what has been stored, and delete it.

19. Tap to enable or disable the SafeSearch Filter that blocks offensive content.

20. Tap to enable or disable high-contrast text if you have a vision disability.

21. Tap to save your changes and return to the main Google Now settings screen.

>>>*Go Further*

HOW TO SET UP NICKNAMES

To set up nicknames for people whom you often call or otherwise communicate with, while Google Now is open, say "OK Google" or tap the microphone and set up a new nickname. You can do this by saying something like "Diane is my mom." Google Now looks in your list of Contacts to find someone with the name of Diane. If Google Now finds more than one Diane it prompts you to choose the correct one. Tap Add Nickname to finish adding the nickname. After you have created the nickname, you can tell Google Now to "Call Mom," and it will know who "Mom" is and make the call for you.

22. Tap to manage how Google Now alerts you when new cards are ready and choose the ringtone that plays when they are ready to view.

23. Tap to enable or disable Now on Tap. See the "What Is Now on Tap?" note for more information.

24. Tap to save your changes and return to Google Now.

What Is Now on Tap?

Now on Tap is a new feature of Google Now that provides contextually relevant information based on what you are looking at on the screen of your Galaxy S7. When Now on Tap is enabled and you press and hold the Home button, Now on Tap activates, but you can still switch to the regular Google Now screen by tapping the Google logo. For example, say I'm playing some Depeche Mode and I activate Now on Tap. It will suggest places on Google Now, Facebook, and YouTube where I can find more Depeche Mode content. It will also provide links to places where I can learn more about Depeche Mode and see and hear more Depeche Mode content on places like YouTube, Instagram, Facebook, and so on.

Tell Google Maps Where You Live and Work

Google Now can be even more effective if you configure your work and home addresses in Google Maps. Google Now uses that information to tell you things such as how long your commute to work will be, whether there is heavy traffic on the route, and so on. See step 3 in the "Configure Google Maps Settings" task later in this chapter for information about how to do that.

Google Maps

Google Maps enables you to see where you are on a map, find points of interest close to you, get driving or walking directions, and review extra layers of information, such as a satellite view.

1. Tap to launch Google Maps.

2. Tap to type a search term, the name of a business, or an address.

3. Tap to speak a search term, the name of a business, or an address.

4. Tap to get walking or driving directions from one location to another. You can also choose to use public transit or biking paths to get to your destination.

5. Tap to switch between the top-down view that always points North and the 3D view that follows the direction your phone is pointing.

6. Tap to explore points of interest near your current location.

7. Swipe in from the left of the screen to reveal the menu.

8. Tap to switch to a different Google account for use with Google Maps.

9. Tap to see your work and home address, plus addresses you have recently searched for.

10. Tap to view and manage your timeline. Your timeline is a map with plot points for all the places you have traveled while carrying your S7.

11. Tap to view and manage your contributions to Google Maps. This includes places you have rated or written reviews about and photos you have taken at places you have visited.

12. Tap to have places of interest appear on the map, allowing you to tap them and quickly get driving directions to those locations.

13. Tap to manage what areas of the map you have downloaded to your S7. When an area is downloaded, you can navigate that area while you're disconnected from the Internet.

14. Tap to explore places of interest in your area.

15. Tap to overlay traffic conditions on the map.

16. Tap to overlay public transportation locations on the map.

17. Touch to overlay cycling paths on the map.

Changing Google Maps Settings

See the "Configure Google Maps Settings" task later in this chapter for more information about customizing Google Maps.

Get Directions

You can use Google Maps to get directions to where you want to go.

1. Tap the search field.

2. Type a search term, place name, or address

3. Tap the destination.

4. Swipe up to see information about the destination.

5. Swipe up to see additional information about the destination.

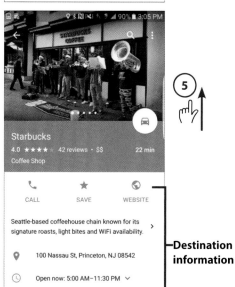

Destination information

6. Tap to return to the map view.

7. Choose your mode of transport. You can choose to drive, take public transportation, walk, or cycle the route.

Public Transportation

If you choose to use public transportation to get to your destination, you have two extra options to use. You can choose the type of public transportation to use, including bus, subway, train, or tram/light rail. You can also choose the best route (fewer transfers and less walking).

8. Tap the Menu icon to change the way the map looks and to set route options. If you don't want to make any changes, skip to step 19.

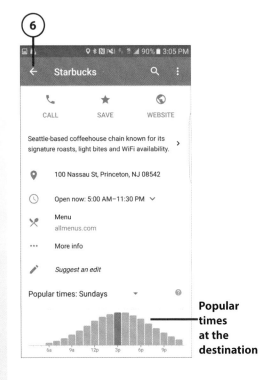

Popular times at the destination

9. Tap to reverse the start and destination points.

10. Tap to share the directions with friends using social media and other methods like email.

11. Tap to overlay traffic conditions on the map.

12. Tap to switch between a satellite image and a regular map.

13. Tap to show terrain on a map view. If you select terrain, the traffic and satellite choices are unchecked.

14. Tap to set route options. If you don't want to make any changes to the route options, skip to step 19.

15. Check the box to calculate the route to the destination while avoiding highways.

16. Check the box to calculate the route to the destination while avoiding tolls.

17. Check the box to calculate the route to the destination while avoiding ferries.

18. Tap Done.

19. Tap to start your turn-by-turn directions. Follow the voice prompts to navigate to your destination.

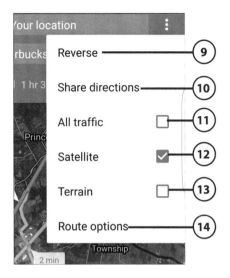

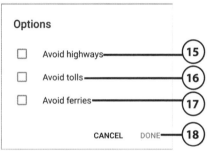

20. Tap the search icon to include gas stations, restaurants, grocery stores, and coffee shops along the route. This is useful if you want to stop in at one of these locations during your trip.

21. Tap to adjust the volume of the voice prompts. You can choose to mute the voice prompts, play them at an increased volume, or play them at the normal volume.

22. Tap to orient the map to always face north, or to follow the direction that you are traveling.

23. Tap the Menu icon to change the turn-by-turn voice prompt settings including choose whether you want voice prompts while on a phone call, whether you want voice prompts to play over Bluetooth, and whether you want to be given an estimated time of arrival (ETA) when you connect to your car's Bluetooth.

Configure Google Maps Settings

1. Swipe in from the left side of the screen.

2. Tap Settings.

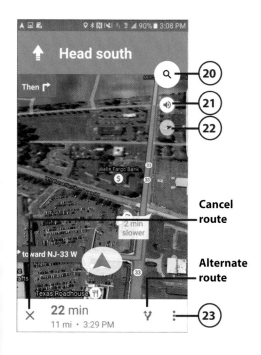

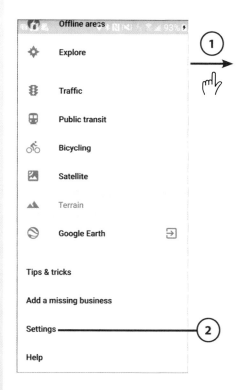

3. Tap to edit your work and home addresses. Telling Maps your home and work addresses is important for Google Now to work efficiently, but it also helps you quickly plan new routes to work and home.

4. Tap to view and manage areas of the map that you have saved offline to your S7.

5. Tap to enable or disable the capability for your phone to report its location. You can also choose the accuracy of your location by changing the mode.

6. Tap to improve your location accuracy if you think that your phone is not reporting it correctly.

7. Tap to see addresses you have looked up and received directions to. You can also delete items in this list.

8. Tap to manage what notifications you receive from Google Maps. These include notifications about traffic events on the planned route.

9. Tap to set the distance unit of measure. You can either set it to automatic so that Google Maps adjusts it based on where you are on the planet, or you can manually set it.

10. Tap to choose whether you want to see a scale on the map always or only when you are zooming in and out.

11. Swipe up for more settings.

12. Turn the switch to on to enable a feature where you can simply shake your S7 to send feedback to Google about Google Maps.

13. Tap to change the navigation settings.

14. Tap to set the unit of measure, or leave it on automatic.

15. Tap to change the voice level of the spoken turn-by-turn directions.

16. Tap to enable or disable playing turn-by-turn voice prompts while you are on a phone call.

17. Tap to enable or disable playing turn-by-turn voice prompts using a Bluetooth headset or your car's Bluetooth connection.

18. Tap to play a test of how loud the voice prompts are.

19. Tap to enable or disable a feature that tilts the map during turn-by-turn directions so that you can see a view from your perspective. Turning this off shows the map from directly above you.

20. Tap to enable or disable a feature that speaks your ETA when your S7 connects to your car's Bluetooth connection.

21. Tap to add a shortcut to "Driving" on your Home screen. Tapping the shortcut in the future will take you straight to the navigation mode, but it will also provide ETAs on trips you have made in the past, such as driving to work or driving home.

22. Tap to save your changes and go back to the previous screen.

Use Offline Google Maps

Google Maps enables you to download small parts of the global map to your phone. This is useful if you are traveling and need an electronic map but cannot connect to a network to download it in real time.

1. Swipe in from the left of the screen.

2. Tap Offline Areas.

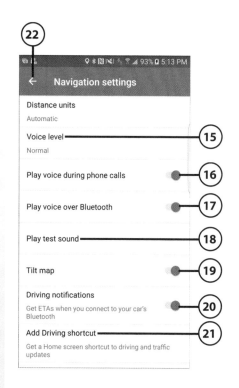

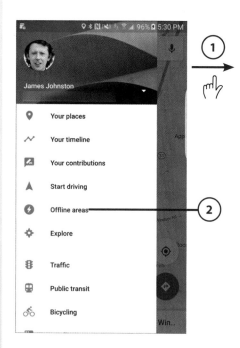

3. Tap the plus symbol to save a new area of the map offline.

4. Pan around to find the area of the map you want to save offline.

5. Pinch to zoom out or unpinch to zoom in to the area of the map you want to save offline. You cannot zoom out past a certain range.

6. Tap Download when you have the area of the map you want to save in the blue viewing area.

7. Type a name for the offline map and tap Save.

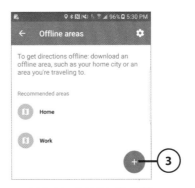

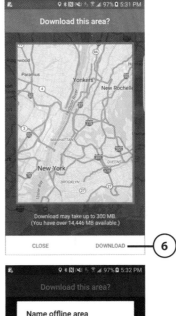

How Much Map Can I Take Offline?

When selecting the area of the map to take offline, you are limited to how far you can zoom out. That equates to around 1.5GB of map data. A saved map is automatically deleted after 30 days.

It's Not All Good

Offline Maps Have Some Limitations

If you download one or more areas of the map, they are saved on your Galaxy S7 and can be accessed in the future when you have no cellular data coverage. Within the saved map areas, when you have no data coverage, you can zoom right in to street level and tap on places to view information about them. You can also get turn-by-turn directions within the saved map areas. However, because your phone is not connected to the Internet, the map will not be able to show you progress nor will it be able to show traffic conditions.

Purchase and download music to your Galaxy S7

Play and manage music from the Google Play Store

Download and manage podcasts

In this chapter, you find out how to get the most out of the audio and music playing capabilities of the Galaxy S7. Topics in this chapter include the following:

→ Purchasing music
→ Playing songs and creating a playlist
→ Adding a podcast app

Playing and Managing Music

Your Galaxy S7 is a digital media player packed with entertainment possibilities. You can play music using the preinstalled Google Play Music app. You can also download apps from the Google Play Store to listen to podcasts and audiobooks.

Purchasing Music in Google Play Music

The Galaxy S7 includes the preinstalled Google Play Music app for finding, previewing, purchasing, downloading, and playing music. This app isn't the only one you can use, however—there are plenty of other music apps available for download in the Google Play Store.

1. Tap the Apps icon on the Home screen.

2. Tap Play Music.

3. Tap Learn More to discover more about adding songs and copying music to your phone.

4. For now, tap No Thanks.

5. From the Listen Now screen, tap the Menu icon in the menu bar.

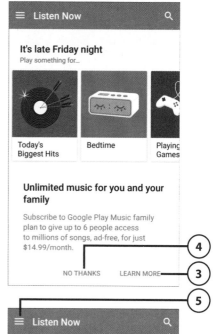

6. Tap Shop in the list to open the Music screen within the Google Play Store.

7. The Music screen shows the latest free music and exclusive videos. Swipe up and down the screen to view more featured songs and albums in a variety of categories.

How Do I Know If a Song Has Explicit Lyrics?

If you don't want to listen to songs with explicit lyrics (and/or don't want your kids to listen to them), you can easily see which songs and albums have explicit lyrics by looking for the Parental Advisory warning within the song or album tile. You also see the word Explicit in the lower-left corner of the song or album tile.

The Parental Advisory warning label in the album tile

8. Tap More to view more songs and albums in the category.

9. Tap Top Songs to view the best-selling songs in the Google Play Store.

10. Tap Top Albums to view the best-selling albums in the Google Play Store.

11. Within the button bar at the top of the page, swipe from right to left to view more options.

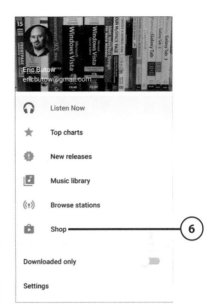

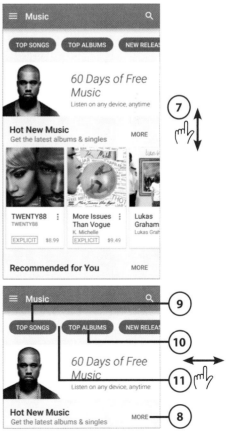

12. Tap New Releases to view the newest albums in the Google Play Store.

13. Tap Genres to view categories of music you can choose from.

14. View all the genres by swiping up and down in the list. When you find a genre you want, tap the genre name in the list.

15. Swipe up and down the screen to view different sections of the genre page.

16. Tap Top Charts.

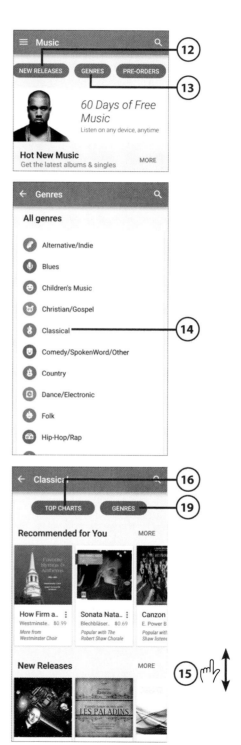

17. Top-selling albums in that genre appear on the screen. Tap a category to view new releases and top songs in the genre.

18. Tap the Back icon to return to the genre page.

19. Tap Genres to view a list of sub-genres within the main genre.

20. Tap a subgenre in the list.

21. Top-selling albums in that sub-genre appear on the screen. Swipe up and down the screen to view all the top albums.

22. Tap New Releases to view newly released songs and albums within that subgenre.

23. Tap Top Songs to view the best-selling songs in the subgenre.

24. Tap the Back icon to return to the genre page.

25. Tap the album or song tile on the screen to view more information.

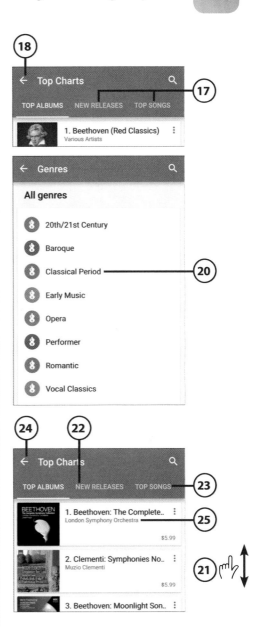

26. The title and album cover appear at the top of the screen. You can purchase the entire album by tapping the orange purchase button that contains the album price.

27. Swipe from bottom to top on the page to view a description of the album and artist, view songs in the album, read reviews from other Google Play users who downloaded the songs or album, see more albums by the artist, and also view similar artists.

28. Swipe up and down the screen if necessary until you see the Songs section, and then tap a song name to play a 90-second snippet of that song.

29. Tap Play All to play all the snippets in the album.

30. Purchase a song on the album by tapping the purchase button that contains the price of that specific song.

A Song Says It's "Album Only." What Does That Mean?

You might not be able to purchase one or more individual songs within the album. Instead, you need to purchase the entire album to hear the song(s). When you see a song in the list that says "Album Only" it means you can't purchase that individual song to download and listen to on your Galaxy S7.

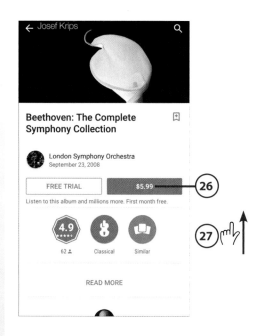

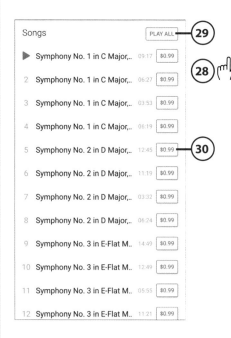

31. Swipe down the screen until you see the album cover and then tap the orange price button.

32. The Google Play window appears with the price of the album and the credit card that the Google Play Store will use to process the transaction.

33. Tap Buy to purchase the album.

34. After you purchase the album, a Shopping bag with a checkmark tells you that you successfully downloaded the album to your Galaxy S7 (not shown).

Playing Songs and Creating a Playlist

The Play Music app makes it easy for you to listen to music from the Google Play Store directly within the app. When you like a song, the Play Music app also makes it easy to add the song to your playlist so you can open the playlist and play your favorite songs whenever you want.

1. Tap Google on the Home screen.

2. Tap Play Music.

3. From the Listen Now screen, tap the Menu icon at the left side of the menu bar, as discussed earlier in this chapter.

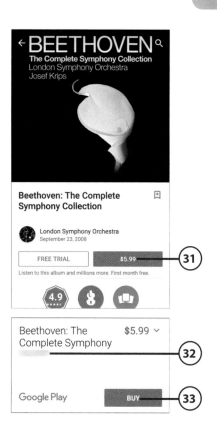

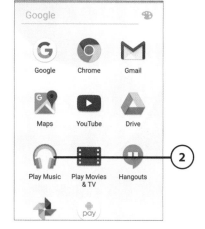

4. Tap Music Library.

5. Within the list of categories in the orange menu bar, the selected category is Songs. Swipe from left to right to view more categories.

6. Swipe up and down the list of songs (if necessary) and then tap the song title in the list.

7. Tap the Pause button while you're playing the song to pause playback.

8. Tap the Play button to resume playing the song (not shown).

9. Tap the Play bar at the bottom of the screen to view more options.

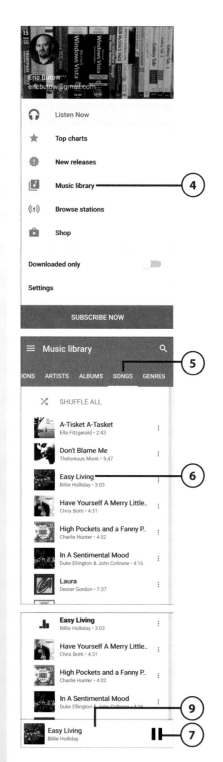

10. By default, the Repeat icon is active so the song will repeat when it finishes playing. Tap the icon to turn off the repeat feature; when the current song finishes playing, Google Music Player begins to play the next song in your queue.

11. Tap the Rewind icon to begin playing at the beginning of the song.

12. Tap the Pause button while you're playing the song to pause playback.

13. Tap the Fast Forward icon to move to the end of the song.

14. Tap the Shuffle icon to play a random song in your library after the current song ends.

15. Rate the song so other Google Play Music users can see your rating by tapping the thumbs up (good) or thumbs down (bad) icon.

16. Tap the Library icon to view all songs in your library; you can listen to another song in your library by tapping the song in the list.

17. Return to the My Library screen by tapping the Back touch button.

18. Open the menu for the song by tapping the Menu icon to the right of the song name.

19. Tap Start Radio to add the song to your own personal radio station that you can then listen to on any Android smartphone, an Apple iPhone or iPod, or on the Google Play Music website.

20. Tap start Instant Mix to have the Play Music app randomly play all songs in the list.

21. Play the next song in the list by tapping Play Next.

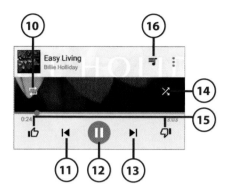

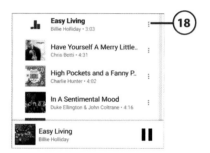

22. Download the song to your Galaxy S7 by tapping Add to Queue.

23. Add the song to a new playlist by tapping Add to Playlist.

24. Within the Add to Playlist window, tap New Playlist to add the song to a new playlist in the New Playlist window.

25. Type the playlist name in the Name field.

26. Type a description of your playlist in the Description field.

27. Share your playlist with all other Google Play Music users who view your profile by sliding the Public slider button from left (off) to right (on). Otherwise, only you are able to hear music in the playlist.

28. Tap Create Playlist. A pop-up box appears at the bottom of the screen that informs you that Play Music added the song to your playlist. Open the song options menu again by tapping the Menu icon to the right of the song title.

29. View all the artist's albums that you've added to your library by tapping Go to Artist.

30. View the album you've added to your library by tapping Go to Album.

31. Tap Delete to delete the song from your Galaxy S7 and from your playlist within the Play Music app.

32. Tap Share to share the song directly with another device using Android Beam, Bluetooth, or Wi-Fi Direct, save the song to your Google Drive account, copy the song link to the clipboard, or share the song as a link within the Email, Facebook, Gmail, Google Hangouts, Memo, or Messages app.

33. Tap Shop This Artist to shop for more music from the artist in the Google Play Store.

34. Tap Buy to purchase the song in the Google Play Store.

35. Tap the Back touch button to return to the main Play Music screen.

Adding a Podcast App

One popular podcast manager is BeyondPod, and the lite version of it is free. The lite version has all the features of the Pro version except that scheduling of updates is disabled, you can update only one feed at a time, and you can download only one podcast at a time.

During the first 7 days after installation you can use the full version of BeyondPod at no charge. If you decide you want all the bells and whistles BeyondPod has to offer, you can purchase an unlock key for $6.99. If not, you can continue to use the free lite version indefinitely.

1. Find the BeyondPod app in the Google Play Store and install it. (Read Chapter 12, "Working with Android Applications," for more information on getting apps from the Google Play Store.) After you have installed the app, tap Open to launch the app.

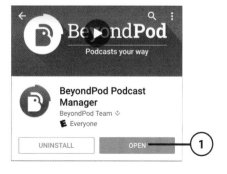

2. Tap Let's Start in the Welcome screen.

3. Swipe up and down in the window and tap one or more podcast categories. After you tap a category, a checkmark appears in the upper-right corner of the category tile. When you're finished, tap Continue.

4. Keep the default settings and tap Finish.

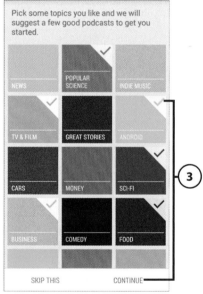

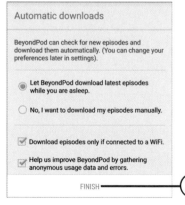

5. Scroll up and down the feeds list in the What to Play window within the My Feeds screen. Tap the down arrow to the right of a feed category name to view podcasts within that category.

6. Tap a podcast to view the episodes.

7. Tap No, Thanks to close the Quick Tour box at the top of the screen.

8. In the My Episodes screen, each recent episode appears as a tile on the screen. Swipe up and down the screen if necessary to view all recent episodes. If you don't see the episode you want, tap See All Published Episodes at the bottom of the list.

9. Add an episode to your episode list by tapping the Menu icon within the episode tile and then tapping Add to My Episodes in the menu.

10. Return to the list of your episodes by tapping the podcast name in the menu bar.

11. Tap Download to download the episode to your Galaxy S7.

12. Tap Add to Playlist to add the episode to your playlist.

13. Tap the Menu icon to view a menu with more options.

14. Tap Delete Episode to delete the episode tile from the My Episodes screen.

15. Tap Set as Favorite to mark the episode as a favorite. After you add the episode as a favorite, the favorite icon (a red heart) appears to the left of the podcast publication date at the top of the tile.

16. Tap Mark Played to mark the episode as one you've already listened to. After you mark the episode as played, the episode tile is gray so you can't play the episode.

17. Tap Share Episode to share the episode link using the Memo app, Android Beam, Facebook, Google Drive, Google Hangouts, the Messages app, Bluetooth, Wi-Fi Direct, Gmail or Email, or to copy the episode link to the clipboard.

18. Tap Play to play the episode.

19. The number of episodes in your playlist appears in the upper-right corner of the podcast tile in the feeds list. View all episodes in your playlist for that feed by tapping the playlist number.

20. Tap the car icon to view a large control area at the bottom half of the screen. This large control area includes a large Play button as well as buttons to rewind, fast forward, go to the beginning of the podcast, or skip to the end of the podcast.

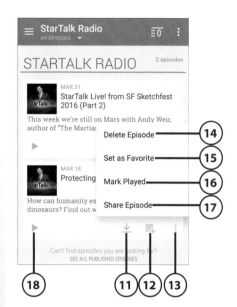

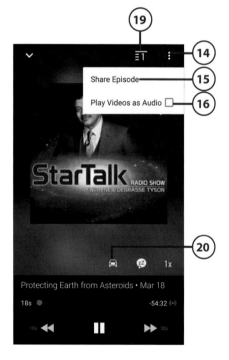

21. Turn on sleep mode to pause the playback automatically after a certain period of time by tapping Sleep and then tapping the amount of time you want to play the podcast before it stops playing.

22. Change the playback speed by tapping 1x. Note that you can't change the speed of streamed podcasts, which are podcasts that play while the podcast app receives the rest of the podcast.

23. Use the slider to shuttle through the podcast. When the podcast ends, BeyondPod begins to play the next episode in the playlist, if any.

24. Use the playback controls to pause, play, or jump forward or backward in the podcast.

25. View a menu with more options by tapping the Menu icon.

26. Tap Share Episode to share the episode link using the Memo app, Android Beam, Facebook, Google Drive, Google Hangouts, the Messages app, Bluetooth, Wi-Fi Direct, Gmail or Email, or to copy the episode link to the clipboard.

27. Tap Play Videos as Audio to play the episode in audio mode only.

28. Return to the My Episodes screen by tapping the down arrow icon.

29. The podcast information appears in the playback box at the bottom of the screen so you can play the episode by tapping the Play icon.

30. View the options menu for the My Episodes screen by tapping the Menu icon.

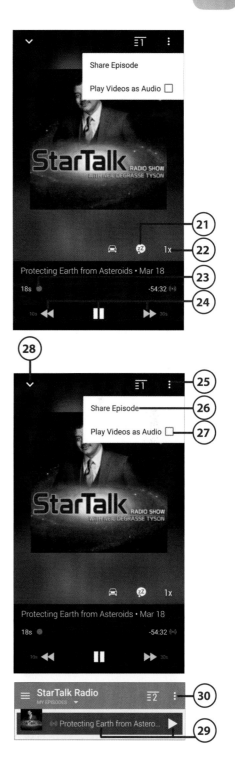

31. Tap Update Feed to refresh the current feed on the page.

32. Tap Sort to sort episodes in the My Episodes list by a variety of criteria, such as listing the episodes alphabetically by name.

33. Tap Filter to filter episodes in the My Episodes list by a variety of criteria, such as viewing only those episodes you downloaded to your Galaxy S7.

34. Tap Share Feed to share the feed link using the Memo app, Android Beam, Facebook, Google Drive, Google Hangouts, the Messages app, Bluetooth, Wi-Fi Direct, Gmail or Email, or to copy the feed link to the clipboard.

35. Tap Edit Feed to edit feed settings such as changing the feed category.

36. Tap Search to search for a feed in the BeyondPod database.

37. Tap Compact Cards to hide the brief description of the episode in each episode tile.

38. Tap Play Videos as Audio to play all episodes within the feed in audio mode only.

39. Close the menu by pressing the Back touch button.

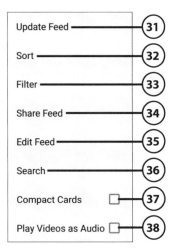

Automatically Updating Feeds

By default, feeds are set to automatically update on a configurable interval. You can change the interval by tapping and holding on the left edge of the screen and then swiping right. Within the menu, tap Settings. In the BeyondPod Settings screen, tap Feed Update Settings to change the interval.

Deleting Feeds

If you want to delete a feed, tap and hold your finger on the left side of the screen and then swipe right. Within the menu, tap and hold on the feed name for a couple of seconds. A pop-up menu displays that includes a Delete Feed option.

Edit and share
photos

Browse, manage, and
share photos

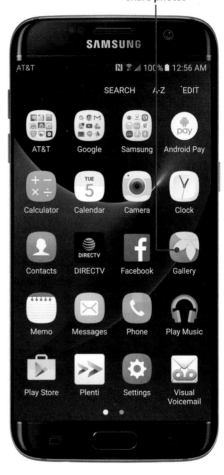

Capture photos

In this chapter, you find out how to capture photos and screenshots, share photos via email and slideshows, and view and manage photos with Gallery.

→ Using the camera
→ Tips for capturing photos
→ Navigating Image Viewer
→ Working with Gallery
→ Editing and sharing images
→ Performing screen captures

Taking and Sharing Photos

Along with transferring images from other sources, such as your computer, to your Galaxy S7, you can also take high-quality photos with your Galaxy S7, which can house thousands of photos organized in categories. You also have the capability to take screenshots of the Galaxy S7 interface.

The high-resolution screen on your Galaxy S7 offers a great way to showcase photos to friends and family, but you don't have to stop there. You can also share pictures via Bluetooth, email, Facebook, Instagram, and more.

Using the Camera

Both the Galaxy S7 and S7 edge use a 12.0-megapixel rear-facing camera located on the back of the device to take photos, along with a 5.0-megapixel front-facing camera that you can use for self-portraits.

Taking a photo can be as simple as choosing a subject, composing your shot, and pressing a button. The Galaxy S7 is also equipped with some helpful features commonly found on dedicated photo cameras, including shooting modes, scene modes, manual exposure, white balance, flash, manual exposure, and ISO settings.

Why Does the Camera App Stop Running on Its Own?

If you don't use the Camera app for two minutes, then the app automatically minimizes and you return to the Home page. This approach helps conserve battery life as the app is resource intensive. You can return to the Camera app by tapping the Recent Apps button and then tapping the Camera tile in the Recent Apps screen.

Change Quick Settings

1. On the Home screen, tap Camera.

2. The first time you start the Camera app, the Location Tags window appears and informs you that location tags will be turned on. Tap OK to continue. The next time you start the Camera app, proceed to step 3.

Location tags

Location tags will be turned on.

Learn more

CANCEL   OK

Vertical or Horizontal View?

You can take pictures in the view that's most comfortable for you: vertical or horizontal. The examples in this section starting with step 3 are in horizontal view, so when you use the Camera app, keep in mind that the location of features on the screen in vertical view will be different from what is described here. For example, in vertical view the Settings icon is in the upper-left corner of the screen, but in horizontal view the icon is in the lower-left or upper-right corner of the screen depending on how you hold the Galaxy S7.

3. The Quick Settings icons appear at the left side of the Viewer screen. Hide the Quick Settings icons by tapping the up arrow.

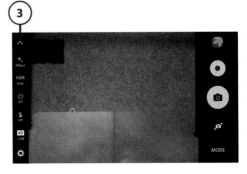

4. View the Quick Settings icons again by tapping the down arrow.

5. Select an effect to apply to your photo after you take the photo by tapping Effect.

6. Tap the Effect tile in the list; the selected effect appears with a checkmark in the center of the tile.

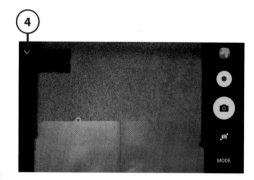

7. Tap Manage to rearrange the Effect icons in the Manage screen.

8. Tap Download to shop for and download another effect in the Galaxy Apps store.

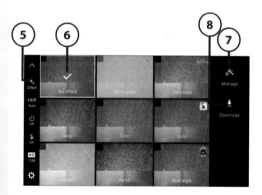

9. An image that is too light or too dark degrades the appearance of your photos. The Galaxy S7 contains the HDR (High Dynamic Range) setting so the device automatically adjusts the brightness level for various bright or dark lighting conditions. HDR automatic mode is on by default, which means the Camera app checks the lighting conditions and applies the HDR feature if needed. Tap HDR Auto to turn the HDR feature on for every photo you take.

10. Tap HDR On to turn the HDR feature off.

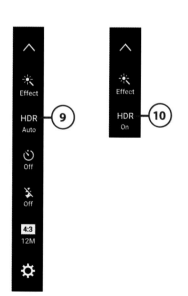

11. Tap HDR Off to return the HDR feature to automatic mode.

12. Tap the Timer icon to designate how long the Galaxy S7 should wait before the camera takes a photo. This is great when you want to set up the shot and then place yourself in the frame.

13. Select the timer option in the Timer window. The default option is Off, but you can select from 2 seconds, 5 seconds, or 10 seconds.

14. The camera flash is off by default. Tap the Flash icon to turn on automatic flash mode, which means the Camera app checks the lighting conditions and applies the flash if lighting is too dim.

15. Tap Flash Auto to turn the flash on for every photo you take.

16. Tap Flash On to turn the flash off.

17. Tap the Picture Size icon to change the picture size and aspect ratio.

18. Select the picture size in the Picture Size window. The default size is a 4:3 aspect ratio; the corresponding image size of the photo and the picture size in pixels appear to the right of the aspect ratio. You can select two different picture sizes in 4:3, 16:9, and 1:1 aspect ratios.

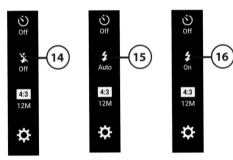

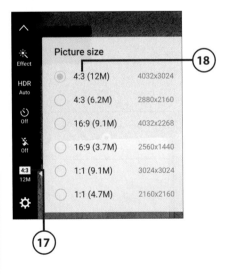

What Is the Aspect Ratio?

The aspect ratio of a screen or image is the proportional relationship between the width and height, and it's expressed as the width and height numbers separated by a colon. For example, a 4:3 screen aspect ratio means the rectangular dimensions of the screen are 4 units wide and 3 units high, and each unit contains 1,008 pixels.

View and Change Pro Settings

By default, the Camera app takes photos in Auto mode so you can take photos and know that they'll look great. If you need more control over how your photos look, you can access Pro settings and make manual changes to the color effect, focus mode, white balance, ISO value, and exposure value.

1. Tap Mode in the lower-right corner of the screen.

2. Tap Pro in the menu screen.

3. The Pro settings appear on the right side of the screen.

4. Tap Standard to apply a color effect after you take the photo.

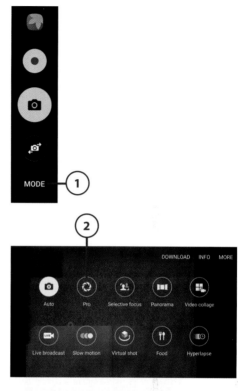

5. Swipe up and down the color effect list to view the effects. The default effect is Standard, which contains the default color settings. The selected effect has a white checkmark in the middle of the color effect tile.

6. Each tile shows you how the photo looks in comparison to the Standard effect.

7. Create a new custom effect by swiping down the list and then tapping Tone 1 or Tone 2. You can add up to two custom effects.

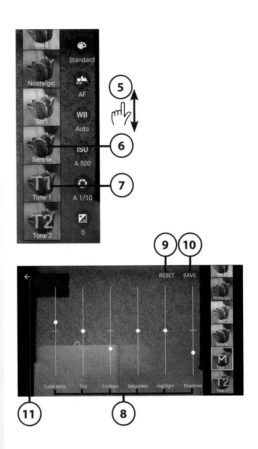

8. Change the effect by moving one or more of the six setting sliders up and down. You can change the color temperature, tint, contrast, saturation, highlight, and shadow levels. As you move each slider, the Viewer changes to show how your color effects will appear in a photo.

9. Reset effect settings to their default levels by tapping Reset.

10. Save your changes by tapping Save.

11. Return to the Viewer without making changes by tapping the Back icon.

12. Tap the Focus Mode icon to manually change the focus. The default is AF, which stands for Auto Focus, but you can slide the button on the slider bar up and down. You can swipe between close focus, which is signified by the flower icon, and broader focus, which is signified by the mountain icon.

13. The focus setting name below the Focus Mode icon (AF in this example) changes to MF, or Manual Focus, after you have manually set the focus.

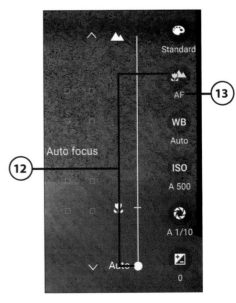

Can I Select a Focus Between Auto and Close?

You can't select a focus on the slider bar between Auto and Close Focus. When you try, after you release your finger from the slider button the Camera app determines the setting to which the slider button is closest and then automatically moves to either the Close Focus or Auto setting in the slider bar.

14. Tap the WB icon (WB stands for White Balance) to adjust the white balance for the camera. The white balance features help accurately reproduce colors when you are shooting in various lighting situations so that neutral colors, such as white and gray, are truly neutral and all colors are rendered without undesired color casts, or tints of colors that affect the entire photo evenly.

15. Move the slider button up and down between Incandescent, Fluorescent, Daylight, and Cloudy white balances. Move the slider button all the way to the top of the slider bar (next to the K icon) to set the white balance level manually.

16. The white balance level appears below the WB icon after you have selected a white balance mode or have set the balance manually.

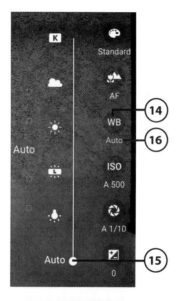

17. Tap the ISO icon to adjust the brightness level in your photo. The default level in the slider bar is Auto, which means the digital sensor in your camera senses the amount of light and changes the brightness level so you have a better chance of getting a good shot.

18. Slide the button in the slider bar up to achieve a proper brightness level in a low-light shooting environment, or slide the button down for a bright shooting environment. You can select from one of five levels: Auto, 100, 200, 400, and 800. If you release your finger from the button between one of the levels, the button moves to the level closest to the button.

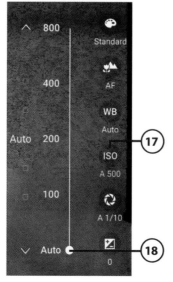

19. The level number appears below the ISO icon after you have selected the ISO level. (It's A 500, which stands for Auto 500, in this example.) The Viewer also changes the light level so you can see whether the selected ISO level is appropriate for your environment.

20. Tap the Shutter Speed icon to change your shutter speed. The speed determines how long the digital sensor in the camera is exposed to light when you take a photo. Slower shutter speeds allow more light in so the photo is brighter, which is ideal for taking photos in dark environments. Faster shutter speeds allow less light in so you can take pictures of fast-moving objects or effects such as a lightning strike. The default speed is Auto, which is 1/10th of a second.

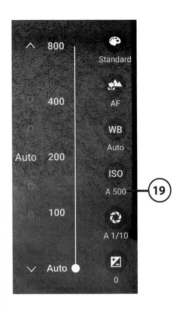

21. Slide the button in the slider bar up to determine how long the digital sensor is exposed to light. You can select from one of five levels: Auto, 1/24000th of a second, 1/500th of a second, 1/10th of a second, and 10 seconds. If you release your finger from the button between one of the levels, the button moves to the level closest to the button. Remember that if the shutter speed is at any level other than Auto, you can't change the exposure value because the Camera app automatically sets the exposure value to the appropriate level for your shutter speed.

22. The level number appears below the Shutter Speed icon after you have selected the shutter speed. (It's A 1/10 in this example.) The Viewer also changes the light level so you can see whether the selected shutter speed is appropriate for your environment.

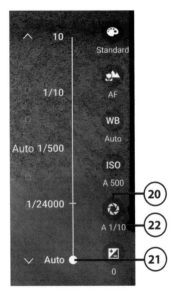

23. Change the exposure value by tapping the Exposure icon. The exposure value determines how much light the camera's sensor receives.

24. Slide the button in the slider bar up if you're in a low-light environment or slide the button down for a bright shooting environment. You can slide to any level between +2 and –2. 0 is the default setting.

25. The value appears below the Exposure icon after you have selected the exposure value. The Viewer also changes the light level so you can see whether the selected exposure value is appropriate for your environment.

26. Tap Metering to set how the camera measures or meters the light source. This setting determines how the camera factors light in a scene to achieve the proper exposure.

27. Change the metering mode in the Metering Modes window.

28. Save all your Pro settings so you don't have to set them each time you use the camera by tapping Custom.

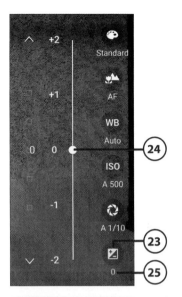

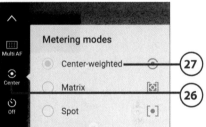

LOOKING AT METERING MODES

The default Metering setting is Center-Weighted. Your other choices are Matrix, which measures light intensity in several points to achieve the best exposure, and Spot, where only a small area in the scene is measured. Matrix metering is usually considered the most accurate form of metering because it measures the entire scene and then sets the exposure according to an average. Spot metering is generally used to capture very-high-contrast scenes, such as when a subject's back is to the sun.

29. Tap Save Current Settings in the Custom Settings window.

30. Tap one of the three custom setting names into which you can save your settings.

31. Tap Save.

32. The custom setting icon appears in the Viewer so you can tap the icon to change to your preferred camera settings automatically.

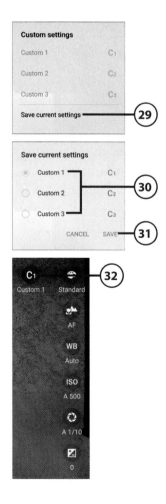

Set Camera Modes

You can apply special effects to your photos by selecting from one of three camera modes. If you don't see the camera mode you want, you can download other modes from Samsung's Galaxy Apps store.

1. Tap Mode in the lower-right corner of the Viewer.

2. If you want to have one or more specific objects in your photo stand out, tap Selective Focus. After you take the photo, you can specify which object(s) have sharper focus and which objects do not.

3. Tap Panorama to take a picture and then use the onscreen guide to move the viewfinder and take seven more shots. Then you can stitch each individual shot together to capture a wide vista, such as landscapes and cityscapes.

4. Tap Virtual Shot to take a series of photos around an object by moving the Galaxy S7 around the object. When the Camera app finishes taking the photos, the app stitches those photos together and creates a brief video that shows a 270-degree view of the object.

5. If you don't see a camera mode that meets your needs, tap Download to shop for other camera modes in the Galaxy Apps store.

6. Return to the Viewer by tapping the Back touch button (not shown).

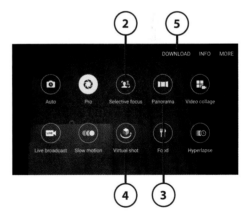

Change Camera Settings

The Camera app contains a variety of settings you can view and/or change. Some of the settings allow you to change the video camera, but this section discusses camera settings only. Refer to Chapter 10, "Watching and Creating Videos," for more information about video settings within the Camera app.

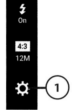

1. In the Viewer, tap the Settings icon to customize camera quick settings.

2. The Camera Settings screen appears with five setting options in the list.

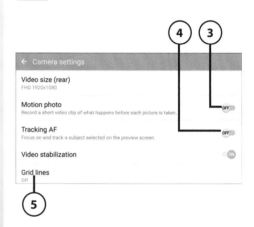

3. Slide the Motion Photo slider from left (Off) to right (On) so the Camera app records a video for three seconds before you tap the Camera button. When you view the photo in the Preview screen, you can preview the video by tapping the Preview icon in the upper-right corner of the photo. Then you can capture a still image from that video if you want.

4. Slide the Tracking AF slider button from left (Off) to right (On) to focus on and track an object. If the object of your photo moves between the time the camera achieves focus and the time the photo is captured, the object will be blurred. With the Tracking AF feature on, the camera follows the moving object and keeps it in focus so your photo isn't blurry.

5. Tap Grid Lines to enable an onscreen grid that can help you with composition.

6. Swipe up on the screen to view the next four setting options.

7. Slide the Location Tags slider to the left (Off) or right (On) to disable or enable, respectively, GPS tagging of the photos you capture. Embedded GPS information can come in handy if you use an application for photo editing and management, such as Photoshop, which enables you to use the location information to manage and showcase photos.

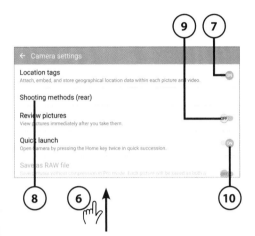

8. If you want to use your voice to take photos on the Galaxy S7, tap Shooting Methods (Rear). In the Shooting Methods (Rear) screen (not shown), slide the Voice Control slider button from left (Off) to right (On). You can use one of four different voice commands to capture a photo: Smile, Cheese, Capture, or Shoot. After you turn on voice control, return to the Camera Settings screen by tapping the Back icon in the upper-left corner of the screen.

9. Slide the Review Pictures slider to the right (On) or left (Off) to turn the review screen on or off, respectively. If Review is turned on, you see a preview of the photo you just shot in the Review screen.

10. By default, you can open the Camera app by quickly pressing the Home key two times. You can turn this feature off by sliding the Quick Launch slider button from right (On) to left (Off).

11. Swipe up on the screen to view the last five setting options.

12. If you have selected Pro mode, slide the Save as RAW File slider to the right (On) or left (Off) to enable or disable, respectively, the ability to save files without compression when you take a picture in Pro mode. RAW pictures are saved in DNG file format and contain untouched pixel information straight from your camera sensor. Each picture you take will be saved in both DNG and JPG format files; you need a special app (like Photoshop) to view DNG files. If you take a burst picture in Pro mode then you can't save the photos in DNG format.

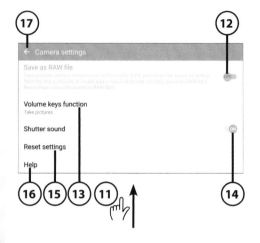

13. Tap Volume Keys Function to determine if the volume key acts as the zoom key, the video recording key, or the camera key. The default is the camera key, shown as "Take pictures" underneath the Volume Keys Function setting name.

14. By default, the Camera app makes a noise similar to an old camera shutter when you tap the Camera button. If you don't want to hear this sound, slide the Shutter Sound slider from right (On) to left (Off).

15. Tap Reset Settings to reset the Camera settings to their defaults.

16. Tap Help to get some quick onscreen help for the Camera app.

17. Return to the Viewer by tapping the Back icon.

What Is Burst Mode and How Do I Use It?

Burst Mode is built right into the Camera app and is useful when you want to take continuous photos within a few seconds, such as when you want to view different facial expressions a person makes over a few seconds. Just tap and hold on the Camera button as you take the shot. The Camera app stops taking photos after you release your finger or after the app has taken 30 photos. You can take up to 30 more photos in Burst Mode by tapping and holding on the camera button again.

Take a Photo

After you view and/or change Camera app settings, it's easy for you to take a photo with your Galaxy S7.

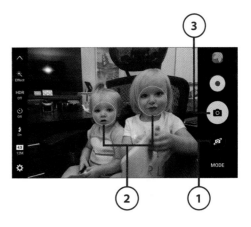

1. In the Viewer, tap to switch between the rear-facing and front-facing cameras. Tap again to return to the previous camera view.

2. Compose the subject in the Viewer. By default, Camera automatically focuses on what is in the center of the Viewer or on the face(s) in your shot, as shown by the yellow circle around the faces in this example.

3. Hold your finger on the Camera button, level the shot, and then remove your finger from the button to capture the image. A thumbnail of the image appears in the Image Viewer.

4. Tap the Image Viewer to review the image you just captured. You can also access your photos by tapping the Gallery icon under Applications from any Home screen.

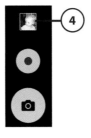

Why Are the Viewer Icons on Opposite Sides of the Screen?

There are two ways to hold your Galaxy S7 in horizontal view: with the Home button to your left or to your right of the screen. Most of the examples in this chapter show the icons when the screen is held in horizontal view with the Home button to the right. When you rotate the screen 180 degrees so the Home button is on your left, the icons switch sides on the screen so the Camera button and Image Viewer are on the right side of the screen, as you see in this example.

Navigating Image Viewer

Image Viewer provides a quick-and-easy way to review the photos you have just taken. It also enables you to quickly share your pictures as soon as you capture them or set them as wallpaper. You can also edit and delete unwanted photos in Image Viewer.

As soon as you take a picture, a thumbnail of that photo appears next to the Camera button. You can tap that thumbnail to review the picture you have taken and browse other photos.

1. Tap the Image Viewer to review the image.

2. The image opens full screen, the controls appear, and then they fade away. Tap the middle of the screen to access the controls again.

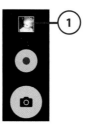

3. Tap to add the photo as a favorite that you can view in the Gallery app, which is covered later in this chapter in the "Working with Gallery" section.

4. Tap to access many options for sharing your photos through services and apps including the Messages app, the Memo app, the Maps app, the Photos app, Android Beam, Wi-Fi Direct, Bluetooth, Facebook, Hangouts, Kindle, Gmail, Email, Google Drive, and any other service (such as file storage) provided by your carrier. You can also view the photo on a connected device and print the photo, such as to a Bluetooth printer.

5. Tap to automatically adjust the photo for best viewing, rotate the photo, and crop the photo. You can also edit the photo in the Photo Editor app or create a collage of photos in the Collage app.

6. Tap to delete the currently displayed photo.

7. Swipe the image from left to right to navigate through all the photos you have captured.

8. Tap Album to view the album of all the photos you captured.

9. Tap More to access other options.

10. Tap to rotate the photo counterclockwise 90 degrees.

11. Tap to rotate the photo clockwise 90 degrees.

12. Tap to view details about the photo, including the time it was taken, the date it was captured, and the location where you took the photo.

13. Tap to begin a slideshow of your photos. After the slideshow begins, you can tap anywhere onscreen to end the slideshow.

14. Tap to set the current picture as a contact photo.

15. Swipe up in the menu to view more options.

16. Tap to set the current picture as wallpaper on your Home screen, Lock screen, or the Home and Lock screens.

17. Close the menu by tapping the Back touch button (not shown).

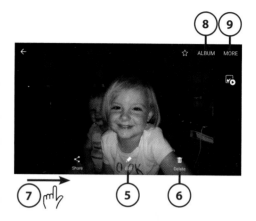

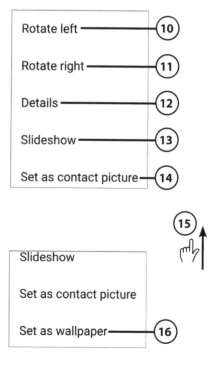

18. With the menu closed, double-tap the image to zoom in. You can double-tap it again to zoom out and return the image to its normal size. You can also touch the screen with two fingers and then move them apart to zoom in on an image.

19. Tap the Preview button to view a preview video of what happened in the three seconds before you took the picture. When the video stops playing, you return to the Image Viewer screen.

20. Tap the Back touch button (not shown) to return to the Camera app and take more pictures.

>>>Go Further

TIPS FOR CAPTURING PHOTOS

Shutter lag is the amount of time that elapses between your press of the shutter release button and the moment the picture is captured. A longer shutter lag is common among most compact cameras and also the Galaxy S7. What this means for you is that you have to be particularly mindful of timing your shots when recording moving subjects. Shutter lag can cause you to miss out on a key action if you do not anticipate the shot.

One important thing to know about your Galaxy S7 is that the shutter does not fire as you place your finger down on the Camera button; the shutter fires when you lift your finger off the button. Use this knowledge to your advantage by pressing your finger on the shutter button and holding while you frame the shot and focus on an object about the same distance as where the subject will pass, to anticipate the shot, and then lift your finger. This means you need to hold your Galaxy S7 completely still for a little bit longer. Anticipating moving subjects to capture dynamic, moving shots can take some practice.

The slow shutter on the Galaxy S7 makes it prone to producing blurry photos if you do not remain perfectly still during capture. Even the smallest movement can have an adverse effect on your photographs; this is especially true in low-light situations. A photo might appear to be fine when you review it on the Galaxy S7 display, but when you download it and view it on a larger display, you can see the problem.

Working with Gallery

Gallery offers a more robust photo and video management system than Image Viewer, but it has similar options for viewing, sharing, and editing photos.

Manage Photos with Gallery

By default, you can access the Gallery icon by flicking the main Home screen from left to right, or you can access it from the Apps menu.

1. Tap the Apps icon on the Home screen.

2. Tap Gallery in the Apps screen.

3. Content is arranged by the time the photos and videos were captured. If you have downloaded photos with your Galaxy S7 and transferred images from your computer, they are in here, too.

4. Tap Time to group your photos and videos in other ways. The name of this particular menu changes depending on which grouping method you have selected.

5. Tap the Time option to arrange photos and videos based on when they were taken.

6. Tap Events to arrange photos and videos by event, such as a birthday party. You can create events within the Events screen by tapping More in the menu bar, tapping Create Event, and then selecting the photos to add to your event.

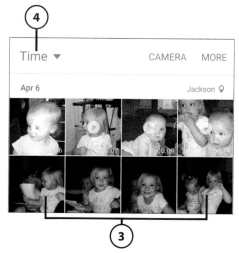

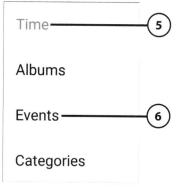

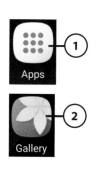

7. Tap Categories to arrange photos and videos based on various categories, such as People to show photos of people.

8. Tap Albums to arrange photos and videos based on how the photos and videos were captured. For example, the Camera album shows all photos and videos taken with the camera and the Screenshots album shows all your screen captures that you'll learn to take later in this chapter. This example shows photos and videos in albums.

9. Tap Camera in the menu bar to access the Camera feature from Gallery and take more photos.

10. Tap More.

11. Tap Edit to select one or more complete albums to delete.

12. Tap Search to search for a photo by typing search term(s) in the Search box, or you can search in different categories such as events and location where the photo was taken.

13. Tap Create Album to create a new album.

14. Tap Help to get quick help for the Gallery app.

15. Close the menu by tapping the Back touch button (not shown).

16. Tap an album to view all photos in it.

17. If you have more photos in the album than can fit on the screen, swipe up and down on the screen to view all thumbnail-sized photos in the album.

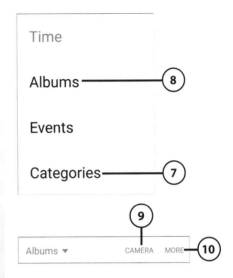

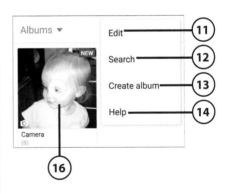

18. Tap and hold your finger on a photo for a couple of seconds to select it. The selected photo has a white checkbox with a black checkmark in the upper-left corner of the photo.

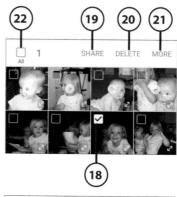

19. Tap Share to view options for sharing the selected image(s) in an email or Gmail message, on Google Drive, to OneNote or a memo, to another device using Samsung Quick Connect or a Wi-Fi Direct or Bluetooth connection, on Hangouts or Skype, Google+ or Facebook, or within the Instagram and Photos apps. You can also use your phone carrier's messaging, mail, and/or file storage services if applicable. And you can print the photo, such as to a Bluetooth printer.

20. Tap Delete to delete the photo from the album and the Galaxy S7 altogether.

21. Tap More to either copy or move the photo to another album.

22. Select all photos in the album by tapping the All checkbox.

23. Turn off the image selection feature by tapping the Back touch button (not shown), and then tap a photo in the album to open it full screen.

24. Touch the middle of the screen to reveal the controls if necessary and then tap the left arrow icon in the menu bar to return to the previous screen.

>>>Go Further
MORE PHOTO-EDITING OPTIONS

The Photo Editor is included in the Camera app and offers many more options for enhancing your photographs. You can edit your photo in Photo Editor by opening a photo full screen, tapping the center of the screen, and then tapping the Edit icon at the bottom of the screen. In Photo Editor you find options to rotate, resize, crop, color, and add effects.

Email Photos from Gallery

Emailing your photos to friends and family can be accomplished in just a few taps on your Galaxy S7. The following instructions presume you have set up an email account. If you haven't, bookmark this page and read Chapter 6, "Email and Text Messages," before you email your photos in the Gallery app.

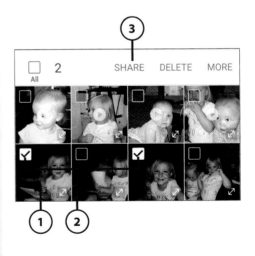

1. Open the album that has the photo you want to email, and then touch and hold your finger on that photo to access more Gallery options.

2. Touch more photos that you want to share. A black checkmark appears within the white checkbox that appears in the upper-left corner of each photo, letting you know that it is selected. Email providers have varying file size limitations, so make sure you are aware of your provider's limitations before emailing photographs.

3. Tap Share to access the options in the Share Via window that appears in the bottom half of the screen. You can access these same Share options even if you are viewing a single photo in full screen mode.

Additional Sharing Options

Keep in mind that as you add an email account or Facebook account on your Galaxy S7, those options also display in the Share Via window.

4. Swipe to the appropriate page with the Email app icon.

5. Tap Email.

6. The Email app opens and displays the email message on the screen. Tap the Back touch button (not shown) to close the keyboard and view the photo files attached to the message.

7. A list of the attached photo files appears below the Subject field and includes a small thumbnail image of each photo as well as the filename.

8. Tap Resize Image to open the Resize Image window and resize all the images when you include them in the email message.

9. Remove the attachment from the message by tapping the red minus icon located to the right of the photo name.

10. Type the recipient's email address into the To field. If you see the name of the recipient in the drop-down list as you type, tap the name of the recipient. After you add a recipient to the list, you can add another one by typing the recipient name; you don't need any separator characters, such as a semicolon.

11. Tap in the Subject field and then type a subject for the email.

12. Tap in the Compose Email field to compose a message.

13. Tap Send to send the message.

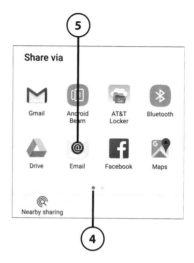

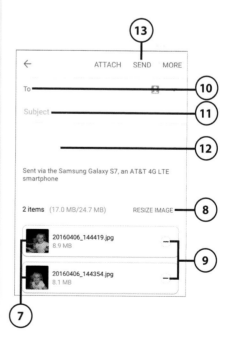

>>>Go Further
EMAILING FROM CAMERA

You can also email a photo from Camera within Image View. After you tap the Camera button to capture the image, a thumbnail of the image appears in the Image Viewer. Tap the Image Viewer to review the image, and then tap the Share icon to access your email. Email providers have varying file size limitations, so make sure you are aware of your provider's limitations before emailing photographs.

Creating Screen Captures

Your Galaxy S7 has a very helpful feature that enables you to take screen captures of its interface. The ability to take screenshots can come in handy for educational purposes, especially if you want to post a few Galaxy S7 tips online.

1. Open the screen that you want to take the screenshot of and position the Galaxy S7 into the orientation in which you want to grab the screen capture: vertical or horizontal.

2. Press and hold the Power button and Home button at the same time, or use your hand to swipe across the screen. Refer to the Prologue to read about the Palm Swipe to Capture feature.

3. You hear the shutter sound effect as it takes the screen capture. The screenshot is saved to the Screenshots folder in the Gallery app, and the image is also saved to the clipboard.

4. Three buttons appear at the bottom of the screen for about three seconds after you capture the screen, from left to right: Capture More (capture any scrollable area on the screen), Share (share the current screenshot), and Crop (crop the current screenshot). The first time you capture a screen, you see the tutorial screen; tap OK to close it. You won't see this tutorial screen with subsequent screen captures.

5. Swipe down in the Status bar to open the Quick Settings and Notification screen.

6. Tap Share to share the selected image(s) in an email or Gmail message, on Google Drive, to another device using Android Beam, Wi-Fi Direct, or Bluetooth connection, on Hangouts or Facebook, upload the link to the Photos app, send the image to your Amazon Kindle app, or as a link within the Maps, Memo, or Messages app. You can also use your phone carrier's messaging, mail, and/or file storage services if applicable.

7. In the Screenshot Captured tile, tap Edit to edit the screenshot in the Gallery app.

8. Tap Delete to delete the screenshot. In the Delete window that appears, finish the deletion process by tapping Delete.

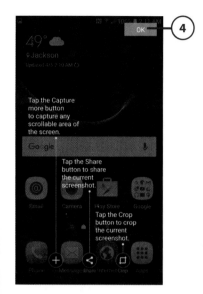

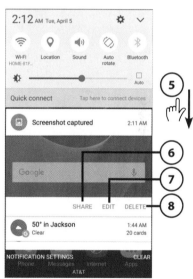

It's Not All Good

Difficulties Taking Screen Captures

It might not be possible to capture some of the Galaxy S7 menus using the Screen Capture function. For example, if you're playing a video, and then press and hold the Power button and Home button at the same time, the app you're using to view the video (such as YouTube) is minimized and the screenshot is not captured. You can resume playing the video by tapping the Recent touch button and then tapping the video app tile in the Recent Apps screen.

Record video

Play and
manage videos

Download and
watch movies
and TV shows

In this chapter, you find out how to get the most out of the video recording and playback capabilities of the Galaxy S7. Topics in this chapter include the following:

→ Purchasing movies and TV shows
→ Playing videos
→ Viewing YouTube videos
→ Recording video

10

Watching and Creating Videos

Your Galaxy S7 allows you to play movies, TV shows, and videos on its high-resolution screen using several preinstalled apps. What's more, the Galaxy S7 is camcorder capable, which you can use to record HD video.

Downloading Movies and TV Shows

The Google Play Store makes it easy for you to browse, purchase, and download the latest music, movies, and popular TV shows to your Galaxy S7. If you want to find movies and television shows within the Google Play Store more quickly than shopping in the Play Store itself, try using the preinstalled Play Movies & TV app.

The Play Movies & TV app enables you to shop for movies and television shows, pay for a movie or show if necessary, download the movie or show, and then watch the movie or show within the app.

Download a TV Show

In this example, you find out how to download a free television featurette.

1. Tap Google on the Home screen.

2. Tap Play Movies & TV.

3. Tap Get Started at the bottom of the introductory screen. If you've opened the Play Movies & TV app before, you won't see this introductory screen and you can skip ahead to step 4.

4. Tap the Menu icon in the menu bar.

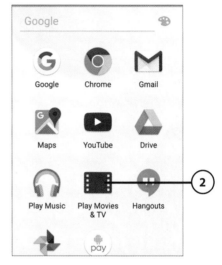

5. Tap Shop.

6. Tap TV in the button bar to view TV shows. This example walks through downloading a free TV show episode.

7. Swipe up in the TV page until you see the Free TV Episodes section. Tap More.

8. Swipe up in the page until you see the tile that contains the featurette you want to download and then tap the tile.

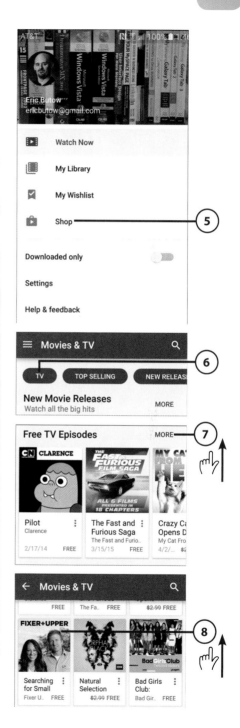

9. In the middle of the page, information about the selected featurette appears below the title, including an image, summary, and reviews from other Google Play Store users who have watched the video. Swipe up in the page to read more reviews and view a list of episodes and featurettes.

10. Tap Free to the right of the episode title.

11. The video begins to play in horizontal screen orientation (not shown).

12. When you finish viewing the featurette, tap the Back touch button. View the episode again by tapping the Last Watched tile.

13. Return to the My Library screen by tapping the Back icon in the menu bar. You'll learn more about the My Library screen in the next section.

Play the TV Show

The TV show you downloaded
appears within the My Library screen
so you can play it whenever you want.

1. The shows you have downloaded
   appear within the My TV Shows
   section. Swipe up and down in
   the screen to view all the TV show
   tiles.

2. Tap a tile to view more information about each video within the
   section.

3. Tap a tile to begin playing the
   video in horizontal screen
   orientation.

Shop for a Movie

It's easy to shop for movies that you
can buy and keep on your Galaxy S7
so you can watch them any time you
want.

1. From the Play Movies & TV app's
   home screen (the title of the
   screen is Watch Now), open the
   menu by tapping the Menu icon
   at the left side of the menu bar.

2. Tap Shop.

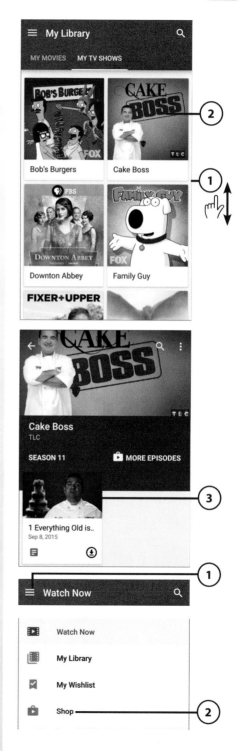

3. In the button bar, swipe from right to left to view the other three buttons on the screen.

4. Tap Genres.

5. Tap the genre you're interested in.

6. Swipe up and down in the page to view all the Top Selling movies in the category you selected. You can view new releases in the category by tapping New Movie Releases.

7. Tap the tile with the movie you want more information about.

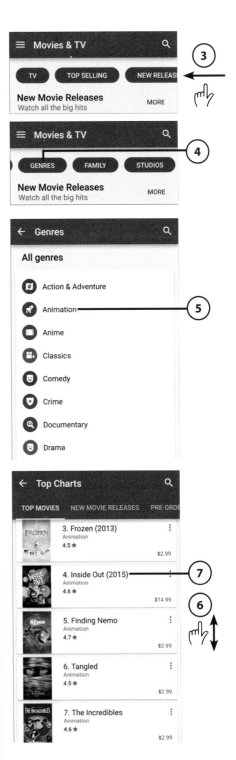

8. The name of the movie, the release year and movie rating, the movie run time, and buttons to either rent or buy the movie at the stated price appear on the screen.

9. Swipe up and down the information area to view the video trailer; rate and review the movie; view user reviews; read the synopsis, cast, and credits; and get rental period information if any.

10. Tap one of the Buy options.

11. The Buy window shows you the credit card that you have saved, which you need in order to buy a movie or TV show (even free ones) from the Google Play Store. If you don't have a card on file, the app takes you through the steps to register your credit card.

12. Buy the movie by tapping Buy. Google Play charges the card you have on file and downloads the movie to your Galaxy S7 so you can view it.

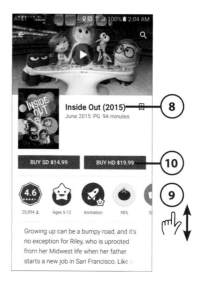

Playing Videos

The Play Movies & TV app makes it easy for you to watch movies and TV shows from the Google Play Store directly within the app.

1. Tap Google on the Home screen.

2. Tap Play Movies & TV.

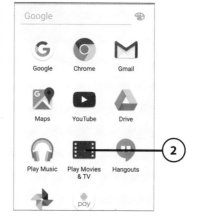

3. Swipe up and down in the Watch Now screen to view movies and TV shows you downloaded as well as get recommendations for movies and TV shows from Google Play.

4. Open and watch the video by tapping the movie or TV episode tile.

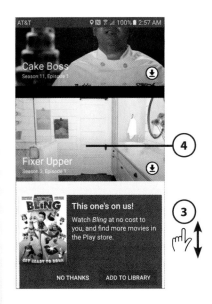

Viewing YouTube Videos

The high-resolution screen of the Galaxy S7, along with its portability and built-in video camera, makes it great for viewing and sharing videos online. The preinstalled YouTube widget gives you the capability to browse and view videos posted by users from around the world. You can also upload videos as soon as you shoot them with your Galaxy S7.

1. Tap the Google icon on the Home screen.

2. Tap YouTube.

3. Skip the promotional message screen by tapping Not Now. Note that the promotional message screen only appears the first time you start YouTube. If you don't see this screen, skip to step 4.

4. Open the Subscriptions screen by tapping the Subscriptions icon in the menu bar.

5. A list of your channels appear as icons within the icon bar that appears below the menu bar.

6. Tap the right arrow icon in the icon bar to view all your channels.

7. If there are new videos within a channel, the number of new videos appears to the right of the channel name.

8. Swipe up in the list and then tap Browse Channels to view channels YouTube recommends for you.

9. View channels by swiping up and down the screen. You can see videos and more information about the artist channel by tapping the channel tile.

10. Return to the Channels screen by tapping the Back icon.

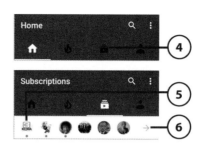

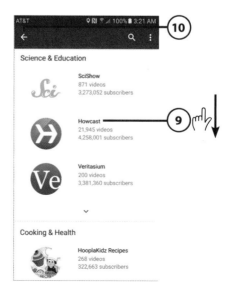

11. Return to the Subscriptions screen by tapping the Back icon.

12. Tap the Search icon to search for a YouTube video.

13. Type the search terms in the Search YouTube field. As you type, a list of potential matches appears under the field.

14. When you're finished typing, tap the Search button in the keyboard.

15. Swipe up and down the list of results in the Search page.

16. Tap the thumbnail image of the video or the video name to view the video on the screen. If you watched the video previously, the Watched box appears in the upper-left corner of the thumbnail image.

17. Return to the Subscriptions screen by tapping the Back icon.

18. Tap the right arrow icon in the icon bar as described in step 6.

19. Swipe up and down in the Channels list and tap the channel name to view videos within that subscription channel.

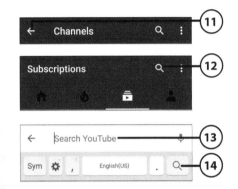

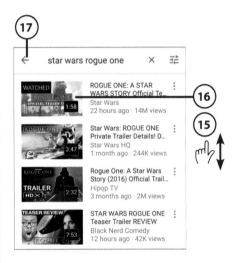

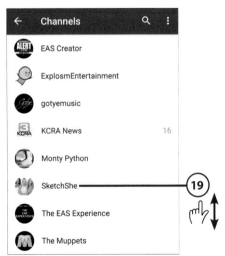

20. Tap the thumbnail image of the video or the video name to view the video on the screen. If you watched the video previously, the Watched box appears in the upper-left corner of the thumbnail image.

21. Tap the Add icon to add the video to an existing playlist or create a new playlist.

22. Tap the Share icon to share a link to the current video using Facebook, Hangouts, Gmail, Messages, Google Drive, Bluetooth, Android Beam, Email, Memo, or Wi-Fi Direct. You can also share your video using your phone carrier's built-in messaging, mail, or storage apps. What's more, you can copy the link to the Clipboard.

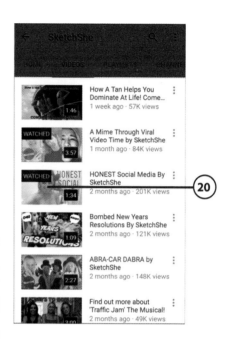

Other Sharing Options

Other sharing options might appear in this list if you have downloaded apps that allow for additional sharing features, such as BeyondPod.

23. Tap the Menu icon so you can turn closed captioning on and off, change the video quality, flag the video for inappropriate content so Google can review it, or watch your video in Google Cardboard view in combination with the Google Cardboard viewer. (You can view more information about the viewer at https://www.google.com/get/cardboard/.)

24. Tap the Full Screen icon to view the video on the entire screen. If you view the full screen video in vertical screen orientation, you'll see black areas above and below the screen.

25. Tap to pause and play the current video.

26. Drag the button in the timeline slider to move through the current video.

27. The video description appears below the video.

28. Tap to visit the channel of the user who posted this video.

29. Swipe up and down in the page to read more about the artists, view similar videos and artists, read comments about this video from other users, and create a response of your own.

30. Return to the channel screen by tapping the Back touch button (not shown).

31. The video continues to play in the window in the lower-right corner of the screen. View the video screen by tapping and holding in the window and then flicking upward. Close the video screen by tapping and holding in the window and then flicking to the right.

32. Return to the Channels screen by tapping the Back icon in the upper-left corner of the screen. Return to the Subscriptions screen by tapping the Back icon in the upper-left corner of the Channels screen as described in step 11.

Recording Video

Your Galaxy S7 is capable of recording HD video with its main 12-megapixel camera, located on the rear of the device. The Galaxy S7 is also equipped with some very helpful features commonly found on dedicated camcorders, including white balance, a video light, manual exposure, and effects.

1. Tap Camera on the Home screen.

2. In the Viewer screen, switch to video mode by tapping the video button. The Camera app starts recording automatically.

3. The timer appears at the bottom of the screen so you can see how long you've been recording your video.

4. Pause recording by tapping the Pause button. After you tap the Pause button, the button changes to a Record button (with a red circle in the center). Resume recording by tapping the Record button.

5. Stop recording by tapping the Stop button.

6. The video you just recorded appears in the Image Viewer in the upper-right corner of the window. Tap the Image Viewer to review the recorded video in the Gallery app.

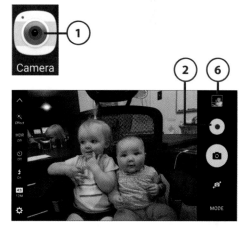

Change Camera App Settings

It's easy to change your app and camera settings so you can have the app work the way you expect each time you use it.

1. Tap the Settings icon.

2. In the Camera Settings screen, tap Video Size (Rear) to set a size for the images you record. You can select from UHD (3,840 x 2,160 pixels), QHD (2,560 x 1,440 pixels), or FHD (1,920 x 1,080 pixels) in 60 fps (frames per second). Alternatively, you can select the standard 30 fps, 1:1 (1,440 x 1,440 pixels), HD (1,280 x 720 pixels), or VGA (640 x 480 pixels). The default selection is FHD. Swipe down in the Video Size (rear) screen to view notes about what features are unavailable when you record in certain video sizes.

3. Slide the Video Stabilization slider button from left (Off) to right (On) to reduce or remove any blurriness that occurs in your video from the shaking of your hand and/or arm as you hold the Galaxy S7 to record your video.

4. Tap Grid Lines to enable an onscreen grid that can help you with the composition of the video.

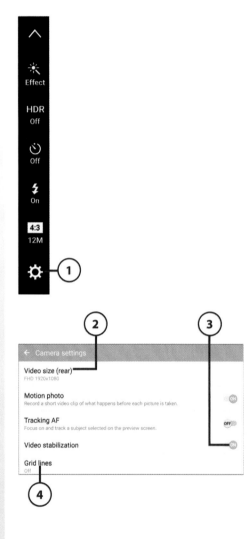

Why Do I See Video Size (Front) Instead of Video Size (Rear)?

If you switch to the front-facing camera by tapping the Switch button on the Viewer screen (it's next to the Camera button), you see Video Size (Front) instead of Video Size (Rear) so you can change the front camera size and resolution. The video sizes for the front camera are limited to QHD, FHD, 1:1, HD, and VGA.

5. Swipe upward to view the next four settings.

6. If you want to use your voice to take videos on the Galaxy S7, tap Shooting Methods (Rear). In the Shooting Methods (Rear) screen (not shown), slide the Voice Control slider button from left (Off) to right (On). You can use one of four different voice commands to capture a video: Smile, Cheese, Capture, or Shoot. After you turn on voice control, return to the Camera Settings screen by tapping the Back icon in the upper-left corner of the screen.

7. By default, you can open the Camera app by quickly pressing the Home key two times. You can turn this feature off by sliding the Quick Launch slider button from right (On) to left (Off).

8. Swipe upward to view the last five settings options.

9. Tap Volume Keys Function to determine whether the volume key acts as the zoom key, the video recording key, or the camera key. In the menu that appears, tap Record Video to tell the Galaxy S7 the volume key is the video recording key.

10. Tap Reset Settings to reset the Camera settings to their defaults.

11. Tap Help to get some quick onscreen help for the Camera app.

12. Return to the Viewer by tapping the Back icon.

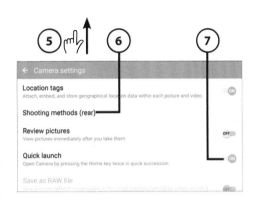

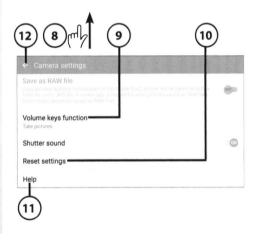

View and Change Basic Settings

Several settings icons appear on one side of the Viewer depending on how you hold your phone. These icons allow you to add effects, change light settings, and set a time before the camera starts to record your video.

1. Tap to add camera effects to your videos as you capture them.

2. Apply an effect by tapping the effect tile. Your choices include Monogram, Delicious, Deep, Film, Gold, Pastel, Retro, and Nostalgia. If you don't see an effect, you can shop for one in the Galaxy Apps app by tapping the Download tile.

Adding Video Effects

Keep in mind that when you use any of the video effects, they become a permanent part of your videos. To give yourself more choices in the future as to how you use your images, consider purchasing a video-editing app that enables you to perform such effects but still maintain your original video.

---

3. Tap the Back touch button (not shown) to close the Effects area.

4. An image that is too light or too dark degrades the appearance of your videos. The Galaxy S7 contains the HDR (High Dynamic Range) setting so the device automatically adjusts the brightness level for various bright or dark lighting conditions. Tap HDR Off to turn on HDR automatic mode, which means the Camera app checks the lighting conditions and applies the HDR feature if needed.

5. Tap Timer to designate how long the Galaxy S7 should wait before the camera starts to record. This is great for allowing time for you to set up the shot and then place yourself in the frame.

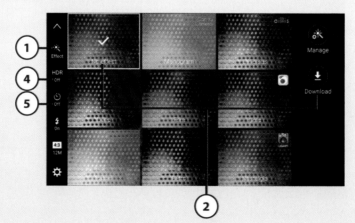

View and Change Pro Settings

By default, the Camera app records videos in Auto mode so you can record videos and know that they'll look great. If you need more control over how your videos look, you can access Pro settings and make manual changes to the color effect, focus mode, white balance, ISO value, and exposure value.

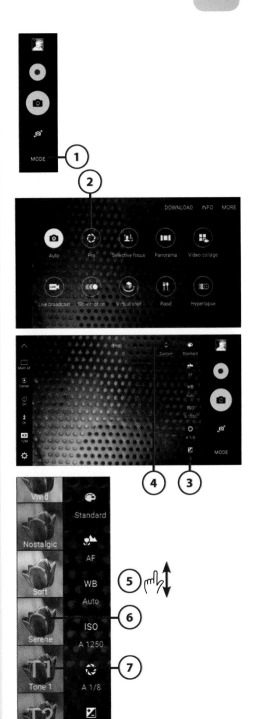

1. Access Pro settings to get more control over how your videos look by tapping Mode in the lower-right corner of the screen.

2. Tap Pro in the menu screen.

3. The Pro settings appear on one side of the screen depending on how you hold your Galaxy S7. In this example, the phone is being held with the Home button to the right of the screen so the Pro settings appear on the right side of the screen.

4. Tap Standard to apply a color effect before you take the video.

5. Swipe up and down the color effect list to view the effects. The default effect is Standard, which contains the default color settings. The selected effect has a white checkmark in the middle of the color effect tile (not shown).

6. Each tile shows you how the video will look in comparison to the Standard effect.

7. Create a new custom effect by swiping down the list and then tapping Tone 1 or Tone 2. You can add up to two custom effects.

8. Change the effect by moving one or more of the six setting sliders up and down. You can change the color temperature, tint, contrast, saturation, highlight, and shadow levels. As you move each slider, the Viewer changes to show how your color effects will appear in your video.

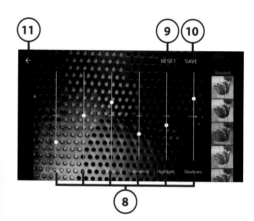

9. Reset effect settings to their default levels by tapping Reset.

10. Save your changes by tapping Save.

11. Return to the Viewer without making changes by tapping the Back icon.

12. Tap the Focus Mode icon to manually change the focus. The default is Auto, but you can slide the button on the slider bar up and down. You can swipe between close focus, which is signified by the flower icon, and broader focus, which is signified by the mountain icon.

13. After you manually set the focus, the focus setting name below the Focus Mode icon (AF in this example, which stands for Auto Focus) changes to MF (which stands for Manual Focus).

Can I Select a Focus Between Auto and Close?

You can't select a focus on the slider bar between Auto and Close Focus. When you try, after you release your finger from the slider button the Camera app determines the setting to which the slider button is closest and then automatically moves to either the Close Focus or Auto setting in the slider bar.

14. Tap the WB icon (WB stands for White Balance) to adjust the white balance for the camera. The white balance features help accurately reproduce colors when you are shooting in various lighting situations so that neutral colors, such as white and gray, are truly neutral and all colors are rendered without undesired color casts.

15. Move the slider button up and down between Incandescent, Fluorescent, Daylight, and Cloudy white balances. Move the slider button to the top of the slider bar (next to the K icon) to set the white balance level manually.

16. After you select a white balance mode or set the white balance level manually, the white balance appears below the WB icon, which is Auto in this example.

17. Tap the ISO icon to adjust the brightness level in your video. The default level in the slider bar is Auto.

18. Slide the button in the slider bar up to achieve a proper brightness level in a low-light shooting environment, or slide the button down for a bright shooting environment. You can select from one of five levels: Auto, 100, 200, 400, and 800. If you release your finger from the button between one of the levels, the button moves to the level closest to the button.

19. After you select the ISO level (A 1250 in this example, which is the Automatic level of 1250) the level number appears below the ISO icon. The Viewer also changes the light level so you can see whether the selected ISO level is appropriate for your environment.

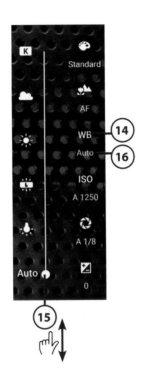

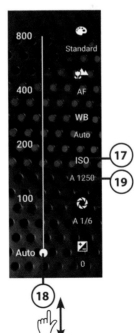

20. Change the exposure value by tapping the Exposure icon. The exposure value determines how much light the camera's sensor receives.

21. Slide the button in the slider bar up if you're in a low-light environment or slide the button down for a bright shooting environment. You can slide to any level between +2 and –2. 0 is the default setting.

22. After you select the exposure value, the value appears below the Exposure icon. The Viewer also changes the light level so you can see if the selected exposure value is appropriate for your environment.

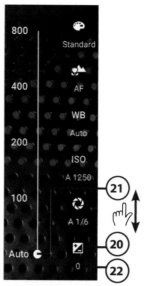

Should I Change the Shutter Speed?

The Shutter Speed icon appears above the Exposure icon, but because the shutter speed is used for taking photos and not videos, you don't need to set the shutter speed. You can learn more about setting the shutter speed in Chapter 9, "Taking and Sharing Photos."

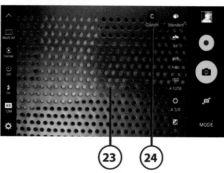

23. Tap in the center of the screen to close the Exposure Value slider bar.

24. Save all your Pro settings so you don't have to set them each time you use the camera by tapping Custom.

25. Tap Save Current Settings.

26. Tap one of the three custom setting names into which you can save your settings.

27. Tap Save.

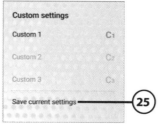

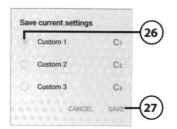

28. The custom setting icon appears in the Viewer so you can tap the icon to change to your preferred camera settings automatically.

View Recorded Videos

After you finish recording a video, view the video you just recorded or a video you recorded earlier by tapping the Image Viewer icon in the upper-right corner of the screen.

In the Image Viewer screen, the Play button appears in the center of the screen and controls appear at the top and bottom of the screen. After a few seconds, the controls on the screen fade away. Access the controls again by tapping anywhere on the screen other than on the Play button.

— The Image Viewer icon

1. Tap to add the video as a favorite that you can view in the Gallery app.

2. Tap Album to view all the photos and videos you captured with your camera in the Camera album.

3. Tap More to access other options.

4. Tap Details to view details of the video such as File Name, Resolution, Size, and Last Modified.

5. Tap to begin a slideshow of all photos and videos in your album. After the slideshow begins, you can tap anywhere onscreen to end the slideshow.

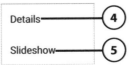

Details — 4

Slideshow — 5

6. Close the menu by tapping the Back touch button (not shown).

7. Tap Share to share the video using the Messages app, the Photos app, Android Beam, Wi-Fi Direct, Bluetooth, Facebook, YouTube, Gmail, Email, and Google Drive. You can also share your video using your phone carrier's built-in messaging, mail, or storage apps. What's more, you can view content on another device.

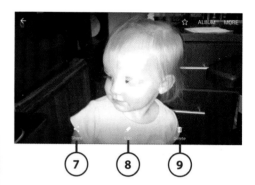

8. Tap Edit to edit the beginning and end of a video by performing a trim, adding an effect, and/or editing the audio. You can also download the Video Editor app from the Samsung Galaxy Apps store so you can edit the video with more powerful tools.

9. Tap Delete to delete the video from the playlist.

10. Swipe from right to left to view more videos in your album, if any. When you find the video you want to watch, tap the Play button in the center of the screen.

11. After the video has started, tap in the middle of the screen to bring up the playback controls.

12. Adjust the volume of the video by tapping your finger on the Volume icon and then sliding your finger on the Volume slider.

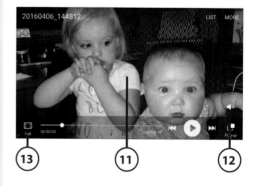

13. Tap the Viewfinder icon to change the size of the video between normal and full screen views.

14. Drag your finger across the Movie Timeline to advance through the video or jump to a new location. You can also tap the timeline in a new location to jump to that location.

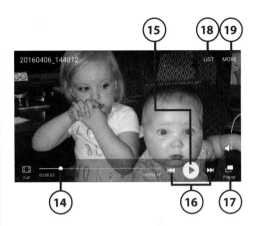

15. The Play button, located in the Playback controls, turns into a Pause button as the video plays. Tap the Pause button to pause the video.

16. Tap the Rewind or Fast Forward button to move to the beginning or end of the video, respectively.

17. Tap the Pop-Up icon to view the video in a small video player window that you can move around on the screen. Though the video player window appears on the Camera screen, you can access any other screen (such as the Home screen) and the video player window still appears.

18. Tap List to view a list of other videos in the album that you can play. Tap a thumbnail image in the list to start playing the video on the right side of the screen.

19. Tap More.

20. Tap Editor to edit the beginning and end of a video by performing a trim, adding an effect, and/ or editing the audio. You can also download the Video Editor app from the Samsung Galaxy Apps store so you can edit the video with more powerful tools.

21. Tap Delete to delete the video from the playlist.

22. Tap Share to share the video using Facebook, Google Drive, Bluetooth, Wi-Fi Direct, Android Beam, YouTube, Instagram, Photos, the Messages app, Gmail, or Email. You can also share your video using your phone carrier's built-in messaging, mail, or storage apps. What's more, you can view content on another device.

23. Tap Turn On Play Audio Only to hide the video on the screen and play only the audio that was recorded with the video.

24. Tap Play Speed to change the play speed of the video so it plays faster or slower than the speed at which you recorded the video.

25. Swipe up in the menu to view more options.

26. Tap Subtitles (CC) to set the app to view closed-captioned subtitles on the screen as you view the video.

27. Tap Details to view details of the video such as File Name, Size, and Resolution.

28. Close the menu by tapping the Back touch button (not shown).

29. Return to the Image Viewer screen to view the videos and photos in the Camera album by tapping the Back touch button twice (not shown).

>>>Go Further

RETURN TO VIEWING THE VIDEO FROM ANOTHER SCREEN

If you open another screen while you're playing a video, such as the Home screen, the video stops playing automatically. Watch the video again by tapping the Recent touch button and then tapping Video Player. Then you can tap the Play button in the Video Player screen.

If you want to return to the screen you were viewing before you returned to the Video Player, which is the Home screen in this example, tap the Back touch button twice. You can return to the Image Viewer screen by tapping the Recent touch button and then tapping the Camera tile in the Recent Apps screen.

Connect to other devices
using Wi-Fi Direct

Connect to the cloud with
the Google Drive app

The Galaxy S7 is a great tool for sharing with other devices directly using Wi-Fi Direct and also for sharing files and media in the cloud. This chapter covers the following topics:

→ Connecting using Wi-Fi Direct
→ Printing wirelessly
→ Using the Google Drive app
→ Finding other cloud services
→ Sharing music and video
→ Backing up and restoring your Galaxy S7

Sharing and Synchronizing Data

The Galaxy S7 enables you to synchronize data with other devices directly by using Wi-Fi Direct so you don't need to buy a cable or even a wireless router to connect your Galaxy S7 to another device. You can store and share data with online services on the cloud, which is file storage available on the Internet. What's more, you can share music and video between your Galaxy S7 and your computer using a USB cable and the Samsung Smart Switch app.

Connecting Using Wi-Fi Direct

If you need to wirelessly transfer data to or connect with another device such as your smartphone, you can use the Galaxy S7 Wi-Fi Direct feature to connect to another device that also has Wi-Fi Direct enabled.

Set Up Wi-Fi Direct

Before you can transfer data
between devices, you have to set up
Wi-Fi Direct on the Galaxy S7 to connect with the other device.

1. On the Home screen, tap Apps.

2. Tap Settings.v

3. Tap Connections in the tab bar.

4. Tap Wi-Fi in the settings list.

5. Tap Wi-Fi Direct in the menu bar.

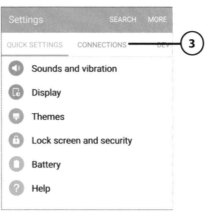

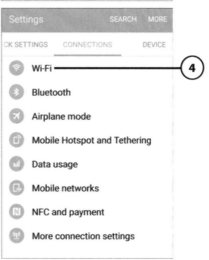

6. The name of your Galaxy S7 appears at the bottom of the list of connections and tells you the device is currently visible to other devices.

7. Tap the device name to which you want to connect.

8. The name of the other device turns blue, which signifies that you're connected to the other device via Wi-Fi Connect.

9. Disconnect from the device by tapping the device name.

10. Return to the Wi-Fi settings screen by tapping the Back icon.

How Do I Know I'm Connected to a Device Through Wi-Fi Direct?

If you're not sure you're connected to another device through Wi-Fi Direct, look in the Status bar at the top of the screen. The Wi-Fi Direct icon appears to the left of the Wi-Fi icon at the right side of the bar.

The Wi-Fi Direct icon

>>>Go Further

TROUBLESHOOTING CONNECTION ISSUES

If the Galaxy S7 can't find your Wi-Fi Direct device, check the other device's Wi-Fi connection and ensure the other device offers Wi-Fi Direct. You should also check the Wi-Fi Alliance website to learn whether your device is Wi-Fi Direct enabled. The Wi-Fi Alliance is a nonprofit group founded in 1999 that was formed to grow Wi-Fi acceptance in the marketplace, support industry standards, and provide a forum so Wi-Fi companies can collaborate and improve Wi-Fi technologies. You can begin searching for products that include Wi-Fi Direct functionality by opening the Internet app and then accessing the Certified Products page at http://www.wi-fi.org/product-finder.

Printing Wirelessly

It's easy to print a file such as a word processing document or spreadsheet from your Galaxy S7. You don't need any cables, and you don't need to transfer your files to another computer, either. There are some limitations to the printing functionality built in to the Galaxy S7, but you can download apps and use web-based services to get around those limits.

Connect a Wi-Fi Printer

Your Galaxy S7 automatically scans for wireless printers that are available through a Wi-Fi connection. Note that you might have to enable a Wi-Fi connection on the printer as well. For this example, I use my Hewlett-Packard (HP) Officejet Pro X576dw printer. This Officejet Pro requires the user to enable HP Wireless Direct functionality on the printer before any device can see it.

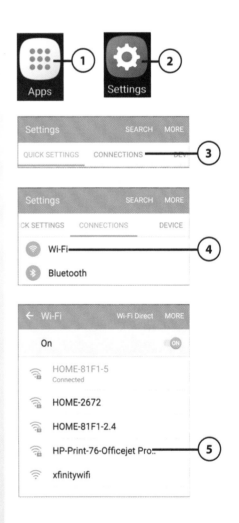

1. On the Home screen, tap Apps.

2. Tap Settings.

3. Tap Connections in the tab bar.

4. Tap Wi-Fi in the settings list.

5. Connect to the printer by tapping the printer name in the Wi-Fi networks list.

6. If you need to enter a password, the password window appears so you can type the password in the Password field.

7. Tap Connect.

8. The Galaxy S7 might take a few seconds to find the printer's IP address; after it does, the printer appears at the top of the Wi-Fi Networks list and displays the Connected status.

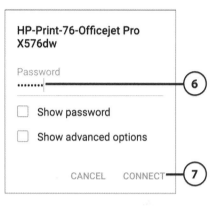

What If the Galaxy S7 Can't Find My Wireless Printer?

If the Galaxy S7 doesn't recognize your wireless printer, you might need to bring your Galaxy S7 closer to it. You can scan for the printer again by tapping Scan in the Settings menu bar that appears at the top of the screen. When the wireless printer appears in the Wi-Fi list, connect to the printer by tapping the printer name.

Connect a Bluetooth Printer

If you have a Bluetooth printer, you can also connect that printer to your Galaxy S7 so you can print wirelessly. The printer in this example is different from the HP Officejet Pro used in the previous section.

1. On the Home screen, tap Apps.

2. Tap Settings.

3. Tap Connections in the tab bar.

4. Tap Bluetooth in the settings list.

5. Turn Bluetooth on by sliding the slider button from left (Off) to right (On).

6. After the Galaxy S7 finds your Bluetooth printer, tap the printer name.

7. If your PIN contains letters or symbols, tap the PIN Containing Letters or Symbols checkbox before you type your PIN.

8. Type the printer's PIN in the Bluetooth Pairing Request window using the keypad (or the keyboard if your PIN has letters or symbols) at the bottom of the screen. If you aren't sure what the PIN is, try 0000 or 1234. If those PINs don't work, you need to consult your printer documentation and/or the printer manufacturer's website to find the PIN.

9. When you're finished, tap Done.

10. Tap OK.

11. The paired Bluetooth printer appears in the Paired Devices section.

12. Tap the Settings icon to the right of the printer name to change the printer name and unpair, or disconnect, the printer from the Galaxy S7.

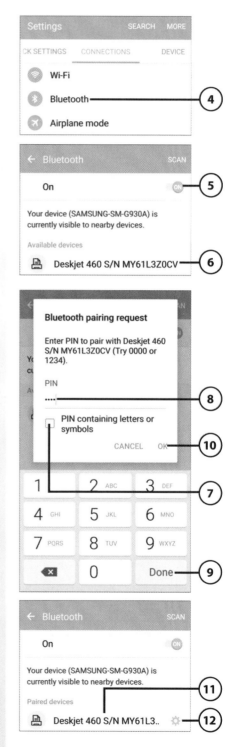

>>>Go Further
DOWNLOAD A PRINT APP

Samsung boasts that you can print directly from within an app on your Galaxy S7 to any compatible printer without having to connect to a Wi-Fi or Bluetooth printer. Unfortunately, what Samsung doesn't tell you is that you can only print to Samsung's printers. You find this out when you try to print from an app for the first time and see the message "You can only print to a Samsung printer." Fortunately, apps are available from the Google Play Store that enable you to print to other printers.

For example, if you have a Hewlett-Packard printer, as I'm using in this example, you can download the HP ePrint app. You can also search for your printer manufacturer in the Google Play Store to see if a printing app is available. There are also apps available from the Google Play Store for printing to a variety of devices. One such app is PrinterShare Mobile Print, which is free.

If you find a printing app in the Google Play Store that doesn't work for you (or doesn't work at all), another option is to use Google's Cloud Print service. This service connects your printers to the Web so any web-enabled device, including the Galaxy S7, can access a printer connected to Cloud Print. As of this writing, Google Cloud Print is still in beta test status, so be aware that the service's performance might not match your expectations.

You can access the Google Cloud Print website in the Internet app at www.google.com/cloudprint/learn. After you open the site, you're invited to log in using your Gmail account. After you log in, you can add a printer that's connected to a laptop or PC, or you can add a Cloud Ready printer, which is a printer that connects directly to the Web.

The Google Cloud Print website

Sharing Files

A "cloud storage" service enables you to upload files onto its server computers. Cloud storage services make it easy for you to share large files with others, especially because the maximum file attachment sizes in email messages can vary depending on the email service you use, and downloading email messages with large file attachments can take a long time.

Use the Google Drive App

The Google Drive app came installed on your Galaxy S7, and you might have set up your Google Drive account when you set up your Galaxy S7. You can give another Google Drive user access to one or more folders in your account so that other users can upload files to and download files from that folder.

What Do I Need to Use the Google Drive App?

These instructions presume that you already have a Google account and you logged into your Google account when you set up your Galaxy S7 or within the Settings screen, and that you already have a Google Drive account. If you don't have a Google Drive account, bookmark this page and set up the account at http://drive.google.com.

Add Galaxy S7 Photos to Google Drive and Create a Folder

When you first start Google Drive, the app takes you step by step through setting up your Galaxy S7 to work with Google Drive. Then you can start adding files.

You may want to start by adding photos on your Galaxy S7 to your Google Drive account so you don't lose them in case something happens to your device. Complete the following steps after you upload one or more photos to your Google Drive account.

1. On the Home screen, tap Google.

2. Tap Drive.

3. Swipe from right to left to view introductory information about Google Drive. Note that if you've already used Google Drive on your Galaxy S7, you can skip ahead to step 5.

4. Tap Done in the last introductory screen.

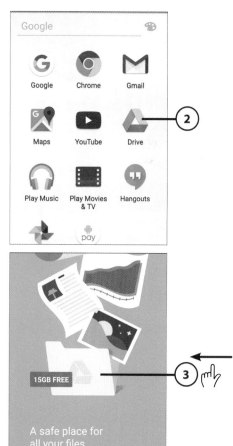

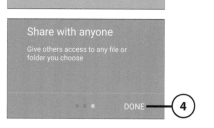

5. Tap Got It to close the informational tile about organizing your files using drag and drop.

6. Tap the Add icon in the bottom-right corner of the screen.

7. Tap Upload in the New window that appears at the bottom of the screen.

8. Tap Images in the Upload list.

9. Tap the folder tile that contains the photos you want to upload to Google Drive.

10. Tap and hold on the first file you want to upload; this example uses photos. The selected photo contains a circle with a white checkmark in the center of the photo.

11. Swipe up and down in the list if necessary and tap each photo tile you want to add.

12. Tap Open.

13. If you see a window on the screen that asks if you want to allow Google Drive to access photos, media, and files on your Galaxy S7, tap Allow (not shown).

14. The photo(s) you added appear at the top of the Files section as a tile. Select the photo by tapping and holding your finger on the photo for a second.

15. The selected photo has a blue circle with a white checkmark in the center of the photo.

16. Select another photo by tapping the photo tile.

17. If you see the Drag to Move Items screen, close the screen by tapping Got It (not shown).

18. Tap the Menu icon in the pop-up window at the bottom of the screen.

19. Tap Move.

20. Tap the New Folder icon in the Select Destination Folder window.

21. Type the name of your album in the New Folder field.

22. Tap OK.

23. Your new folder appears in the window and shows you there are no items in the folder.

24. Tap Move.

25. The new folder appears in the Folders section. Tap the folder to open files within the folder.

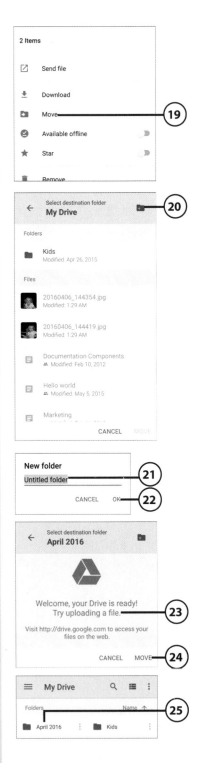

View and Share Files in Google Drive

The Google Drive home screen contains all files and subfolders within the Google Drive folder.

1. View files within a folder by tapping the folder name within the Folders section.

2. Swipe up and down in the screen if necessary to view all the files within the folder. When you find a file that you want to view, tap the tile to view it. If the file is a photo or image file, as in this example, then the file opens within the built-in Google Drive image viewer.

3. After a couple of seconds, the menu bar at the top of the image disappears so you can view the image in its entirety. Open the menu again by tapping the image.

4. Tap the Menu icon.

5. Tap Add People to give permission to another Google Drive user to access the file so they can either view, comment on, or edit the file.

6. Tap Share Link to share or copy a link to the file. You can share using Android Beam, Bluetooth, Wi-Fi Direct, Email or Gmail, Hangouts, Facebook, the Messenger app, or your phone carrier's preinstalled messaging or mail apps. You can also share with another Google Drive account. What's more, you can copy the link to a memo to access in the Memo app or copy the link to the clipboard.

7. Tap Send File to send the file using an app or service. You can send the file to a Gmail or Email message, a memo you can access with the Memo app, Photos, Hangouts, Facebook, the Messages app, the Maps app, Amazon Kindle, or your phone carrier's preinstalled messaging or mail apps. You can send the file to another device using the Android Beam, Bluetooth, or Wi-Fi Direct services. You can also send the file to another Google Drive account.

8. Swipe up within the menu to view more options.

9. Tap Open With to view the photo in either the Gallery or Photos app.

10. Tap Download to download the file to your Galaxy S7.

11. Tap Move to move the file to a different folder. You can also create a new folder as described earlier in this chapter and then move the file into the new folder.

12. Slide the Available Offline slider button from left (Off) to right (On) to save a copy of the photo to your Galaxy S7 so you can still view the photo in Google Drive when you're not connected to the Internet.

13. Slide the Star slider button from left (Off) to right (On) to add the file as a favorite to your Starred list. Read the "Access Menu Options" section later in this chapter for more information about the Starred list.

14. Tap Rename to rename the file in the Rename File window.

15. Print the file, such as to a connected Bluetooth printer.

16. Tap the Info icon to view details about the file and perform more tasks.

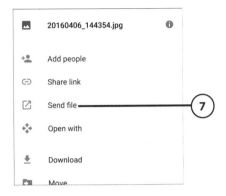

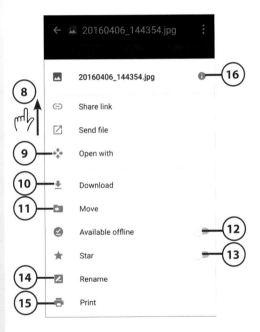

17. Swipe up and down to view information about the file, who has access to the file, and any activity related to the file. You can also add people who can access your file as you learned about in step 5.

18. Return to the image screen by tapping the Back icon.

19. Return to the folder screen by tapping the Back icon.

20. In the folder screen, return to the main Google Drive folder by tapping the Back touch button (not shown).

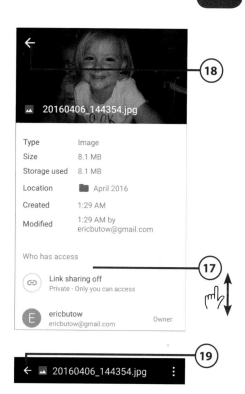

Access Menu Options

You can access a variety of tools and settings for the Google Drive app from within the menu bar at the top of the My Drive screen.

1. Tap the Menu icon at the left side of the menu bar.

2. Tap Shared with Me to view files and folders within other Google Drive users' accounts that those users are sharing with you.

3. Tap Google Photos to view, add, and delete photos and albums in your Google Photos account.

4. Tap Recent to order all files in your Google Drive account by the time it was last viewed. The most recently viewed files appear at the top of the list and the oldest files appear at the bottom of the list.

5. Tap Starred to view all the files you marked as Starred as you learned about earlier in this chapter.

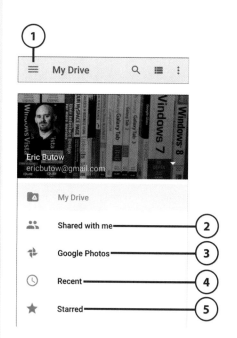

6. Tap Offline to view all files in your Google Drive account that are also stored on your Galaxy S7.

7. Tap Uploads to view all files uploaded from your Galaxy S7 to your Google Drive account.

8. Tap Trash to view all deleted files contained in your Trash folder within your Google Drive account.

9. Tap Upgrade Storage to open the Drive Storage screen to view the current amount of storage space used, view the total amount of storage available in your account, and add more storage.

10. Swipe up within the menu to view more options.

11. Tap to view notifications generated by Google Drive, such as the addition of a new file in a shared folder.

12. Tap Settings to get information about your account, change your account settings, and learn more about Google Drive.

13. Tap Help & Feedback to get answers to your most common questions about Google Drive.

14. Close the menu by tapping My Drive.

15. Tap the Search icon to search for files in Google Drive.

16. Type your search term(s) in the Search field.

17. As you type, files matching the description appear as tiles underneath the Search field.

18. If you don't see the search results you want, or there are more tiles than can fit on the screen, tap the Search button in the keyboard.

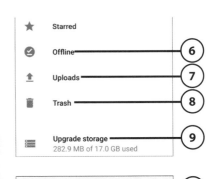

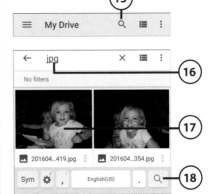

19. Swipe up and down the screen to view all the files in the list. Tap on a tile to view the contents of the file on the screen.

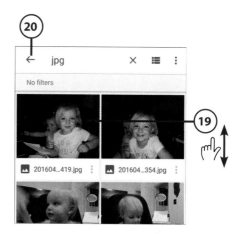

20. Return to the File Types screen by tapping the Back icon.

21. In the File Types screen, tap the Back icon in the upper-left corner of the screen (not shown).

22. Tap the List View icon to view all the files in a list. After you tap the icon, the icon changes to the Tile View icon; return to the tile view by tapping the Tile View icon.

23. View more options by tapping the Menu icon.

24. Tap Sort By to change the sort order. The default is by title, but you can also sort by the files' last modified date, when you last opened the file, when you last edited the file, or how much of your file storage quota was used.

25. Tap Select to select one or more files and/or folders in the My Drive screen. If you want to deselect all the files you selected, tap the Menu icon and then tap Clear Selection.

26. Tap Select All to select all files and folders in the My Drive screen. You can deselect all the files and folders by tapping the Menu icon and then tapping Clear Selection.

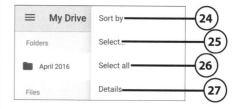

27. Tap Details to get information about your activities on My Drive. Activities are sorted from the most recent activity at the top of the Details list to the oldest activity at the bottom.

>>>Go Further

GET MORE GOOGLE DRIVE SPACE

Google gives you 15GB of space on its servers for storing photos on Google+ photos, storing your email messages on Google Mail, and storing files in Google Drive. If you find you need more storage, you can choose from five different monthly plans that give you from 100GB ($1.99 per month) to 30TB ($299.99 per month) of total storage. Google doesn't offer annual storage plans as of this writing.

When you visit the Google Drive Storage website (https://www.google.com/settings/storage), you'll see how much total space you have and how much of that total space is in use. You also see different ways to add more space to your account. After you choose your monthly plan, the Drive Storage website takes you through the checkout process.

Find Other Cloud Services

If you prefer to use a cloud storage app other than Google Drive, you can shop the Google Play Store for cloud storage apps that are optimized for the Android operating system.

1. Tap Play Store on the Home screen.

2. Tap the Google Play box.

3. Type cloud storage in the Search Google Play field.

4. Tap the search button in the keyboard.

5. Swipe up and down within the list of apps in the search results screen. Tap a tile to view more information about the app. You learn more about shopping for apps in the Play Store in Chapter 12, "Working with Android Applications."

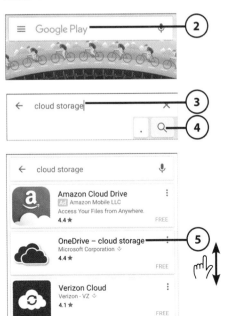

Sharing Music and Video

You have a number of ways to share your music and video between different devices or between your computer and your Galaxy S7. If you have a computer that runs Windows, you can connect the Galaxy S7 to your computer and copy files with Windows Media Player. You can also connect your Galaxy S7 to your Windows computer and tell Windows that your Galaxy S7 is a storage device. One other alternative is to connect your PC or Mac to your Galaxy S7 using Samsung's free Smart Switch application.

Copy Files with Windows Media Player

When you connect your Galaxy S7 to your PC with the data cable, you can choose how you want to connect and/or synchronize media files with your Galaxy S7. One option is to sync your PC and your Galaxy S7 with Windows Media Player. This example connects the Galaxy S7 to a PC running Windows 8.1.

1. Connect the data cable from the Galaxy S7 to the USB port on your PC. If an AutoPlay window opens, click the window and then click Sync Digital Media Files to This Device: Windows Media Player in the list. If you don't see this window, open the Windows Media Player app on your PC.

2. Click the Sync tab within the Windows Media Player window.

3. Click and drag the music file(s) you want to copy to the Sync list.

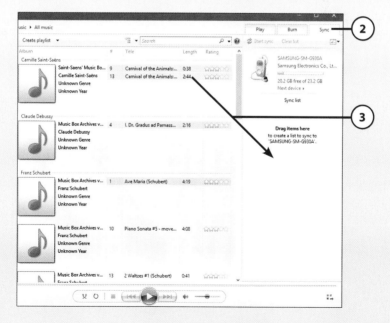

4. The list of music files you select appears in the Sync list. You can deselect any files you do not want to copy by right-clicking the filename and then clicking Remove from List in the pop-up menu that appears.

5. Tap Start Sync to begin copying the files from your PC to your Galaxy S7.

6. After sync is complete, you can view the music files within the My Files app on your Galaxy S7. Start by tapping Apps in the Home screen.

7. Tap Samsung.

8. Tap My Files.

9. Tap Audio.

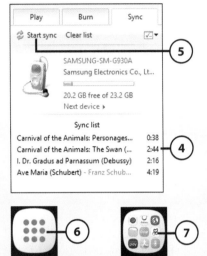

10. The songs you synced appear in the list of audio files. Begin playing a song by tapping the song filename.

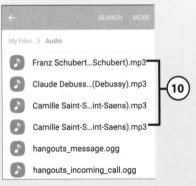

Connect as a Mass Storage Device

You can drag and drop files from a PC to your Galaxy S7 by connecting as a removable disk. Follow these steps to transfer music files from your PC to your Galaxy S7 using the Mass Storage USB mode.

1. Connect the data cable to the Galaxy S7 and the USB connector to the USB port on your computer. If an AutoPlay window opens, click the window and then click Open Device to View Files: File Explorer in the list. If you don't see this window, open the File Explorer app on your computer.

2. Your Galaxy S7 appears as a removable disk in the folder tree within the File Explorer window. Double-click the SAMSUNG-SM-G930A entry in the tree.

3. Open the list of folders on the Galaxy S7 by double-clicking the Phone folder in the tree.

4. Double-click the Music folder in the tree. The list of music files and subfolders appears in the file pane.

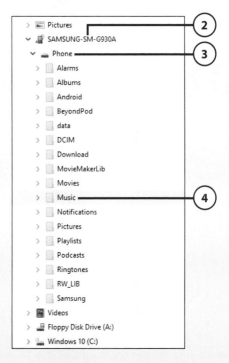

5. Locate the files you want to transfer from your computer and then drag them to the Music folder on your Galaxy S7. The files are copied to the device.

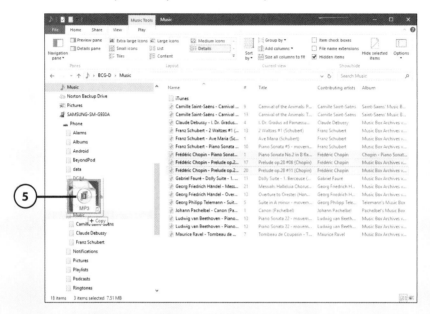

6. After you have finished copying files to your Galaxy S7 from your computer, remove the USB cable from the PC.

7. Open the My Files app as you learned to do earlier in this chapter and then tap Audio.

8. The music you have transferred is available for playback. Play a song by tapping the song filename in the list.

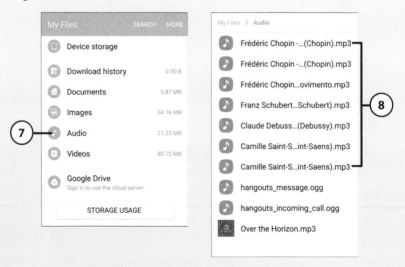

>>>Go Further
CONNECTING TO A MAC

You need extra software to connect your Galaxy S7 to a Mac. Android File Transfer is an application for Macs running OS X 10.5 or later that enables you to view and transfer files between your Mac and Galaxy S7. This application works with Android devices running Android 3.0 or later. You can download Android File Transfer from www.android.com/filetransfer/.

Samsung Smart Switch for PCs and Macs

The Samsung Smart Switch application makes it easy for you to back up data to your computer and restore that backed up data to your Galaxy S7. The Smart Switch app is already installed on your Galaxy S7.

When you connect your Galaxy S7 to your PC or Mac, Samsung Smart Switch enables you to copy files from your computer and other devices (such as another smartphone) to your Galaxy S7. You can download Smart Switch for your PC or Mac on the Samsung website at www.samsung.com/us/support/smart-switch-support/.

Can I Use Samsung Kies?

Previous models of Samsung smartphones used the Kies app to synchronize data. With the Galaxy S6 and Galaxy S7 smartphone families, Samsung requires that you use Smart Switch. If you try using Kies on your computer with your Galaxy S7, a dialog box appears in Kies that informs you that you can only use Smart Switch with the device. After you close the window, Kies doesn't recognize the Galaxy S7 and asks you to connect a device. You need to close Kies before you can run Smart Switch.

Now that you've installed Samsung Smart Switch onto your computer, you can use Smart Switch to match your media files between your smartphone and your computer.

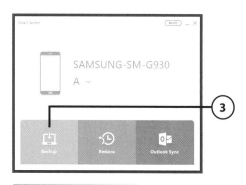

1. Connect your Galaxy S7 to a Bluetooth port PC or Mac.

2. Launch Samsung Smart Switch on your computer. If Smart Switch doesn't find your Galaxy S7 right away, disconnect your smartphone from your computer and then connect the Galaxy S7 into the Bluetooth port again.

What's This Message I See About iTunes Backup Data?

If you see a pop-up window that states that Smart Switch has found iTunes backup data, you don't need to bother as you're backing up your Galaxy S7. So close the window by clicking the Close icon in the upper-right corner of the pop-up window.

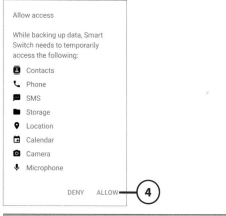

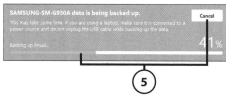

3. Click Backup.

4. In the Allow Access window on the Galaxy S7, tap Allow.

5. The progress bar shows you how much of the backup is complete. If you want to stop the backup, click Cancel.

6. After the backup process is complete, you see a summary of the data that was backed up. Click OK.

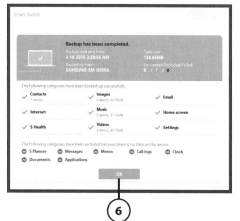

7. Restore your backed up data by clicking Restore.

8. You can select a different backup to restore by clicking Select a Different Backup and then selecting the date and time of the backed up data in the Select a Backup to Restore screen (not shown).

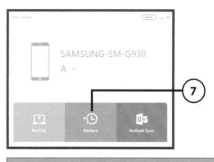

9. Restore the most recent backup by clicking Restore Now.

10. In the Allow Access window on the Galaxy S7, tap Allow.

11. The progress bar shows you how much of the restoration is complete. If you want to stop the restoration, click Cancel.

12. Click OK. On your Galaxy S7, you may have to restore some features such as the data within the Weather widget that appears on the Home screen.

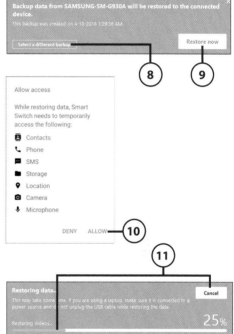

13. You can sync your Outlook contacts, calendar, and to-do lists on your computer with your Galaxy S7. Start by clicking Outlook Sync.

14. Click Sync Preferences for Outlook because so far you haven't specified what Outlook data you want to sync.

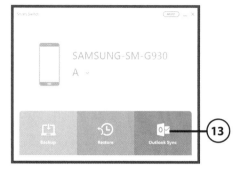

15. Click the Contacts, Calendar, and/or To Do checkboxes. By default, you select all contacts, calendar, or to-do items.

16. Choose one or more folders to sync by clicking the appropriate Selected button and then clicking Select to open the appropriate window and choose the folder. In this example, select Contacts folders by clicking the Selected Contacts Folder button and then clicking Select. Now you can select the folder(s) in the Outlook Selected Contacts window (not shown).

17. When you're done selecting your folder(s) to sync, click OK.

18. Start syncing by clicking Sync Now.

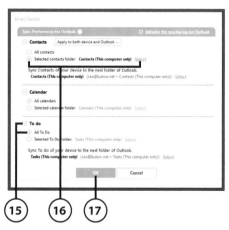

19. The progress bar shows you how much of the sync is complete. If you want to stop the sync, click Cancel.

20. When the sync process is complete, click Confirm. Now you can check the Contacts and/or Calendar apps on your Galaxy S7 to ensure the inclusion of your contacts, calendar, and/or to-do lists from Outlook.

21. Click More to view menu options.

22. Within the menu, you can recover and initialize your Galaxy S7 system software, reinstall a malfunctioning device driver on your Galaxy S7, change Smart Switch preferences, as well as view Smart Switch help and information.

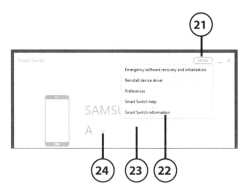

23. Close the menu by clicking a blank area outside the menu.

24. View basic information about the Galaxy S7 by clicking the down arrow icon next to your smartphone's model name.

25. The list under your smartphone's model name tells you if the system software is up to date and also lists the model name, phone number, Android version, how much internal memory has been used, and the amount of free memory on your Galaxy S7.

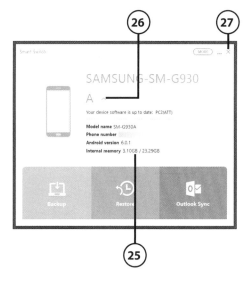

26. Hide the basic information list by clicking the up arrow icon.

27. Close Smart Switch by clicking the Close icon.

Backing Up and Restoring Your Galaxy S7

Backing up the contents of your Galaxy S7 is a good practice for securing your important information and multimedia content. You can ensure that your contacts, photos, videos, and apps are copied to your PC or Mac in case something happens to your Galaxy S7.

Ensure Automatic Google Account Backup

Your Google account information—such as your Gmail inbox, Contacts list, and Calendar app appointments—automatically sync with Google servers, so this information is already backed up for you. To ensure that your Google account information is being automatically backed up, follow these directions.

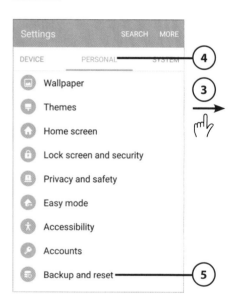

1. On the Home screen, tap Apps.

2. Tap Settings.

3. Swipe from right to left within the tab bar.

4. Tap Personal.

5. Tap Backup and Reset.

6. Make sure the status for the Back Up My Data option is on. If Back Up My Data is not on, tap Back Up My Data and in the Back Up My Data screen (not shown), slide the slider button from left (Off) to right (On) and then tap the Back icon to return to the Backup and Reset screen.

7. Make sure the slider button for the Automatic Restore option is in the On position. If Automatic Restore is not on, slide the slider button in Automatic Restore from left (Off) to right (On). When the Back Up My Data and Automatic Restore options are on, the information associated with your Google address is now automatically backed up.

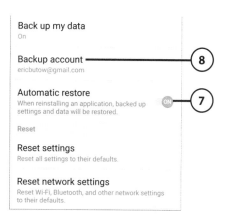

The Automatic Restore Option

Having the Automatic Restore option on ensures that any data or settings placed on third-party apps are restored when you restore those apps to your Galaxy S7.

8. If you want to change your backup account to a different Google account, tap Backup Account.

9. Tap Add Account in the Set Backup Account window. Then follow the steps to add another Google Account in the Add Your Account screen.

>>>*Go Further*

MANUALLY BACKING UP

When connected to your PC or Mac as a mass storage device, you can open File Explorer in Windows or Finder in Mac OS to view all of the data on your Galaxy S7's internal storage. The content is categorized into specific folders that you can copy from your card and internal storage such as DCIM, Download, Music, Pictures, Movies, Podcasts, and more. You can also copy all folders that have the names of apps installed on your Galaxy S7, such as Facebook, to your PC or Mac.

See the top apps

Search for apps

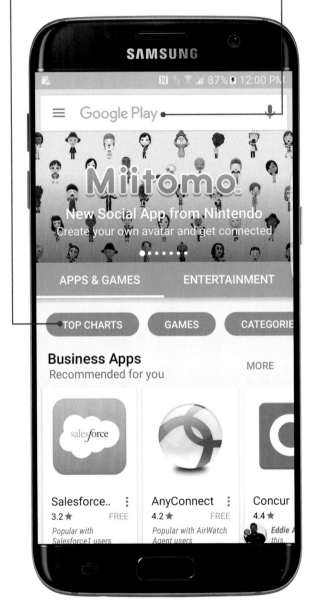

In this chapter, you find out how to purchase and use Android applications on your Galaxy S7. Topics include the following:

→ Setting up Google Wallet
→ Finding applications with the Google Play Store
→ Working with the Galaxy Apps Store
→ Purchasing applications

Working with Android Applications

Your Galaxy S7 comes with enough applications to make it a worthy phone. However, wouldn't it be great to play games, update your Facebook and Twitter statuses, or even keep a grocery list? Well, you can use the Google Play Store to find these types of applications. Read on to discover how to find, purchase, and maintain applications.

Configuring Google Wallet

Before you start buying apps in the Google Play Store, you must first set up your Google Wallet account. If you plan to download only free applications, you do not need a Google Wallet account.

1. From a desktop computer or your Galaxy S7, open the web browser and go to http://wallet.google.com (not shown). Sign in using the same Google account you used to set up your phone.

2. Click or tap Payment Methods.

3. Click or tap Add a Payment Method, and select either Add a Credit or Debit Card or Link a Bank Account.

4. Enter the required information to add your payment method (not shown).

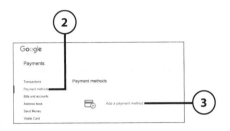

Navigating the Google Play Store

The Google Play Store is the place where you can search for and buy Android applications for your phone.

1. Tap the Play Store icon.

2. Swipe in from the left bezel to see Google Play Store actions.

3. Tap to see any apps you have already purchased or downloaded.

4. Tap to see entertainment related content. Entertainment content is a listing of movies, TV shows, books, and newspapers and magazines related to entertainment.

5. Tap to switch from Apps & Games to Movies & TV, Music, Books, or Newsstand.

6. Tap to manage your payment methods, subscriptions, unused rewards, and see your order history.

7. Tap to redeem a Google Play gift card.

8. Tap to see your wish list. This list shows all apps, music, books, and movies that you have placed on your wish list.

9. Tap to see people you know on Google+ and see the apps they like.

10. Tap to change the settings for Google Play. See the "Adjust Google Play Settings" section later in this chapter for more information.

11. Tap anywhere outside the menu to return to the Google Play Store main screen.

12. Tap Apps & Games to see only Android apps and games.

13. Swipe left and right to move between different views including Top Charts, Games, Categories, Family, and Editor's Choice.

14. Tap to search the Google Play Store. You can also tap the microphone icon and speak your search. This searches everything available in the store, including apps, music, movies, and books.

15. Tap Categories to see apps organized by Category.

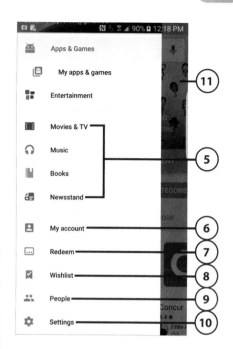

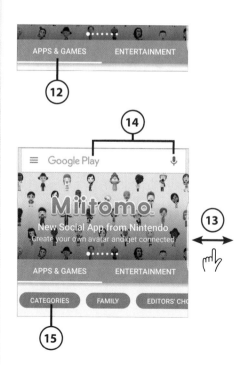

16. Swipe left and right to scroll through the top categories.

17. Swipe up to see all categories.

18. Tap to exit the Categories view.

Install Free Applications

You don't have to spend money to get quality applications. Some of the best applications are free.

1. Tap the free application you want to install.

2. Swipe up to read about the app's features, reviews by other people who installed it, and information on the person or company who wrote it. Swiping up also enables you to share a link to the app with friends.

3. Swipe left and right on the app screen shots to see all of them.

4. Tap Install to download and install the app.

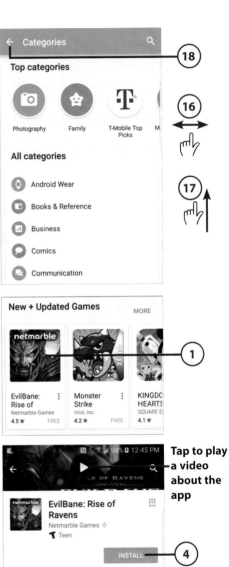

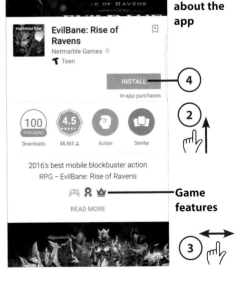

Tap to play a video about the app

Game features

5. Tap Open to launch the app once it has been downloaded.

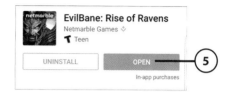

Buy Applications

If an application is not free, the price displays next to the application icon. If you want to buy the application, remember that you need to have a Google Wallet account. See the "Configuring Google Wallet" section earlier in the chapter for more information.

1. Tap the application you want to buy.

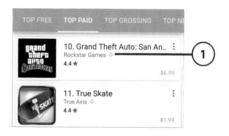

What if the Currency Is Different?

When you browse applications in the Google Play Store, you might see applications that have prices in foreign currencies, such as in Euros. When you purchase an application, the currency is simply converted into your local currency using the exchange rate at the time of purchase.

2. Swipe up to read the application features, reviews by other people who installed it, and information on the person or company who wrote the application. Swiping up also enables you to share a link to the app with friends.

3. Swipe left and right on the app screen shots to see all of them.

4. Tap the price to purchase the app.

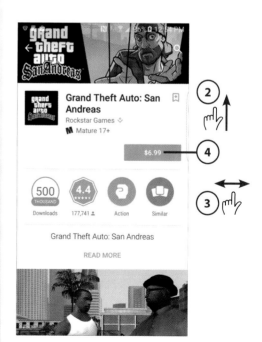

What Are In-App Purchases?

An app you install that is either free or costs little may offer extra features that you need to pay for later if you want to take advantage of them. For example, an app might provide ways to edit photos and add effects to them, but some effects are not available until you pay extra for them. This is considered an in-app purchase.

5. Tap to accept the app's requested permissions and proceed to the payment screen.

6. Tap Buy to purchase the app. You receive an email from the Google Play Store after you purchase an app. The email serves as your invoice.

Checking App Permissions Anytime

To see what permissions you have granted to any app, swipe down from the top bezel, tap the Settings icon (the cog), tap Applications under the Device section, and tap Application Manager. Tap any app and scroll down to Permissions to see what permissions you previously granted for the app. Tap each permission to read a description of what it allows, and in some cases how it affects your device.

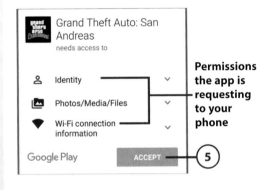

Permissions the app is requesting to your phone

Tap to change the payment method

Some cellular providers allow billing your account for purchases

>>>Go Further

HOW APP PERMISSIONS HAVE CHANGED

Your Galaxy S7 is running version 6 of Android, also known as Marshmallow. In previous versions of Android (versions 5 and below), when you installed an app, the app would show you a list of permissions that it needed before you installed it. It was all or nothing for accepting or rejecting this list of permissions; you couldn't selectively choose which permissions to allow and which to deny. You also had to accept all of the permissions before installing the app, or it wouldn't install.

In many situations, after the app was installed, it would never make use of these permissions, and if it did, you had no way of knowing. For example, if you installed an app that required use of your microphone, and you accepted it, then the app could use your microphone anytime it wanted. In most cases the request for this permission was so that the app could provide you functionality that you wanted—for example, to record a video—but in some cases, it could be an app that really had no reason to be using your microphone, and it could have been spying on you.

In Android version 6.0, apps can take advantage of the new permissions system, which does not require you to accept a full list of app permissions when you install an app. Instead the app is installed with no permissions initially, and as the app needs a particular permission it will ask for it at the time it needs it. For example, if you install an app that allows you to record a video, the very first time you try and record a video, the app asks for permission to use your camera and microphone. You can then make the correlation between an action you took and the app requesting the permission. Some older apps that have not been updated to support Android version 6's app permissions will still ask you to accept the full list of permissions before they are installed.

Manage Apps

Use the My Apps & Games section of the Google Play Store to update apps, delete them, or install apps that you have previously purchased.

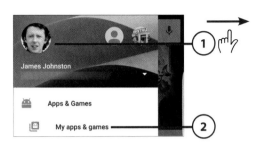

1. Swipe in from the left of the screen.

2. Tap My Apps & Games.

3. Tap All to see all apps that are currently installed or previously were installed on all your Android devices.

4. The word Free indicates a free app that you previously downloaded but that is not installed on this phone. Tapping the app enables you to install it again for free.

5. The word Purchased indicates an app you previously purchased and installed but that is no longer installed on this phone. Tapping the app enables you to install it again for free.

Tap to see only apps you have installed on this device

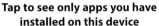

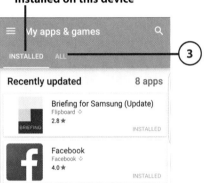

App is already installed

Allow an App to Be Automatically Updated

When the developer of an app you have installed updates it to fix bugs or add new functionality, you are normally notified of this in the System Tray so that you can manually update the app. Google Play enables you to choose to have the app automatically updated without your intervention. To do this, open the My Apps screen, and tap the app you want to update automatically. Tap the Menu icon and make sure that Auto-Update is checked. Automatic Updating is suspended if the developer of the app changes the permissions that the app requires to function. This enables you to review them and manually update the app.

Uninstalling an App

When you uninstall an app, you remove the app and its data from your Galaxy S7. Although the app no longer resides on your Galaxy S7, you can reinstall it as described in steps 4 and 5 because the app remains tied to your Google account.

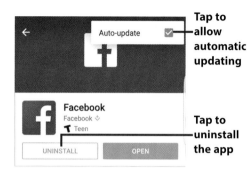

Tap to allow automatic updating

Tap to uninstall the app

Adjust Google Play Settings

1. Swipe in from the left of the screen.

2. Tap Settings.

3. Tap to choose whether apps are updated automatically, and over what types of networks they are updated. For example, you can set your apps to update automatically at any time, which means they will update over the cellular data network or Wi-Fi. Because cellular data charges apply, you may choose to have your apps only update over Wi-Fi.

4. Check the box to create an app shortcut icon to appear on your Home screen for each app that you install.

5. Tap to clear the Google Play Store Search History. This removes the log of searches you have made in the Google Play Store on this device only.

6. Check the box to enable notifications of app or game updates.

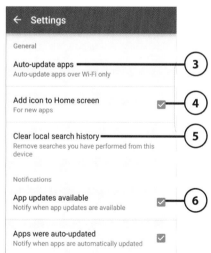

7. Check the box to enable notifications when apps or games have automatically updated.

8. Swipe up for more settings.

9. Check the box to allow the Google Play Store app to see the itineraries in your Gmail account to better recommend apps for you.

10. Tap to set content restrictions on this phone. You can set restrictions on apps, movies, TV shows, books, and music. You can restrict based on the game rating, or movie and TV show age restriction. This is useful if you have purchased your Galaxy S7 for a child and want to restrict what they can download and purchase.

11. Check the box to use your fingerprint to make purchases from the Google Play Store.

12. Tap to choose whether you want to enter your Google password for every Google Play Store purchase, or only every 30 minutes. If you choose 30 minutes, you can enter your password one time and then purchase content in the store for 30 minutes without retyping your password. After 30 minutes have elapsed, you are prompted to enter your password for your next purchase.

13. Tap the Back icon to return to the main screen.

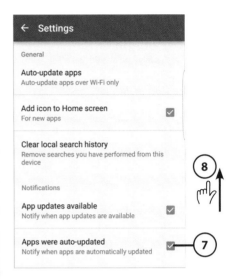

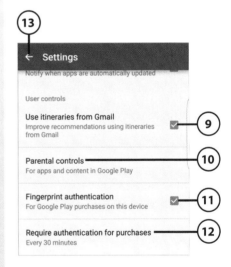

Accidentally Uninstall an Application?

What if you accidentally uninstall an application or you uninstalled an application in the past but now decide you'd like to use it again? To get the application back, go to the My Apps view in the Google Play Store. Scroll to that application and tap it. Tap Install to reinstall it.

Install Apps Not from the Google Play Store

Although it is not recommended that you install Android apps not found in the Google Play Store, there is a way to do it. Open Settings, tap Lock Screen and Security, and tap the switch next to Unknown Sources. If you use your phone for work, your company's Mobile Device Management (MDM) system will likely require this setting to be enabled so that it can push down the MDM Agent app and enable you to install your company's internal apps. Outside the requirement to install non-Google Play Store apps for your company, it is dangerous to install non-approved apps. You open yourself up to apps that may contain malware, spyware, or viruses.

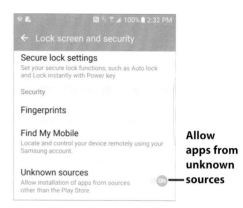

Allow apps from unknown sources

Galaxy Apps

Although you can find the majority of Android apps in the Google Play Store, Samsung has its own app store especially for the Galaxy phones. There are some apps that are exclusive to the Galaxy Apps Store; however most apps in the Galaxy Apps Store are also in the Google Play Store, with some possible price differences between the two stores for the same app.

1. Tap the Galaxy Apps icon.

2. Swipe left and right to see apps grouped by Categories, Staff Picks, Samsung Galaxy Exclusives, Gear smartwatch apps and watch faces, and Top apps.

3. Tap to search for an app.

4. Tap More to see apps you have previously downloaded and to change the Galaxy App Store settings.

Add a Payment Method for Galaxy Apps

Before you start buying apps in the Galaxy Apps Store, you must first set up a payment method. If you plan to download only free applications, you do not need to follow these steps.

1. Tap More.

2. Tap My Apps.

3. Tap Payment Methods.

4. Tap Credit Card.

5. Tap Register to register a new debit or credit card.

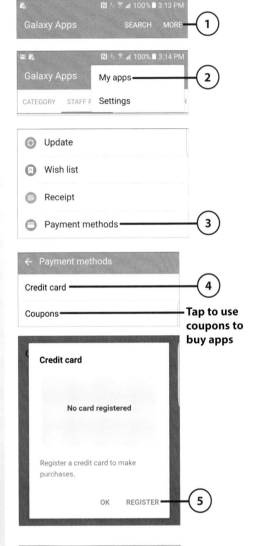

Tap to use coupons to buy apps

Install Free Applications

You don't have to spend money to get quality applications. Some of the best applications are free.

1. Tap the free app you want to install.

2. Swipe up to read about the app's features, reviews by other people who installed it, and information on the person or company who wrote it.

3. Tap to share a link to the app with friends.

4. Tap Install to download and install the app.

5. Tap Open to launch the app once it has downloaded.

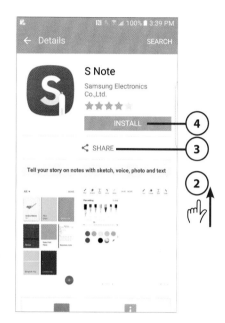

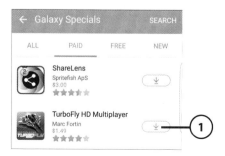

Buy Applications

If an application is not free, the price displays next to the application icon. If you want to buy the application, remember that you need to have set up a payment method, such as a credit card. See the "Add a Payment Method for Galaxy Apps" section earlier in the chapter for more information.

1. Tap the app you want to buy.

2. Swipe up to read the application features, reviews by other people who installed it, and information on the person or company who wrote the application. Swiping up also enables you to share a link to the app with friends.

3. Tap to add the app to your Wish List.

4. Tap the price to purchase the app.

5. Tap to accept the app's requested permissions and proceed to the authentication screen.

6. Place one of your registered fingers over the Home button to authenticate that it is you who is making the app purchase. If you have chosen not to use your fingerprint as authentication for the Galaxy Apps Store, you will be prompted to enter your Samsung account password on this screen.

7. Choose a payment method.

8. Tap Buy to purchase the app.

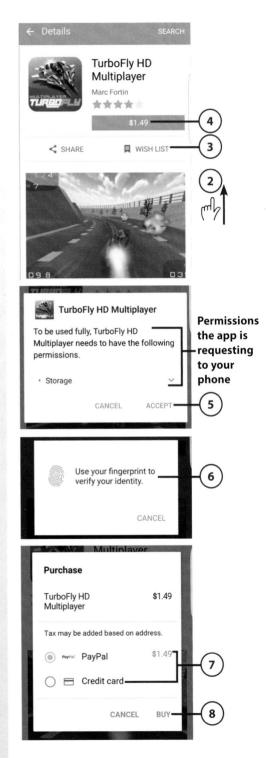

Using Amazon.com to install apps

Your Galaxy S7 comes preinstalled with the Amazon.com app. With this app you can find and purchase items from Amazon.com, but it also allows you to purchase Android apps. Apps that appear in the Amazon.com app store are the same as apps that appear in the Google Play Store, however they may be discounted or free. Before you start using the Amazon.com app, make sure that you have a payment method set up in your Amazon.com account. To do this, log in to your Amazon.com app, tap the icon on the top left of the screen, and tap Add a Credit or Debit Card. To purchase apps and games, tap the icon on the top left of the screen, tap Underground Apps, and tap All Apps & Games to see apps that Amazon.com is selling. Similar to buying apps from the Google Play Store or the Galaxy Apps Store, simply search for an app and tap Buy to buy it.

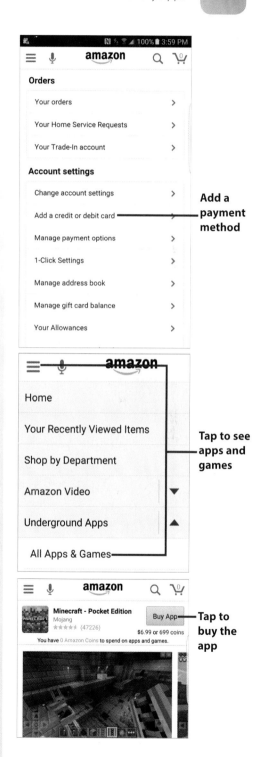

Add a payment method

Tap to see apps and games

Tap to buy the app

Tap a book to read it

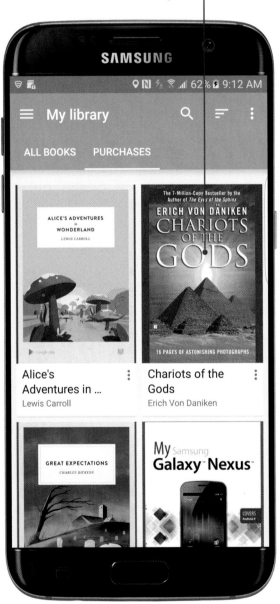

In this chapter, you find out how to buy books, read books, and subscribe to your favorite magazines. Topics include the following:

→ Buying and reading books
→ Buying and reading magazines

13

Books and Magazines

This chapter covers how you can use your Galaxy S7 for reading books and magazine subscriptions.

Books

The Google Play Store has a section that enables you to purchase (and, in some cases, get free) books in eBook form. After you have an eBook, you can read it at your leisure and even bookmark your favorite pages.

Navigate the Play Books App

The Play Books app enables you to read your books, bookmark pages, and find and purchase more books.

1. Tap to launch Play Books. You see the Read Now screen that shows books you have recently opened and books that Google recommends you read.

2. Swipe in from the left of the screen.

3. Tap Shop to find and purchase more books.

4. Tap to see books already in your library.

5. Tap to change the Play Books app settings.

6. Move the switch to the on position to see only books that have been physically downloaded to your phone as opposed to all books you have purchased, some of which may still be stored in the Google cloud.

7. Tap to return to the Read Now screen.

Buy Books

The procedure is the same for downloading a free book and buying a book. The only difference is a free book shows a price of zero.

1. Swipe in from the left of the screen.

2. Tap Shop to open the Google Play Store to the Books section. Bear in mind that at this point you are exiting the Google Books app and opening the Google Play Store.

Searching for a Book

Finding books in the Google Play Store is easy. You can swipe left and right in the white area near the top of the screen to switch between different groupings of books including Top Selling, Deals, New Releases, Genres, Comics, Children's Books, and Top Free Books. You can also swipe up to see books recommended for you, books that you can preview, books less than $10, and so on. You can also use the search icon to find books. When you choose to search, remember that you can also speak your searches.

---

3. Tap a book to open it.

4. Swipe up to read reviews on the book.

5. Tap to read a free sample of the book before you purchase it.

6. Tap to purchase the book.

Search for books

Swipe up to see more options

Add book to your wish list

7. Tap to change the method of payment if you need to.

8. Tap to buy the book. The book immediately starts downloading to your phone and appears in the Read Now screen.

Read Books

As you read a book, you can bookmark certain pages, jump to different chapters, and even change the font size.

1. Tap a book to open it.

2. Swipe left and right across the screen to flip forward and backward through the book. Alternatively, you can also tap on the left and right sides of the screen to flip backward and forward through the book.

3. Tap near the middle of the screen to reveal the formatting controls and controls for quickly moving to specific pages.

4. Swipe down from the top bezel to reveal only the formatting and other controls.

Indicates book has completed downloading

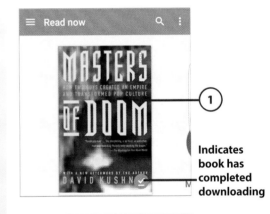

Jump to Pages Quickly

After you tap the middle of the screen you can quickly move to specific pages in the book.

1. Drag left and right to quickly jump to a specific page.

2. Swipe left and right to skim through the pages.

3. Tap a page to return to the reading view.

Formatting and Other Controls

After you tap the middle of the screen, swipe down from the top bezel, or swipe up from the bottom bezel, you can control the way the book is presented on the screen.

1. Tap to search the entire book for a word or phrase.

2. Tap to list all the chapters in the book and jump to them, see notes you may have taken, and bookmarks that you previously set.

3. Tap to change the way the book appears on your screen.

4. Tap to see more options.

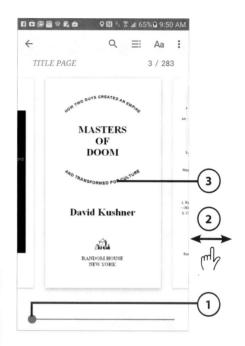

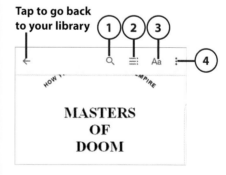

Tap to go back to your library

Control the Visuals

Tap the Font icon to reveal ways to control how the book appears on your screen. You can choose black text on a white background (typically used during the day), white text on a black background (typically used at night), or a simulation of real paper color. If you are viewing the book using the Flowing Text Mode, you can also change the typeface, text alignment, brightness, line height, and font size. Read more about what Flowing Text is in the "What Are Original Pages?" note later in this chapter. Turn on the Night Light feature to let your S7 gradually reduce the blue light on the screen, replacing it with amber light as it gets darker. This makes it easier to read but could also help you fall asleep faster.

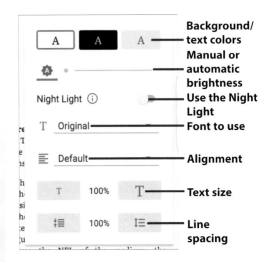

Background/text colors
Manual or automatic brightness
Use the Night Light
Font to use
Alignment
Text size
Line spacing

5. Tap to switch between Original Pages and Flowing Text (if the book supports it).

6. Tap to share a link to the book you are reading via social media, email, and other methods.

7. Tap to add or remove a bookmark.

8. Tap to change the settings for the app.

What Are Original Pages?

When you read a book on your phone, the app defaults to showing the book using Flowing Text. This means that the text of the book is all there, but it's not structured in its original format per page. When viewing the book using Flowing Text you are able to change the font, font size, alignment, and so on. Some books allow you to switch to Original Pages, which makes it possible for you to page through the book as it was originally laid out, using the original typeface and alignment. When reading the book using its original format, you are unable to change the font, font size, line spacing, and alignment.

>>>Go Further

TRANSLATING TEXT AND TAKING NOTES

As you read through your book, you might need a translation of some foreign text, or you might want to highlight some text and make notes about it. To do either thing, touch and hold the text you want to translate or make a note on, and then drag the markers left and right until you have selected all the text you want. Tap the appropriate icon in the toolbar.

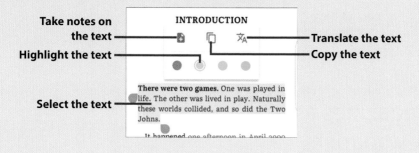

>>>Go Further

SAVE YOUR BOOK TO YOUR PHONE

When you buy and read a book, it is downloaded to your phone and stays there while you are reading it. If you know that you will be reading more than one book in an area with no Internet access (such as on a plane), you should first manually download any books you think you will be reading so that they are available. In the My Library screen, tap the Menu icon under the cover image of each book you want to download and then tap Download. A blue checkmark indicates that the book has been downloaded.

Book already downloaded

Tap to download the book

Magazines and Newspapers

You can subscribe to magazines and newspapers on your phone and have them delivered in electronic form to read anytime. The Play Newsstand app enables you to subscribe to and read your magazines.

1. Tap to launch the Play Newsstand app. The first screen you see is the Read Now screen. This screen shows stories from different publications that you can read without subscribing to those publications.

2. Tap a highlight to read it.

3. Swipe up to see more highlights.

4. Tap to search for magazines and newspapers to subscribe to.

5. Swipe left and right to scroll through the categories of stories. Highlights are a mixture of stories from all categories; other categories include News, Business, Entertainment, Sports, Technology, World, and Automobile.

Purchase or Subscribe to Publications

You can subscribe to publications or just purchase a single edition.

1. Swipe in from the left of the screen.

2. Tap Explore.

3. Tap a category. This example uses the Food & Drink category.

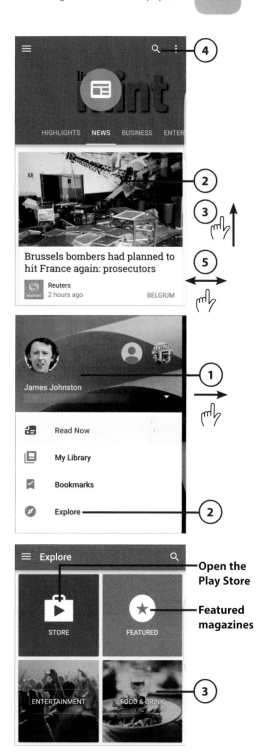

4. Tap a publication.

5. Tap Buy to buy only the latest edition of the magazine, or tap Subscribe to buy a subscription to the magazine.

6. Tap Subscribe to complete the transaction. If you chose to buy only the latest issue, the button is instead labeled Buy.

Why Would I Download a Magazine?

When you open and read magazines, they are temporarily downloaded to your phone, but you are still required to be connected to the Internet before you read them. If you are going to be in an area with no Internet access (such as on a plane) and you want to read a magazine, while you are still connected to the Internet you need to manually download it. To do this, tap the menu icon under the magazine's cover and tap Download. A blue checkmark indicates a downloaded magazine.

Read a Publication

1. Swipe in from the left of the screen.

2. Tap My Library.

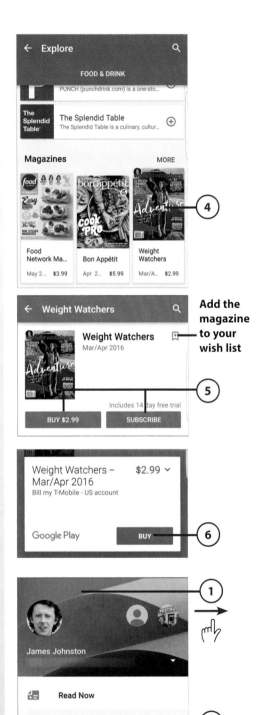

Add the magazine to your wish list

3. Tap the appropriate tab for the type of publication. This example uses a purchased magazine, which is on the Magazines tab.

4. Tap the publication to open it.

5. Swipe up to see all of the magazine's articles.

6. Tap the magazine cover to open the magazine at the cover, or tap one the articles to open them.

Comparing Article Mode and Page Mode

If you tap the blue icon in the top-right of the screen, you can switch between viewing the magazine as it is laid out in the print version, page by page, or in Article mode, which reformats the magazine so that you can move between the articles and scroll through the content of each article. The format is not how it was originally printed, but it is easier to read on your phone. When in Page mode, if you tap on a page to jump to it, you can then continue to swipe left and right to page back and forth through the magazine. When in Article mode, if you tap an article, you must scroll up and down to scroll through the article, and when you swipe left and right you can switch between articles. While reading the magazine, if you want to switch between Page mode and Article mode, just tap in the middle of the screen to reveal the Page/Article mode switch.

Indicates magazine has been downloaded

Switch between page view and story view

Page mode

Scroll left and right through the pages

Article mode

Scroll left and right to switch articles

Scroll up and down through the article

Pair Bluetooth devices
with your Galaxy S7

Troubleshoot Galaxy S7 software,
hardware, and accessories

This chapter covers how to get the most from your Galaxy S7 using hardware accessories. It also explains ways that you can properly maintain your Galaxy S7 or S7 edge and troubleshoot basic software or hardware problems. Topics covered in this chapter include:

→ Finding Galaxy S7 and S7 edge accessories
→ Pairing Bluetooth devices
→ Maintaining your Galaxy S7
→ Updating the Galaxy S7 software
→ Extending battery life
→ Solving Galaxy S7 issues
→ Troubleshooting connected devices
→ Getting help

Optimizing and Troubleshooting

Your Galaxy S7 is fully capable of providing an amazing multimedia experience right out of the box, but whether you are viewing movies, capturing photos and video, or composing a long email, you want your Galaxy S7 to be versatile. Accessories such as covers, Bluetooth headsets, battery packs, and wireless chargers can offer some much needed practical support for your Galaxy S7 use.

Although problems concerning the Galaxy S7 software, hardware, and accessories are rare, on occasion you might experience incidents where your Galaxy S7 or S7 edge does not perform properly. There are a few fixes you can try if you experience the occasional glitch that can occur with any hardware device.

Although your Galaxy S7 or S7 edge is a sophisticated piece of hardware, it is less complex than an actual computer, making any issue that might arise more manageable.

Finding Accessories

You can find accessories for the Galaxy S7 and S7 edge models in electronics stores such as Best Buy, or you can also shop your phone carrier's website, as they may offer accessories for the Galaxy S7 and S7 edge.

Online stores, such as Samsung.com and Amazon.com, are also great places to find hardware accessories for the Galaxy S7 and S7 edge. In the U.S., visit the accessories page for the Samsung website at http://www.samsung.com/us/mobile/cell-phones-accessories/. If you're in another country, visit the Samsung Global website at http://www.samsung.com/countries so you can select your country and then view Galaxy S7 accessories in your country page.

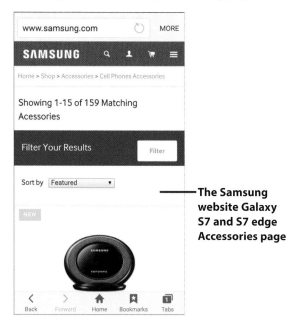

The Samsung website Galaxy S7 and S7 edge Accessories page

Always make sure that you pick the right accessory for your Galaxy S7 model. As of this writing, none of the previous Galaxy S smartphone series accessories work with the Galaxy S7 or S7 edge.

It's Not All Good

Limited Accessories to Date

This section covers accessories that were available as the book was written. It's likely that shortly after this book finds its way onto shelves there will be new accessories for both Galaxy S7 models. For example, Samsung does not currently offer a desk charging dock for the Galaxy S7, but as of this writing desk docks from other companies are available for pre-order. We encourage you to keep up to date on what is available for your device by periodically checking the Samsung website, Amazon.com, and tech forums.

Pairing Bluetooth Devices

Along with the many other comfort features and conveniences found with the Galaxy S7, your Galaxy S7 gives you the capability to connect some external hardware devices wirelessly. The Galaxy S7 is equipped with Bluetooth 4.1 technology, enabling you to connect cable-free with Bluetooth-capable devices. By default, Bluetooth is enabled on your Galaxy S7. If you have already played with this setting, you can tell if Bluetooth is turned on by verifying that the Bluetooth symbol is visible in the status bar at the top of the screen.

Pair a Bluetooth Device

You can easily connect your Galaxy S7 to a Bluetooth device in two phases: discovering and pairing.

1. Turn on the wireless device that you want to pair with your Galaxy S7 and make it discoverable.

Discoverability

Bluetooth devices broadcast their availability only after you instruct them to do so. If necessary, refer to your device's manual to learn how to make it discoverable.

2. Tap the Apps icon on the Home screen.

3. Tap Settings.

4. Tap Connections in the tab bar.

5. Tap Bluetooth.

6. Tap your Bluetooth device in the list. (If you don't see your device, tap Scan in the menu bar above the list.) Your Galaxy S7 attempts to pair with the device.

7. The device appears under a newly created Paired Devices list.

8. If you need to refresh the list of devices, tap Scan.

Entering or Confirming Passcode May Be Required

You may need to enter a passcode for the Bluetooth device you're trying to pair with, such as a printer. For other Bluetooth devices, such as the Galaxy Tab S2 in this example, you may only need to tap OK in the Bluetooth Pairing Request window on both devices to confirm that each device has the same pairing passkey number.

Paired Bluetooth Device Settings

After you have successfully paired your device to your Galaxy S7, a Settings icon appears next to the name of the Bluetooth device within the Paired Devices list. Tap that Settings icon to rename or unpair your device.

Maintaining Your Galaxy S7 and S7 Edge

Regular maintenance of your Galaxy S7 or S7 edge not only helps extend the life of your Galaxy S7, it also helps ensure peak performance. It's important that you make sure your Galaxy S7 software is up to date and that you understand basic troubleshooting concepts.

Properly cleaning and protecting the body of your Galaxy S7 or S7 edge can be equally important. The Galaxy S7 and S7 edge were designed to be sturdy, but, like any other electronic device, they can collect dust, and a simple drop on the sidewalk can prove disastrous. The first step in maintaining your Galaxy S7 or S7 edge is prevention. You can start by purchasing a protective case.

A sturdy case designed for the Galaxy S7 or S7 edge is important for the overall protection of your device. A number of companies have created a variety of cases for the Galaxy S7 and S7 edge, including Samsung. If you don't like Samsung's offerings, search the Internet or go to Amazon.com to see what's out there. The more padded the case, the better it can absorb a shock if you happen to drop your phone.

A case can also help protect your Galaxy S7 or S7 edge from dust and keep it dry if you happen to get caught in the rain. Make sure you keep the inside of your case clean. Dust and sand can find a way into even the most well-constructed cases. Instead of using your sleeve to wipe off your Galaxy S7 display, invest in a microfiber cloth; you can find one in any office supply or computer store.

Your first instinct might be to wet a cloth to clean your Galaxy S7 touchscreen. Don't use liquids to clean the touchscreen, especially if they include alcohol or ammonia. These harsh chemicals can cause irreparable damage to the touchscreen, rendering it difficult to view content. Consider purchasing a screen protector at a local store or your favorite online retailer to keep the touchscreen dust and scratch free. Some screen protectors also come with a microfiber cleaning cloth.

Updating Galaxy S7 Software

Every so often, Google releases software updates for your Galaxy S7's Android operating system. To get the most from your Galaxy S7, it is good practice to update soon after an upgrade has been released. When an update is available, you receive a notification that indicates you can download a system upgrade. At that point, you have the option to initiate the software update. You can also check for system updates manually.

1. Tap the Apps icon on the Home screen.

2. Tap Settings.

3. Swipe from right to left within the tab bar.

4. Tap System.

5. Tap About Device.

6. Tap Software Update.

7. Tap Check for Updates.

8. You see the Software Update screen for your specific carrier, which is AT&T in this example. Tap OK.

9. If the software is up to date, tap OK to return to the About Device screen. If an update is available, follow the provided directions to upgrade your software.

AT&T Software Update

Current software is up to date

OK — 9

Updating Firmware

The Android operating system is not the only software you need to update on your Galaxy S7. Your Galaxy S7 also uses software called *firmware* to run its internal functions. When an update is available, use your own discretion as to whether you want to update right away, just in case there are any issues with the update.

Extending Battery Life

Your Galaxy S7 is capable of up to at least 9 hours of battery life, depending on the model you have. Battery life can also vary depending on how you use the Galaxy S7. Strenuous tasks, such as playing HD video, dramatically lower your battery life more than surfing the Web does.

You can monitor your battery power at the top of the screen in the Status area. The white battery status icon located on the right side of the Status bar lets you keep an eye on how much battery power you have left.

AT&T   N ⧆ ⧎ 100% ▮ 3:47 AM

The battery status icon in the Status bar

When the battery gets low, a warning appears, informing you of the percentage of battery power you have left and instructing you to connect the charger. When the battery is too low, your Galaxy S7 automatically shuts down. There are a few things you can do to extend the life of your Galaxy S7 battery between charges.

Monitor Power Usage

On the Galaxy S7, you can use the Battery Usage screen to see which of the apps you use consumes the most power, and then you can reduce the use of those apps. Your battery power savings are small, but if you're running low on power with no way to recharge, every little bit counts. Follow these directions to access the Battery Usage screen.

1. Tap the Apps icon on the Home screen.

2. Tap Settings.

3. Swipe from right to left within the tab bar.

4. Tap System.

5. Tap Battery.

6. The screen shows you how many hours you have left on your current battery charge and how long it's been since your battery was fully charged.

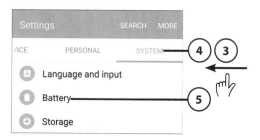

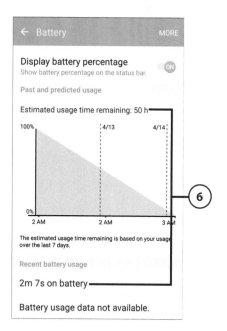

Adjust Screen Brightness

The high-quality touchscreen of the Galaxy S7 can consume plenty of battery power. The higher the brightness level set on your Galaxy S7, the more power the touchscreen uses. If you are viewing the screen in very bright conditions, you probably do not need a very high brightness setting. Consider dimming the screen to extend the battery life.

1. Tap the Apps icon on the Home screen.

2. Tap Settings.

3. Swipe from right to left within the tab bar.

4. Tap Device.

5. Tap Display.

6. Slide the slider button to the left to lower the brightness level or to the right to increase the brightness level.

7. Change the brightness level to the default level by tapping the Auto checkbox.

8. Return to the Device settings list by tapping the Back icon.

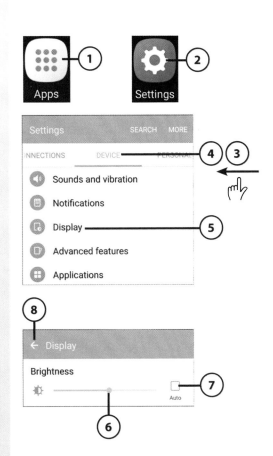

Quick Settings for Brightness

The Galaxy S7 offers a quicker way for you to access the brightness controls by changing the brightness level in the Quick Settings and Notification screen. Open the Quick Settings and Notification screen by swiping down from the top of the screen and then use the slider below the settings button row to adjust screen brightness.

Utilize Sleep Mode

Your Galaxy S7 goes to sleep after a specified period of inactivity, but you don't have to wait for it to fall asleep—you can put it to sleep manually. When your Galaxy S7 is awake, it is consuming battery power. Press and then immediately release the Power button on the side of your Galaxy S7 when you have finished using the device to conserve battery power.

Conserve Power by Turning Off Wi-Fi

When the Wi-Fi antenna is activated on your Galaxy S7, your device is incessantly looking for available Wi-Fi networks to join, which uses battery power. To see if Wi-Fi is turned on, check the right side of the status bar of your Galaxy S7 for the Wi-Fi symbol. If you do not need a Wi-Fi connection, turn it off to conserve battery power. If you are not wandering and are using Wi-Fi in a single location, look for a power outlet and plug in your Galaxy S7.

1. Tap Settings in the Apps screen as you learned to do earlier in this chapter.

2. Tap Connections in the tab bar.

3. Tap Wi-Fi.

4. Turn off Wi-Fi by sliding the Wi-Fi slider button to the left.

5. The slider button displays the word Off with a gray background, and the screen asks you to turn on Wi-Fi to see available networks.

Quick Settings for Wi-Fi

The Galaxy S7 offers an even quicker way for you to access the Wi-Fi setting in the Quick Settings and Notification screen. Simply swipe down from the top of the screen; within the Quick Settings and Notification screen tap the Wi-Fi button with the green Wi-Fi icon to turn it off. When the icon turns gray, tap the Wi-Fi button to turn Wi-Fi on again.

Conserve Power by Turning Off Bluetooth

When Bluetooth is activated on your Galaxy S7, your device is constantly checking for other Bluetooth devices, which drains battery power. To see if Bluetooth is turned on, check the status bar in the top-left corner of your Galaxy S7 for the Bluetooth symbol. If you are not using a Bluetooth device, turn this function off. There are also security reasons why you should turn off Bluetooth when you are not using it, so get in the habit of turning Bluetooth off as soon as you finish using a wireless device with your Galaxy S7. You can easily deactivate Bluetooth in the notification panel.

1. Tap Settings in the Apps screen.

2. Tap Connections in the menu bar.

3. Tap Bluetooth.

4. Turn off Bluetooth by sliding the Bluetooth slider button to the left.

5. The slider button displays the word Off with a gray background, and the screen asks you to turn on Bluetooth to see paired and available devices.

Quick Settings for Bluetooth

The Galaxy S7 offers an even quicker way for you to access the Bluetooth setting in the Quick Settings and Notification screen. Swipe down from the top of the screen to open the Quick Settings and Notification screen. Then turn off Bluetooth by tapping the Bluetooth button with the green Bluetooth icon at the right side of the button bar. When the icon turns gray, tap the Bluetooth button to turn Bluetooth on again.

Conserve Even More Power Using Power Saving Modes

If you would rather not tweak individual settings to save battery life, the Galaxy S7 comes with two power saving modes: Power Saving Mode and Ultra Power Saving Mode. Each mode restricts the performance of the Galaxy S7 and requires few setting changes on your part.

Set Up Power Saving Mode

By default, Power Saving Mode is turned off. When you turn on Power Saving Mode, the Galaxy S7 begins saving power immediately by limiting maximum CPU performance, reducing the screen brightness and frame rate, and turning off the touch key lights and vibration feedback. What's more, the device turns off the screen more quickly after you receive a notification.

You can change when Power Saving Mode goes into effect based on how much battery life you have left.

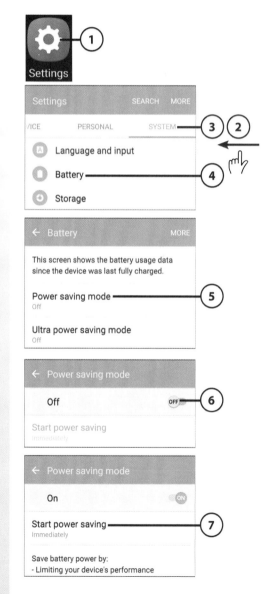

1. Tap Settings on the Apps screen.

2. Swipe from right to left within the tab bar.

3. Tap System.

4. Tap Battery.

5. Tap Power Saving Mode.

6. Slide the slider from left (Off) to right (On).

7. Tap Start Power Saving.

8. Tap the appropriate battery power level in the menu to determine when you start power saving; the default level is Immediately. You can select between 5%, 15%, 20%, and 50% battery power. This example uses 50% power.

9. The Start Power Saving setting shows that the Galaxy S7 will go into Power Saving Mode when your battery life reaches 50%.

10. Turn off Power Saving Mode by sliding the slider button from right (On) to left (Off).

11. Return to the Battery screen by tapping the Back icon.

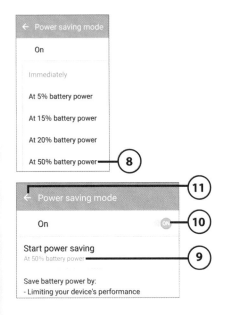

Set Up Ultra Power Saving Mode

Ultra Power Saving Mode automatically puts your display in grayscale mode and goes further by severely limiting the apps and services you can use on the Galaxy S7. These services include mobile data, Wi-Fi, and Bluetooth.

If you already have Power Saving Mode active, the Galaxy S7 closes Power Saving Mode so you can get the benefits of Ultra Power Saving Mode.

1. Tap Settings on the Apps screen.

2. Swipe from right to left within the tab bar.

3. Tap System.

4. Tap Battery.

5. Tap Ultra Power Saving Mode.

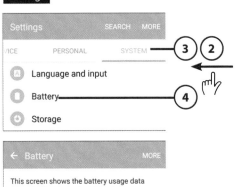

6. Swipe up in the screen to view more information about Ultra Power Saving Mode.

7. Slide the slider from left (Off) to right (On).

8. The Galaxy S7 turns on Ultra Power Saving Mode by dimming the screen, placing the screen in grayscale mode, and turning off the screen after 15 seconds of no activity. The Ultra Power Saving Mode screen appears, and this screen opens every time you wake the Galaxy S7 from sleep mode.

9. The Ultra Power Saving Mode window tells you what your current battery percentage is and the maximum number of days your Galaxy S7 can stay in standby (another word for sleep) mode.

10. By default, you can use the Phone, Messages, and Internet apps. Run the app by tapping the app icon; when you finish using the app, tap the Back touch button.

11. Add an app to the list of apps you can run by tapping one of the Add (+) buttons. In the Add Application window that appears, tap Calculator, Clock, Email, Facebook, or Memo. After you select the application, the app icon appears, replacing the Add icon.

12. Tap More to open the menu so you can remove one or more apps from the list of apps you can run; change various settings including Wi-Fi, Bluetooth, Airplane Mode, Location, Sound, and Brightness; and turn off Ultra Power Saving Mode.

13. When you select to turn off Ultra Power Saving Mode, there's a delay of a few seconds and then the Home screen appears in full color. All apps and services return to normal operation.

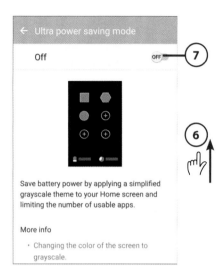

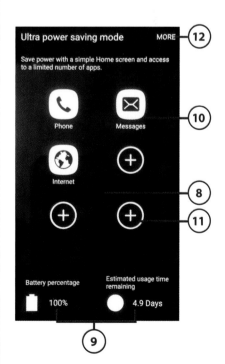

Solving Random Galaxy S7 Issues

The occasional hardware or software glitch happens to even the best of electronic devices. You might encounter an issue, although rare, where an app you are using freezes, a wireless device proves difficult to pair with your Galaxy S7, the touchscreen becomes unresponsive, or landscape orientation is not available at all times. Fortunately, it is not very difficult to troubleshoot some of these issues. If you should happen to come across a problem that you can't solve yourself, there are plenty of channels for you to find technical support.

Difficulty Turning Your Galaxy S7 On or Off

On rare occasions, you might find that your Galaxy S7 is stubborn when you try to turn it on or off. It might appear that the device has locked or become unresponsive. If this happens to you, hold the Power button for 8 seconds to see if it responds. If this does not work, you might need to let your Galaxy S7 sit for a few seconds before you again try holding the Power button for 8 seconds.

Touchscreen Becomes Unresponsive

This tip assumes that your Galaxy S7 and any app you are using is responsive, but the touchscreen is not responding to your touch. If you attempt to use your Galaxy S7 touchscreen while wearing conventional gloves, it does not work. This can prove inconvenient on a very cold day, so you might want to consider a capacitive stylus for your Galaxy S7.

Your Galaxy S7 uses a capacitive touchscreen that holds an electrical charge. When you touch the screen with your bare finger, capacitive stylus, or special static-carrying gloves, it changes the amount of charge at the specific point of contact. In a nutshell, this is how the touchscreen interprets your taps, drags, and pinches.

The touchscreen might also be unresponsive to your touch if you happen to have a thin coat of film on your fingertips. So no sticky fingers, please.

Force Stop an App

Sometimes an app might get an attitude and become unruly. For example, an app might provide a warning screen saying that it is currently busy and is unresponsive, or it might give some other issue warning to convey that a problem exists. If an app is giving you problems, you can manually stop the app.

1. Tap Settings on the Apps screen.

2. Swipe from right to left within the tab bar.

3. Tap Device.

4. Tap Applications.

5. Tap Application Manager.

6. Swipe up and down on the screen if necessary until you see the problem app in the list.

7. Tap the app name.

8. Tap Force Stop. The app stops running.

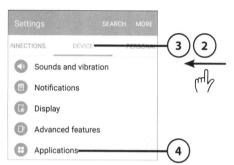

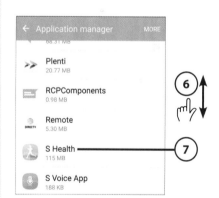

Battery Does Not Charge

If you find that your battery is not charging, first start with the power outlet. Is the outlet supplying power? Is the power strip turned on? Plug something else into the outlet to see if it works, or try another outlet.

Make sure that everything is connected properly. Is the adapter secure on both ends? If the outlet supplies power and the cables are connected properly, but the battery still does not charge, try another cable. If this does not solve the issue, your battery might be defective. Contact Samsung technical support. (See the "Getting Technical Help" section later in this chapter for more information about how to contact Samsung.) There is no way for you to remove the battery yourself.

Overheating

Overheating is rare, but if your Galaxy S7 becomes too hot and regularly turns itself off, you might need to replace the battery. You can tell if your Galaxy S7 is getting too hot by holding it in your hands. Use caution.

Landscape Orientation Does Not Work

The orientation setting on your Galaxy S7 could be set so that your Galaxy S7 stays in either portrait (vertical) or landscape (horizontal) mode, regardless of how you hold the device. If your Galaxy S7 no longer utilizes landscape orientation, first check the setting for screen orientation.

The Galaxy S7 has a Screen Rotation setting that must be selected for the screen to adjust from portrait to landscape mode, depending on how you hold the device. You can easily confirm that the Screen Rotation setting is selected from the Quick Settings and Notification screen.

1. In the Home screen, open the Quick Settings and Notification screen by tapping and holding on the top edge of the screen and then swiping downward.

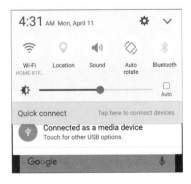

2. Locate the Auto Rotate setting icon and confirm that the icon is blue. If the icon is gray, activate the setting by tapping the Auto Rotate icon. Your screen should now adjust to the orientation in which you hold the device.

Landscape Orientation and Apps

Not every app in the Google Play Store was developed to take advantage of the landscape orientation of your Galaxy S7. If you notice this issue while using an app, close the app and then see whether your Galaxy S7 can situate itself in land-scape orientation. If so, launch the app again and see how it works.

Troubleshooting Wi-Fi Accessibility Problems

Your Galaxy S7 provides you the convenience and flexibility of wireless Internet access via Wi-Fi connectivity. Along with this convenience and flexibility comes the potential for connectivity issues regarding wireless networks. If you are unable to access a Wi-Fi network, or if your connection is sporadic, there are some troubleshooting tips you can use to pinpoint basic accessibility options.

Make Sure Wi-Fi Is Activated

First and foremost, make sure that the Wi-Fi antenna is on. You can determine this by looking on the right side of the Status bar at the top of your Galaxy S7 screen to see whether the Wi-Fi icon is visible. If it is not on, you can open the Quick Settings and Notification screen by swiping down from the top of the screen and then activate Wi-Fi by tapping the Wi-Fi button.

The Wi-Fi icon in the Status bar

Check Your Range

If Wi-Fi is activated on your Galaxy S7 and you still cannot connect, take note of how far away you are from the Wi-Fi access point. In general, you can be only 150 feet from a Wi-Fi access point indoors or 300 feet from an access point outdoors before the signal becomes weak or drops altogether. Structures such as walls with lots of electronics can also impede a Wi-Fi signal.

However, the type of wireless protocol you're using in your Wi-Fi network also affects your range. For example, if your wireless network uses the 802.11n protocol, which the Galaxy S7 supports, you'll have much better range and signal coverage than with the older 802.11a/b/g protocols. If you still have trouble, check your network information for protocol and coverage data. Also, make sure you are close to the access point or turn on the access point's range booster, if it has one, to improve your connection.

Reset Your Router

The issue of Wi-Fi accessibility might not be related to your distance from the Wi-Fi access point, a signal-impeding barrier, or your Galaxy S7. As a last resort, you might need to reset the router. After you reset your router, you have to set up your network from the ground up.

Reset the Galaxy S7 Device

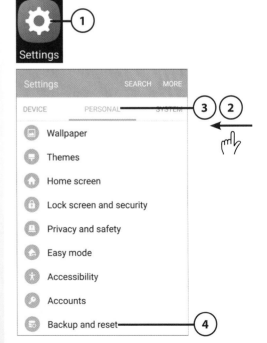

If all else fails and your technical problems still persist, as a last-ditch effort you might need to reset the Galaxy S7. Resetting your Galaxy S7 deletes all data stored on the device and restores your Galaxy S7 to the factory defaults, just like when you took it out of the box for the first time. Consider contacting support before you reset your Galaxy S7, but if you must, follow these directions to reset the device:

1. Tap Settings on the Apps screen.

2. Swipe from right to left within the tab bar.

3. Tap Personal.

4. Tap Backup and Reset.

5. Tap Factory Data Reset.

6. Tap the Reset Device button.

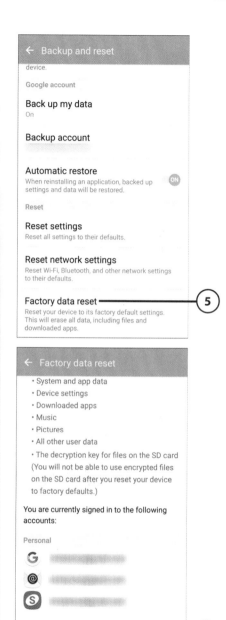

7. If you use a password to log in to your Galaxy S7, type the password in the Confirm Password field.

8. Tap Next.

9. Tap the Delete All button to confirm. Your Galaxy S7 is returned to its factory default state.

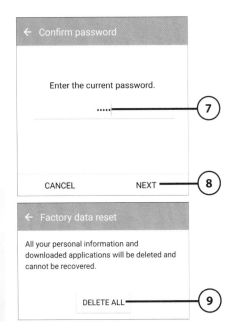

Getting Technical Help

Many outlets are available where you can find help if you run across a Galaxy S7 technical problem that you can't seem to beat. Although limited, the user's manual is a good place to start. You can download the correct manual for your Galaxy S7 model online from the Samsung website (www.samsung.com), in the form of a PDF, and scan the table of contents or perform searches in the document for words that pertain to your problem. In most user manual PDFs, topics in the table of contents are linked to the section they pertain to within the document, so when you find what you are looking for, just click the topic to jump to the pertinent page.

Websites and Galaxy S7 forums are also a great way for you to get support for your device. Type a search phrase, such as "Galaxy S7 Google Calendar sync problem," into your favorite search engine. Chances are plenty of other people are experiencing the same issue. Doing some online research of your own could save you a few minutes on the telephone with technical support and help you solve your problem more quickly.

Contact Your Cellular Provider or Samsung

The Samsung website is a great resource for getting help with technical issues with your Galaxy S7. The Samsung website (www.samsung.com/us/support/) offers support via Twitter, Facebook, Google+, as well as by phone (1-800-726-7864). Before you call, you need to have your device's model number so that you can give it to the technical support representative.

Locate the Galaxy S7 Model Number

You can find the model number on the box that your Galaxy S7 shipped in, and you can also find it in the Settings menu.

1. Tap Settings on the Apps screen.

2. Swipe from right to left within the tabs area in the menu bar.

3. Tap System.

4. Tap About Device.

5. Locate your Galaxy S7 model number in the About Device list.

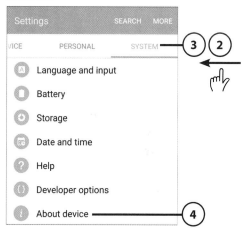

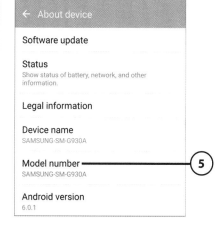

Swipe up to read

In this chapter, you discover how to set up your Android Wear smartwatch and use it with your Samsung Galaxy S7. Topics include the following:

→ Setting up your Android Wear watch
→ Choosing settings and navigating the watch
→ Using the Android Wear watch's apps

Using Your Samsung Galaxy S7 with an Android Wear Smartwatch

To get the most out of your Galaxy S7, you can link it to an Android Wear smartwatch. Android Wear watches are sold by vendors such as Samsung, LG, and Motorola and act as a companion for any Android smartphone, including your S7. The Android Wear watch enables you to display essential information, make phone calls, and allow simple interactions with apps without taking your Galaxy S7 out of your pocket.

Setting Up Your Android Wear Watch

To set up the Android Wear watch, you need to use your Galaxy S7.

1. Unpack the Android Wear watch and identify its components: the Android Wear watch itself, a charging dock/clip, and the charger.

2. Fully charge your Android Wear watch.

3. Turn the Android Wear watch on by pressing and holding its button for a moment. The button is on the right side of the Android Wear watch.

4. Tap to choose your preferred language on the watch screen.

5. When you see a screen on your watch telling you to install the Android Wear app on your phone, switch to your S7 for steps 6–14.

6. Search the Google Play Store for the Android Wear app. When you find it, tap Install.

7. Tap Accept to accept the permissions that the Android Wear app needs to run correctly. After the app installs, run it to start setting up your watch.

8. Tap the right arrow to start setting up your watch.

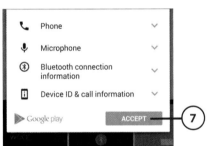

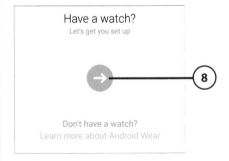

9. Tap Accept to accept that the Android Wear app will synchro-nize data between your watch and your S7.

10. Tap the name of the watch you want to use. In this example, it is a Samsung Gear Live, listed as "Gear Live 2P1R."

11. When prompted, accept the Bluetooth Pairing PIN on both your S7 and your watch. The PIN should be the same on both devices.

12. When your watch and S7 are paired over Bluetooth, you see a screen preparing you to configure Android to allow the Android Wear app to have access to notifi-cations. Tap Enable Notifications.

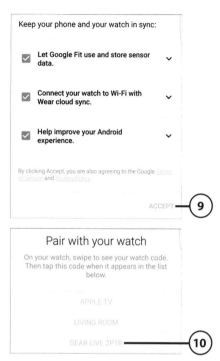

Keep your phone and your watch in sync:

☑ Let Google Fit use and store sensor data. ⌄

☑ Connect your watch to Wi-Fi with Wear cloud sync. ⌄

☑ Help improve your Android experience. ⌄

By clicking Accept, you are also agreeing to the Google Terms of Service and Privacy Policy.

ACCEPT — ⑨

Pair with your watch

On your watch, swipe to see your watch code. Then tap this code when it appears in the list below.

APPLE TV

LIVING ROOM

GEAR LIVE 2P1R — ⑩

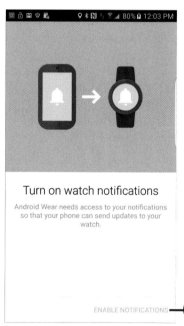

🔲 📷 ✉ ▽ 📑   ♀ ✳ Ⓝ 💹 📶 80% 🔋 12:03 PM

Turn on watch notifications

Android Wear needs access to your notifications so that your phone can send updates to your watch.

ENABLE NOTIFICATIONS — ⑫

13. Move the slider from left (Off) to right (On) to allow the Android Wear app to receive access to Android notifications.

14. Tap OK to verify that you want the Android Wear app to have access to all Android notifications.

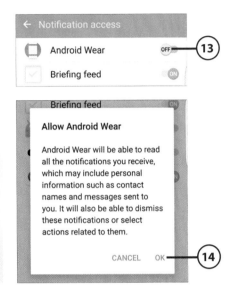

Android Wear Smartwatches Explained

Android Wear is a framework that Google created to support smartwatches connecting to Android devices. This enabled different vendors to create and sell smartwatches that have their own unique look and build quality but can all be compatible with any Android device as long as the owner installs the Android Wear app. Smartwatches that use the Android Wear framework can have square or round faces. Examples of Android Wear watches that have a round face are the Motorola Moto 360 and the LG G Watch R. Examples of Android Wear watches that have a square face are the Asus ZenWatch, Sony SmartWatch 3, Samsung Gear Live, and the LG G Watch. No matter whom you buy your Android Wear–based smartwatch from, and regardless of whether it has a square or round face, the instructions and guidance in this chapter are relevant.

Choosing Settings for Your Android Wear Watch

After pairing your Android Wear watch with your Galaxy S7, you'll probably want to spend some time customizing the Android Wear watch. You can use the Android Wear app on your Galaxy S7 to configure overall settings for the Android Wear watch, as explained in this section. To configure other settings, you use the Settings app on the Android Wear watch itself, as discussed in the following section.

Navigate the Android Wear App

The Android Wear app gives you access to features and settings for configuring and managing your Android Wear watch.

1. Tap to launch the Android Wear app.

2. Tap a watch face to change it on your watch.

3. Tap to see all watch faces you have installed and find more.

4. Swipe up to see all voice actions and what apps are launched when the voice action triggers.

Set Voice Actions

Voice actions are voice commands you speak to your watch. Based on what you say, your watch either launches an app or takes an action, or it tells your S7 to launch an app. Some voice actions can be customized to make use of third-party watch apps that you install. Voice actions that are gray are voice actions that cannot use third-party watch apps, or you have not installed a third-party watch app to make use of them.

1. Your watch shows your agenda.

2. Your watch launches the Google Maps Micro watch app and enables you to get turn-by-turn directions. The Google Maps Micro watch app also launches the Google Maps app on your S7, which actually provides the navigation to your watch.

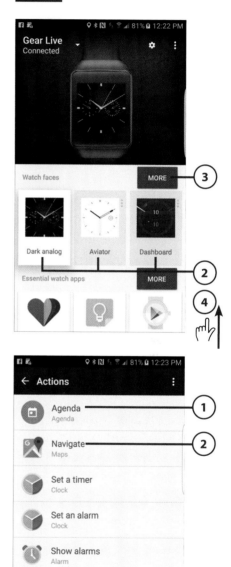

3. Sets a timer on your watch.

4. Sets an alarm on your watch.

5. Shows the alarms set on your watch.

6. Shows your heart rate. Tap to choose which watch app launches to show your heart rate.

7. Shows how many steps you have walked with your watch on.

8. Swipe up for more voice actions.

Why Is the Icon Gray?

In the following steps, many of the voice actions shown in the figure have a gray Google Play icon next to them. That icon indicates that there is currently no app installed to handle the function provided by the voice action. After you install an appropriate app on your S7, these actions will be available.

9. Starts a stopwatch on your watch. Tap to select which watch app launches to start the stopwatch.

10. Call a car to pick you up. Install an app such as Uber or Lyft to make this voice action available. If you have two apps installed that both handle this function, tap Call a Car to choose the app you prefer to use.

11. Allows you to launch an app to start a bike ride. Install an app such as RunKeeper to make this voice action available. If you have two apps installed that both handle this function, tap Start a Bike Ride to choose the app you prefer to use.

12. Allows you to launch an app to start a run. Install an app such as RunKeeper to make this voice action available. If you have two apps installed that both handle this function, tap Start a Run to choose the app you prefer to use.

13. Allows you to launch an app to start a workout. Install an app such as RunKeeper to make this voice action available. If you have two apps installed that both handle this function, tap Start a Workout to choose the app you prefer to use.

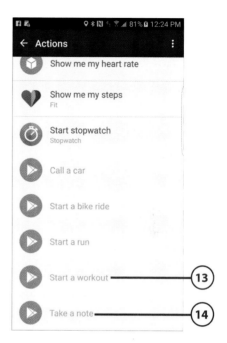

How to Handle Riding, Running, and Workouts

Start a Bike Ride, Start a Run, and Start a Workout are functions that will not work until you install an app on your S7 to handle them. It is your choice which apps you want to install to handle these functions. The one used for writing this chapter was RunKeeper. It just so happens that RunKeeper handles all three functions; however, that does not mean that you need to use just one app for all three functions. You can install three different apps to handle each of the three functions separately. Your favorite app that you already use for tracking bike rides, for example, might already support Android Wear. If that is the case, you will select that app to support the bike ride function. If you have two apps installed that handle one or more of the functions, tap the function to choose which app you want to use. For example, to change what app handles Start a Bike Ride, tap Start a Bike Ride and choose the app.

14. Allows you to launch an app to take a note. If you do not install an app to handle this voice action, when you use this feature, the note you dictate is emailed to your Gmail address. Installing an app such as Chaos Control allows this voice action to launch your favorite note-taking app.

Choose a Watch Face

Your watch comes with some pre-installed watch faces, and you can use the Android Wear app to choose which one you want to use. You can also browse the Google Play Store for more. Some are free; some you must purchase.

1. From the main Android Wear app screen, tap one of the three most recent watch faces to set your watch to use it.

2. Tap More to see all watch faces you have installed.

3. Select a watch face to use.

4. Scroll down to the bottom of the screen and tap Get More Watch Faces to find more watch faces in the Google Play Store.

5. Tap to install a watch face.

6. Once your new watch face has been installed, it automatically downloads to your watch and is visible in the Android Wear app. Tap the watch face to make your watch start using it.

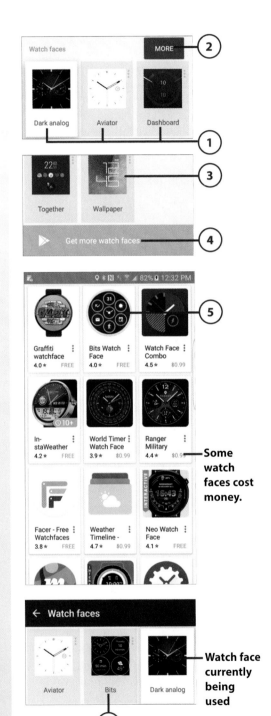

Some watch faces cost money.

Watch face currently being used

7. Some watch faces have configuration options. If the watch face has settings that you can change that affect the way it works, the Settings icon displays over the watch face. Tap it to adjust the watch face's settings.

8. Tap to return to the main Android Wear app screen.

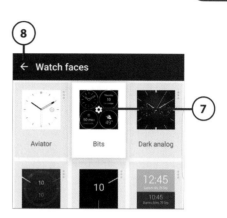

Adjust the Android Wear App's Settings

The Android Wear app does allow for some configuration, and it also provides ways for you to view your watch's battery life and available memory.

1. From the main Android Wear app screen, tap the gear icon to see the settings.

2. Tap to choose which calendars you want to show event cards for on your watch.

3. Tap to choose apps that you no longer want to receive notifications for on your watch. By default, every notification from every app is sent to your watch. Use this setting to select which ones you really care about.

4. Tap the on/off button to mute any alerts and phone call alerts on your S7 while it is connected to the watch. Having this enabled helps cut down on having alerts vibrate your S7 and your watch at the same time.

5. Tap the on/off button to choose whether you want to see tips on your watch describing new features for your watch.

6. Tap to manage the Together feature. The Together feature works with special Together watch faces and allows you to choose a friend to keep in-sync with and share sketches, photos, stickers, and fitness information.

7. Tap the name of your watch to see watch-specific settings.

8. Tap to disconnect your S7 from your watch. Tap again to reconnect.

9. Move the switch to the On position to set your watch to keep a low-resolution monochrome version of the screen on at all times, even when it goes to sleep.

10. Move the switch to the On position to set your watch to wake up when it detects that you're tilting your wrist.

11. Move the switch to the On position to allow a preview of an alert to be displayed on the bottom of the watch screen. If you move the switch to the Off position, there will be no alert previews; however, you can still swipe up to view alerts.

12. Tap to manage the voice actions for your watch.

13. Tap to see how your watch's battery is performing and how much power each app is taking. Using this screen can help you identify apps that are draining the battery.

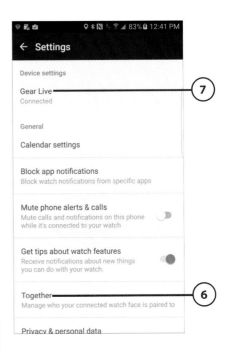

Watch Battery Usage

Viewing your watch's battery performance can help to determine how much longer your watch will last on its current charge based on current usage. You can also see which apps and watch faces are using the most battery time. Watch faces with a lot of animation can use a lot of battery charge. If you see a watch face or watch app that is using a lot of battery charge, you may choose to uninstall the app or stop using the watch face to help your watch last longer on a single charge.

14. Tap to see your watch's memory usage, and how much memory each app is using.

Watch Memory Usage

Viewing your watch's memory usage can help you see if your watch is running out of space, and if it is, which apps and watch faces are using the most memory.

15. Tap to resynchronize apps between your Galaxy S7 and your watch. You don't normally need to do this, but if you suspect that an app you recently installed on your S7 has not installed a mini-app on your watch, you can tap here.

16. Tap to return to the previous screen.

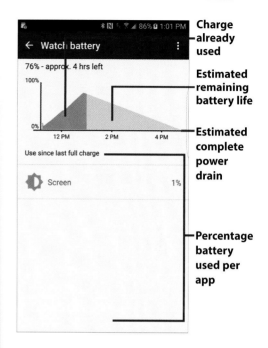

Charge already used

Estimated remaining battery life

Estimated complete power drain

Percentage battery used per app

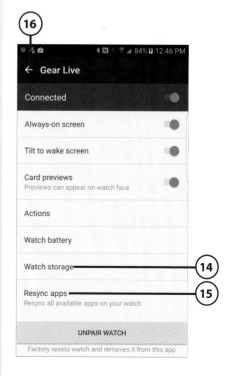

Install Apps on the Android Wear Watch

Some apps installed on your S7 automatically install a watch app on your watch that helps you interact with the app from your watch. There are also dedicated watch apps that you can install from the Google Play Store.

1. In the Android Wear app, tap More next to Essential Watch Apps.

2. Swipe up to see all of the categories of watch apps. The categories are Watch Faces, New Year, Tools, Social, Productivity, Communication, Health & Fitness, Entertainment, Travel & Local, and Games.

3. Tap More to see more apps in a specific category.

4. Tap an app you want to download. Some apps cost money. This example uses 2048 for Android

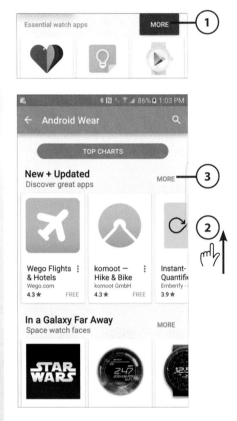

5. Tap Install.

6. Tap Accept to accept any device or information permission the app needs to run. In this example, the app does not need any permissions.

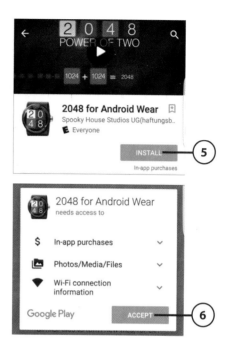

Using Your Android Wear Watch

Now that we have covered how to set up your watch via the Android Wear app, and you've installed some watch faces and apps, let's take a look at using the watch itself.

Watch Features

Your Android Wear watch actually runs on the Android operating system. As of the writing of this book, the version of Android running on Android Wear watches is Android 5.1.1 (Lollipop). Your watch either has a round or square face, includes an accelerometer to detect movement, a capacitive touchscreen so you can perform gestures such as tapping and swiping, and a microphone to listen for voice commands. Your watch probably also has a sensor to monitor your heart rate and a pedometer to measure your activity. Your watch relies on your S7 for the majority of its functions, including voice commands, so you must always have your S7 close by to use your watch. Although most Android Wear watches include a physical button, some do not.

Navigate Your Watch

Your watch responds to taps and swipes that allow you to navigate the interface, run apps, and see and respond to onscreen information.

1. While your watch is not being used, the screen becomes low resolution, monochrome, and dimmed to save energy.

2. Lift your arm to view your watch, and the screen turns to full color.

3. Swipe notifications up to read them, and in some cases take actions on them. If you have more than one notification, swipe up repeatedly to read all of them.

4. Tap the preview of the notification to show more of it, and scroll down to read all of it.

5. Swipe the notification to the left to see any actions that you can take on the notification. This includes an option to block the app so that you don't see notifications from it again.

6. Swipe the notification to the right to dismiss it. To dismiss most apps while using them on your watch, swipe to the right.

7. After you dismiss a notification, if you decide that you didn't want to, you can quickly swipe up from the bottom of the screen to see a dismiss timer. Tap the timer to undo the dismiss before the time runs out.

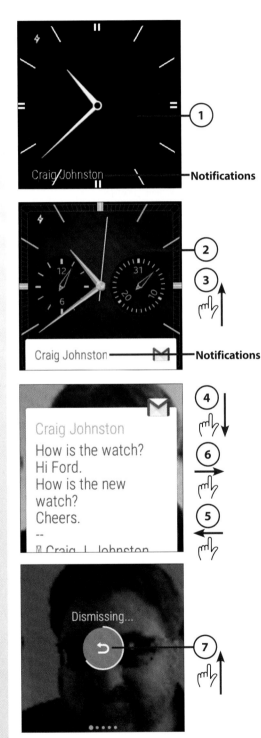

8. Swipe down from the top of the screen to see options and settings.

9. Tap to toggle Do Not Disturb mode on or off.

10. Swipe left to see more options.

11. Tap to put your watch in Theater mode. When in Theater mode, the screen remains blank, you receive no notifications, and the action of lifting your arm to look at your watch is deactivated. Press the watch button to exit Theater mode.

Alternative Method of Activating Theater Mode

If you double-press your watch's button, you set it to Theater mode. Pressing the button again makes the watch exit Theater mode.

12. Swipe left to see more options.

13. Tap to set your watch to Brightness boost for five seconds. Brightness boost sets the screen brightness to the maximum for five seconds to help with bright sunlight or other situations where it is difficult to see the watch screen.

Alternative Method of Activating Brightness Boost

If you triple-press your watch's button, Brightness Boost is engaged for five seconds.

14. Swipe left to see more options.

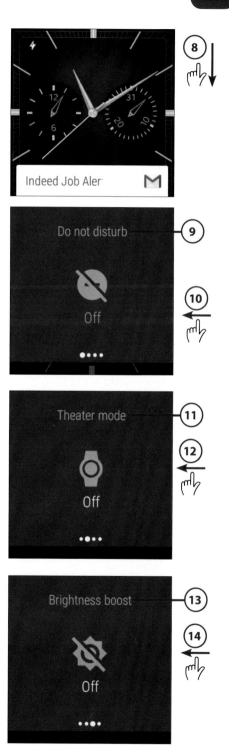

15. Tap to change your watch's settings. See the next section for a description of all settings.

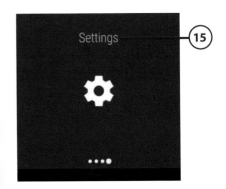

Adjust Your Watch's Settings

Use this section to adjust your watch's settings. To enter your watch's settings, you can either swipe down from the top of the screen and swipe left until you see the Settings icon, or tap your watch screen and scroll down to Settings.

1. Tap to manually adjust the brightness of your watch's screen.

2. Tap to change your watch face.

3. Tap to change the size of the font used on your watch.

4. Swipe up for more settings.

5. Tap to manage what Wi-Fi network your watch connects to. Your watch automatically connects to the same Wi-Fi network that your S7 is connected to, but you can switch Wi-Fi networks.

6. Tap to pair your watch with Bluetooth devices such as Bluetooth speakers.

7. Tap to toggle Always-on Screen on or off. When this is off, your watch screen no longer switches to the low-resolution mode when it goes to sleep; instead, it turns off completely.

8. Swipe up for more settings.

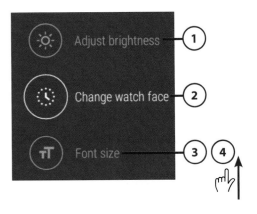

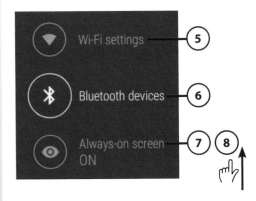

9. Tap to turn Wrist Gestures on or off. Wrist Gestures allow you to scroll forward and backward through cards on your watch by flicking your wrist. To see how to use Wrist Gestures, watch the video at https://youtu.be/_R0qbB4hVbU.

10. Tap to toggle Airplane mode on or off. When in Airplane mode, your watch is not able to communicate using Bluetooth to your S7.

11. Tap to mange whether you want to enable large fonts or the magnification gesture on your watch.

12. Swipe up for more settings.

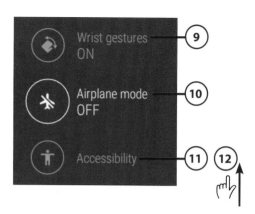

13. Tap to choose whether you want your watch to automatically lock itself when you take it off your wrist. If this is the first time you are enabling this feature, you are asked to draw an unlock pattern. You need to use this pattern to unlock your watch when you put it back on your wrist.

14. Tap to reset your watch. This puts the watch back to the way it came out of the box, and all your saved information will be lost.

15. Tap to restart your watch. All your information remains untouched; your watch just restarts.

16. Swipe up for more settings.

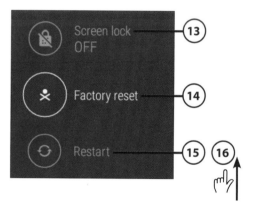

17. Tap to power off your watch.

18. Tap to see information about your watch, as well as whether there is an update for it.

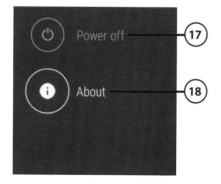

Use Your Watch and Run Watch Apps

Your watch was designed to be used with your voice. However, you can also manually select functions and apps by tapping and swiping on the screen.

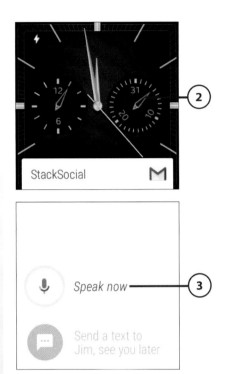

1. Wake up your watch by lifting your arm. Alternatively, you can tap your watch's screen to wake it up.

2. After your watch wakes up and the screen turns to full color, say "OK Google." Alternatively, you can tap the watch screen.

3. Your watch is now listening for a command. Say a command to perform an action or start an app. Use the next section to learn how to use each command and launch watch apps.

Use Watch Functions and Watch Apps

Your watch is designed for voice commands. However, if you don't speak, your watch stops listening and allows you to select functions and run apps using the touchscreen. It's your choice how you want to perform the following functions—either by speaking or by touching.

1. Say "Settings," or tap to see the Settings screen.

2. Say "Start app name" to start an app. For example, say "Start Reversi" to start the Reversi app. Alternatively, you can tap the app icon to start it. Remember that with watch apps like Reversi you must say "Start." You can also start watch apps by saying "Run" (for example, "Run Reversi").

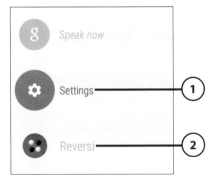

3. Say "Start Stopwatch," or tap to start the Stopwatch watch app.

4. Say "Take a note," or tap and speak the text of the note, to take a note. For example, you can say "Take a note to drink more water" and a new note is created with the text "Drink more water." If you have previously installed an app that handles notes, the note is saved to that app. Otherwise, your note is emailed to your Gmail account.

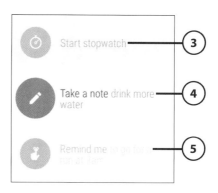

5. Say "Remind me," or tap and speak the reminder to add. For example, you can say "Remind me to go for a run at 7 a.m." and a new reminder is created labeled "Go for a run" set for 7:00 a.m. the next day. You can also set recurring reminders. For example, you can say "Remind me to make coffee at 8 a.m. every weekday."

6. Say "Start a run," or tap to launch the app you installed to handle your runs. Start running and use the watch app you installed to monitor your run.

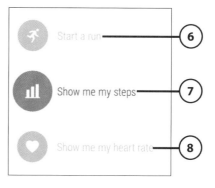

7. Say "Show me my steps," or tap to show how many steps you have walked. Your watch uses its built-in pedometer to keep track of your steps.

8. Say "Show me my heart rate," or tap to activate your watch's heart rate monitor. Follow the instructions to allow your watch to take your heart rate.

9. Say "Send text," or tap and speak the name of the recipient and the text message to send a text message to someone. For example, you can say "Send a text to Jim, see you later" and a new text message is created to Jim with the text "See you later." If the contact has more than one phone number, you need to say the phone number to use, for example "Send a text to Jim mobile."

Contact Recognition

You must enable contact recognition for the Send a Text and Send an Email functions to work. To do this, on your S7, tap Settings, Accounts, Google, Accounts & Privacy, and check the box next to Contact Recognition.

---

10. Say "Email," or tap and speak the name of the recipient and message. For example, you can say "Email Jim, you free on Friday?" and a new email will be created to Jim with the body of the message set to "You free on Friday?" If you have more than one person with the same name, and you are not specific, you are prompted to say the person's full name. If the person has more than one email address, you are prompted to say the one to use (for example, Home or Work).

11. Say "Agenda" or tap to see your agenda for today.

12. Say "Navigate," or tap and speak the desired destination to start turn-by-turn directions to your desired destination. You can say things like "to a pizza place nearby" or "home" or "work," or you can speak an address. Turn-by-turn directions start on your S7, with a mini version of them being displayed on your watch.

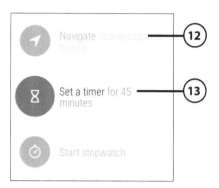

13. Say "Set a timer," or tap and speak the time the timer must use. For example, you can say "Set a timer for 45 minutes." The timer starts on your watch.

14. Say "Set an alarm," or tap and speak when the alarm must be set for. For example, you can say "Set an alarm for 6 this evening." The alarm will be created. Before the alarm is finished being created, you can tap Edit to edit the alarm and even make it recurring by selecting certain days of the week when it must trigger.

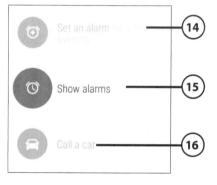

15. Say "Show alarms," or tap to show the alarms that have been set on your watch. You can edit or remove individual alarms by using the touchscreen.

16. Say "Call a car," or tap to launch the car pickup service you installed on your S7 that supports Android Wear, such as Lyft.

17. Say "Play music," or tap to start playing an "I'm feeling lucky" mix on your S7. You can also say "Play Depeche Mode" to start playing all songs by Depeche Mode on your S7. See the "Playing Music from Your Watch" sidebar at the end of this chapter for more information.

18. Say "Settings," or tap to see your watch's settings.

19. Say "Start," or tap and say the name of a watch app you have installed. For example, if you installed an app called Eat 24, you would say "Start Eat 24."

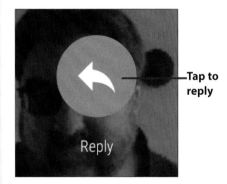

Reply to an Email Using Your Voice

When you receive a new email notification on your watch, you can reply to the email using your voice. To do this, swipe up the email notification. Swipe the notification to the left twice and tap Reply. Speak your reply. When you stop speaking, your watch sends the reply using the message you dictated.

Tap to reply

Speak your reply

>>>Go Further

MORE ABOUT NOTIFICATIONS

If there is more than one notification from an app (this is common for email notifications), you see a plus (+) symbol and a number indicating how many more notifications there are from this app. Tap the number, and all the notifications are shown. Tap the one you want to interact with.

Tap to see all notifications from the app

Some notifications you see come from apps that do not provide any way to interact with them. Your only choice is to have your watch tell your S7 to open the corresponding app. You can then continue interacting with the app on your S7. To do this, swipe the notification to the left and tap Open on Phone.

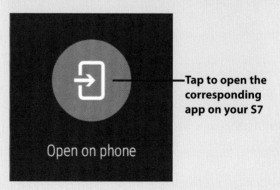

Tap to open the corresponding app on your S7

>>>Go Further

PLAY MUSIC FROM YOUR WATCH

It's easy to command your watch to play music that is stored on your S7; however, you can also store music on your watch. To do this, open the Google Play Music app, open Settings, and turn on the switch next to Download to Android Wear to download a copy of any music that you choose to your Android Wear watch. To switch to playing music from your S7 to your watch, after you say "OK Google, Play music," tap the blue X and tap Android Wear. This then allows you to play only music that is stored on your watch. To hear the music, you need to have a Bluetooth speaker paired with your watch. To switch back to playing music on your S7, say "OK Google, Play music," tap the blue X, and tap Phone.

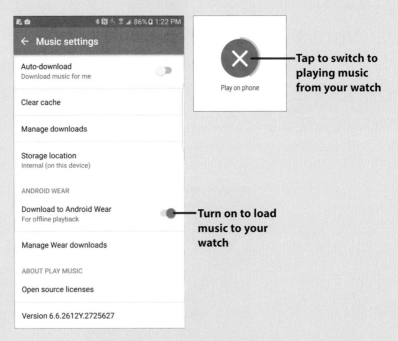

Tap to switch to playing music from your watch

Turn on to load music to your watch

When you choose to play music from your watch, swipe up and down to scroll through the albums. When you find an album you want to play, swipe left to choose to shuffle the songs on the album. Swipe left again to see the songs on the album. Scroll through the songs and tap one to start playing it. If you try to play music from your phone before you have paired a Bluetooth device capable of receiving the audio, you are prompted to complete the pairing process.

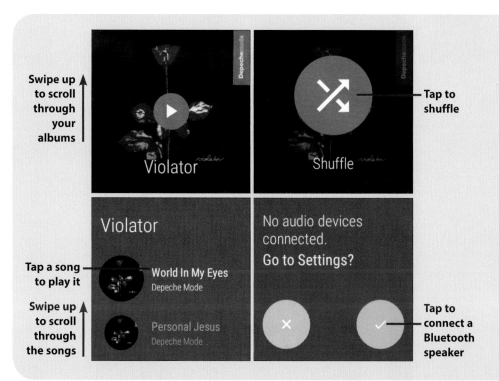

Swipe up to scroll through your albums

Tap to shuffle

Tap a song to play it

Swipe up to scroll through the songs

Tap to connect a Bluetooth speaker

>>>Go Further

THE TOGETHER FEATURE

Android Wear watches support a feature called Together. Together uses special watch faces to allow you to share sketches, photos, emojis, stickers, and your fitness information with someone else who has a Together-enabled device.

To start, you need to pair with someone. You do this from the Android Wear app on your S7. Under Watch Faces, tap Together. Tap Pair with a Friend, and choose the method you'd like to use to invite them to pair with you.

After your friend accepts your Together invite, his picture appears on your Together watch face. Tap the picture to send your activity, draw a quick sketch, or send emojis, stickers, or photos.

Track your health status
and fitness activities

This chapter covers how to use the preinstalled S Health app on your Galaxy S7 or S7 edge to track your health and fitness activities. Topics discussed in this chapter include:

→ Starting the S Health app
→ Synchronizing your health data and changing settings
→ Working with activity trackers
→ Connecting with related third-party apps and accessories
→ Setting activity goals and running programs

Getting Fit with S Health

As you'll probably have your Galaxy S7 or S7 edge with you as you go places, the preinstalled S Health app makes it easy to use the device to track your current health. If you don't like what you see and decide to improve your health with physical activity, you can tell S Health what activity (or activities) you want to track using your Galaxy S7.

You can also set health goals for S Health to track over a period of time. The S Health app contains a number of built-in goals and programs you can set up to create a fitness plan that's right for you. Then, over time, you can see the effects of your fitness plan on your overall health from within the app.

Working with S Health

By default, S Health tracks the number of steps you take and your running times and trends. You can add or remove trackers to track as many as 16 different health details, including how you walk, your caffeine intake, and your blood pressure.

Start S Health

Before you can use S Health, you have to start the app; accept the app terms, conditions, and privacy policy; and learn about the S Health dashboard.

1. Tap Apps on the Home screen.

2. Tap Samsung.

3. Tap S Health.

4. Tap Start.

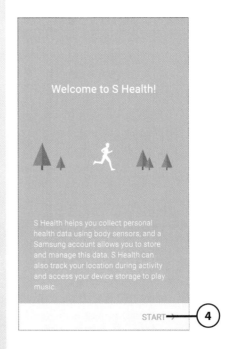

5. Tap the I Agree checkboxes on the Terms, Conditions, and Privacy Policy screen. After you tap each checkbox, the checkbox turns green and includes a white checkmark. Note that this screen opens only when you run the app for the first time. If you don't see this screen, proceed to step 7.
6. Tap Next.
7. Tap Setup.
8. Slide the Auto Sync slider button from left (Off) to right (On).
9. After you turn on Auto Sync, S Health synchronizes your health data with your Samsung account so you have your health data available on other devices or if you have to reset your Galaxy S7.
10. By default, you sync your S Health data with your Samsung account only using your Wi-Fi connection. If you want to sync using your carrier's data network, slide the Sync Via Wi-Fi Only slider button from right (On) to left (Off).
11. Return to the S Health home screen by tapping the Back icon.

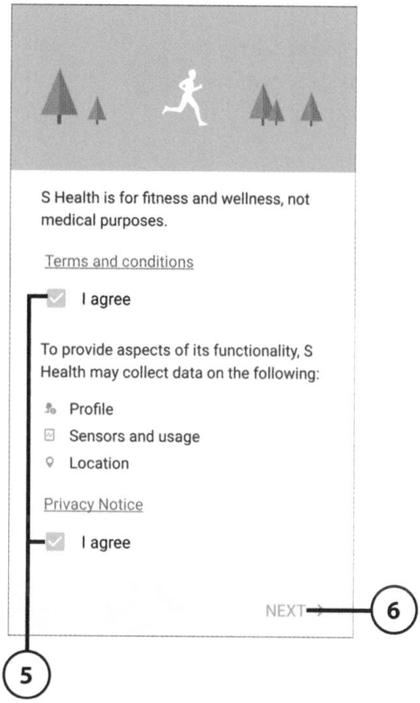
S Health is for fitness and wellness, not medical purposes.
Terms and conditions
I agree
To provide aspects of its functionality, S Health may collect data on the following:
Profile
Sensors and usage
Location
Privacy Notice
I agree
NEXT
6
5

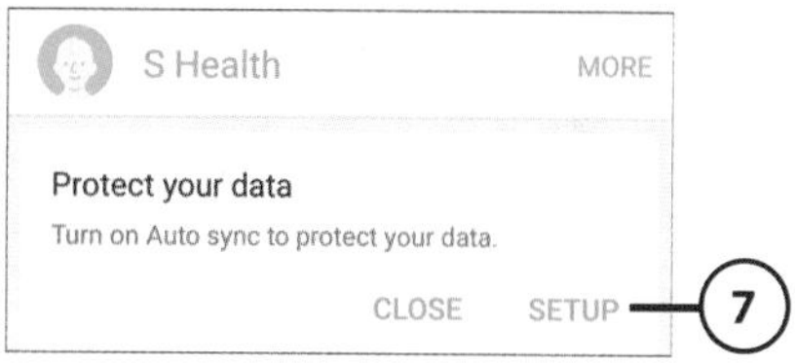
S Health
MORE
Protect your data
Turn on Auto sync to protect your data.
CLOSE
SETUP
7

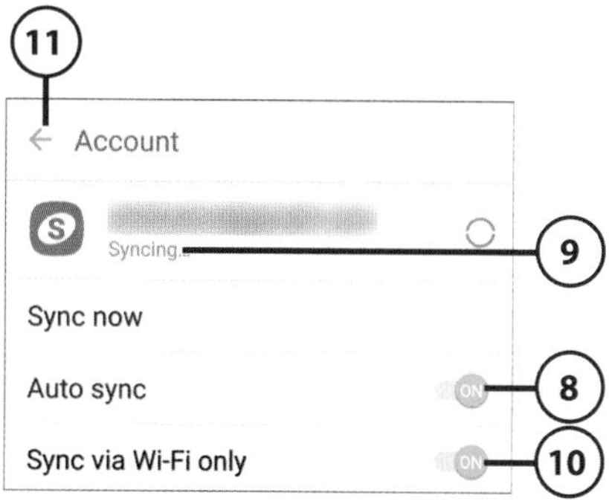
11
Account
Syncing...
9
Sync now
Auto sync
8
Sync via Wi-Fi only
10

12. Tap More in the Flexible Dashboard Layout tile to view more information.

13. Swipe up and down in the screen to learn how to customize the S Health home screen, which S Health calls the Dashboard.

14. Return to the Dashboard by tapping the Back icon.

15. Tap Close to close the Flexible Dashboard Layout information tile.

Add and Remove Trackers

1. In the S Health screen, tap More.

2. Tap Manage Items in the menu.

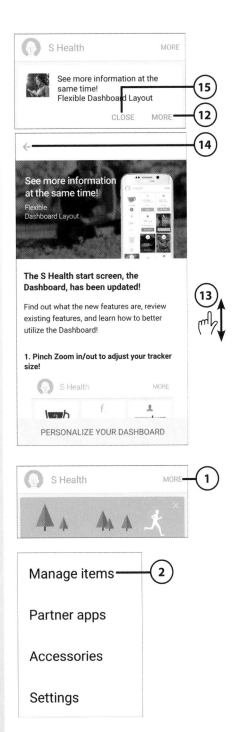

3. In the Trackers tab, the only three trackers turned on by default are the Steps, Walking, and Running trackers.

4. Turn the tracker off by sliding the slider button from right (On) to left (Off).

5. Swipe up and down in the list to view all the trackers you can add.

6. Add a tracker by sliding the slider button from left (Off) to right (On). This example adds the Sleep tracker that you'll learn to use later in this chapter.

7. When you finish adding and/or removing trackers, tap the Back icon.

Sync Your Health Data and Change Settings

After you set up your S Health account, you may see a notification from the app in the Status bar. The notification icon looks like the S Health icon you saw in the Apps screen. When you open the Quick Settings and Notification screen, you see a reminder to synchronize your health data with your Samsung account.

If you have a Samsung account, you can synchronize your health data when you view and/or change other account settings. This example presumes that you set up a Samsung account before you launched the S Health app.

1. Tap More in the menu bar.

2. Tap Settings.

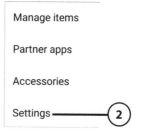

3. Tap Account to turn on synchronization with your Samsung account.

4. Tap Password to set a password you must type every time you start the S Health app.

5. Tap Unit to change the units of measure for height, weight, distance, temperature, and blood glucose levels.

6. Tap Notification to turn notification of S Health events on or off, and also set the notifications to report.

7. Tap Detect Workouts to turn detection of your workouts on and off. S Health automatically detects and records your workout such as duration, distance, and burned calories after you start walking or running for 10 minutes. You can also map your workout location and see the map, such as a section of the city where you walk, after your workout ends.

8. Tap Data Permissions to allow the S Health app to share specific data with third-party apps. You find out more about third-party apps you can use with S Health later in this chapter.

9. Tap Reset Data to erase all S Health data you have accumulated since the time you either started tracking or the last time you erased your data. You need to enter your Samsung account password to erase your data.

← S Health settings

General

Account — ③
Sync your health data with your Samsung account.

Password — ④
Protect your S Health data with a password.

Unit — ⑤

Notifications — ⑥
Receive notifications of new events on the status bar.

Advanced

Detect workouts — ⑦
Detect and record your workout performance.

Data

Data permissions — ⑧
Allow S Health functions and third-party apps to read and write specific data.

Reset data — ⑨
Erase all of your S Health data.

Information

What Happens When I Reset Data?

When you erase all data, you do so both on the Galaxy S7 and in your Samsung account. After the S Health app finishes erasing your data, the app closes and you need to open it again. After you open the app, you'll see the Terms, Conditions, and Privacy screen that you learned about earlier in this chapter.

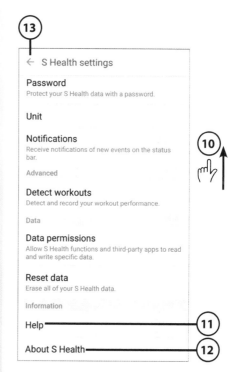

10. Swipe up in the screen to see the last two setting options within the Information section.

11. Tap Help for quick information about using S Health.

12. Tap About S Health to view information about the S Health app and check for app updates.

13. Return to the S Health screen by tapping the Back icon.

Using Activity Trackers

After you set up your activity trackers, you can begin using one or more trackers to monitor your physical activities. This example uses the Steps and Sleep trackers because those are two common physical activities.

Set Daily Step Goals and Track Your Steps

When you track your daily steps, you can see how many steps you've taken over a 24-hour period. What's more, you can see how the number of steps you've taken in a day compares with the number of steps you've taken in recent days as well as your daily activity goal.

1. Tap the Add button in the Be More Active tile.

2. Begin tracking your activity by tapping Start.

3. Tap the Be More Active tile.

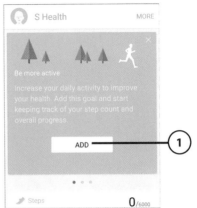

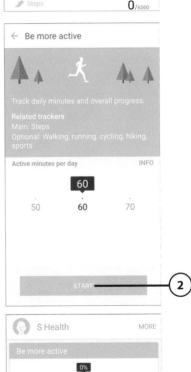

4. Tap Info to get more information about how to be more active.

5. Swipe upward in the list to view a summary of your daily activity, number of calories burned, the distance you've traveled all day, and the longest period of active minutes.

6. Tap the Trends tab to view your recorded activities for the current day and for each day over the previous week to see how the number of steps each day compares with other days and with your daily goals during the weeklong period.

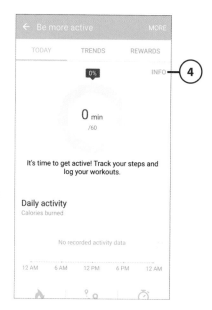

7. Tap the Rewards tab to view any rewards that S Health gives you for meeting goals. If you have no rewards, you see "No rewards" on the screen.

8. Tap More to open a menu with more options.

9. Tap View Goal Details to view information about your fitness goal.

10. Swipe left and right within the timeline to change the number of minutes per day you want to be active. The default number of minutes is 60.

11. Tap Info to get recommendations for the number of minutes you should be active each week.

12. Tap Cancel Goal to cancel your goal of being more active and return to the S Health screen.

13. Tap the Back icon to return to the Be More Active screen.

14. In the Be More Active screen, tap the Back icon to return to the S Health screen.

15. Tap the Steps tile to view how many steps you've taken.

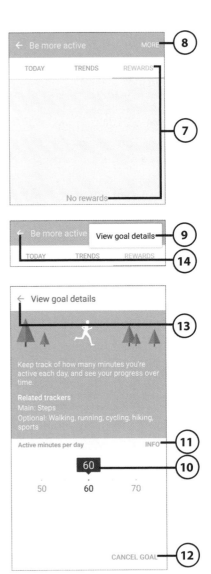

16. Tap Info to get tips about how many steps you need to take for good fitness.

17. View the number of steps you've taken today and compare them with the targeted number of steps.

18. View the number of steps you've taken over the last 24-hour period in the chart.

19. Tap Mobile Phone to select another device, such as a Samsung Gear smartwatch, that you want to use as the device that counts your steps.

20. Swipe up on the screen to view more Steps data.

21. View the current distance you've traveled, how many calories you've burned, and how many steps you've taken at a healthy pace (100 steps per minute for 10 minutes).

22. Tap the Trends tab to view your recorded steps over the period of one week and see how the number of steps each day compares with other days and with your daily goals during the weeklong period.

23. Tap the Rewards tab to view any rewards that S Health gives you for meeting your step goals. If you have no rewards, you see "No rewards" on the screen.

24. Tap More to open a menu with more options.

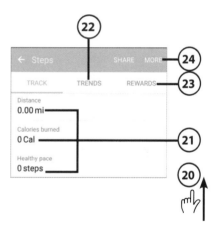

25. Tap Set Target to set your daily target for number of steps in a day.

26. Tap Source Data to View to select another device, such as a Samsung Gear smartwatch, that you want to use as the device that counts your steps.

27. Tap Pause Counting Steps to have S Health stop counting the number of steps until you tell it to resume by tapping More as you did in step 24 and then tapping Start Counting Steps.

28. Close the menu by tapping the Back touch button (not shown).

29. Return to the S Health screen by tapping the Back icon.

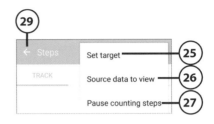

Track Your Sleep

Earlier in this chapter, you learned how to add the Sleep tracker to your Dashboard. Getting a good night's sleep is important for everyone, and if you're concerned about your sleep patterns, you can tell S Health when you go to sleep and when you wake up. After a period of time, you'll be able to see your sleep pattern and determine if you need to make changes to your sleep schedule.

1. In the S Health screen, swipe down the screen until you see the Sleep tile.

2. Tap the Sleep tile.

3. View sleep data for the previous or following day by tapping the left and right arrows on either side of the date. If the date is the current date, then the right arrow is disabled.

4. Tap the date button to change the date within the Set Date window that appears at the bottom of the screen (not shown).

5. Record your sleep times by tapping the Record Manually button.

6. Tap, hold, and drag the Sleep button around the perimeter of the clock until you reach the time of day you went to sleep. As you move the icon, the time you went to sleep appears in the middle of the clock and changes in 10-minute increments as you move the icon so you can set your bedtime more accurately.

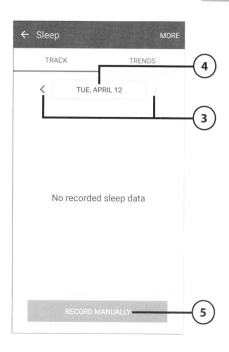

What Do the Number Marks Around the Clock Mean?

The 0 mark on the clock signifies midnight of the current day. If the Sleep button appears before midnight, then S Health presumes you went to bed at your selected time during the previous day. The 6 mark means 6 a.m., the 12 mark means 12 p.m., and the 18 mark means 6 p.m.

7. Tap, hold, and drag the Wake Up button around the perimeter of the clock until you reach the time of day you woke up. As you move the icon, the time you woke up appears in the center of the clock. The default wake-up time is the current time, which is 4:34 a.m. in this example.

8. After you set the sleep and wake-up times, the sleep date(s) and times appear in the center of the clock.

9. The total amount of time you slept appears below the clock.

10. Rate your sleep quality by tapping the appropriate star. For example, if you had a pretty good sleep and you want to give that sleep four stars, tap the fourth star from the left and the first four stars appear in gold and only the last star (the one on the right) remains gray.

11. Tap Save to save your bedtime and wake-up data.

12. Tap Cancel to return to the Sleep screen without setting your bed-time and/or wake-up time.

13. Tap Trends to view sleep data over the past few days.

14. Swipe left and right in the Days chart to view sleep data for each day during the past month.

15. Tap Days to change the chart monitoring period between Days, Weeks, and Months.

16. Return to the S Health screen by tapping the Back icon.

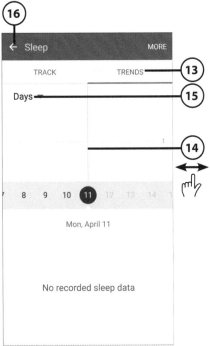

Viewing Partner Apps and Settings

Samsung has partnered with a variety of hardware and app accessories that work with S Health to enhance your monitoring experience and give you even more tools to stay active and healthy.

1. In the S Health screen, swipe up in the screen until you see the partner tiles.

2. Tap one of the partner tiles to learn more about the partnership offer in your preferred web browser app.

3. Tap More.

4. Tap Partner Apps in the menu.

5. Swipe up and down the screen to view all the partner app tiles.

6. Each partner app tile contains the name of the app, the company that produced the app, and a brief description.

7. You can get more information about the app and download it within the Google Play Store by tapping the download icon.

8. Return to the S Health screen by tapping the Back icon.

9. Tap More as you did in step 3 and then tap Accessories in the menu.

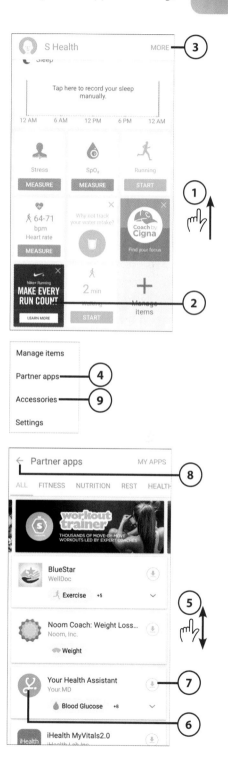

10. Swipe up and down the screen to view fitness hardware accessories from Samsung and partner companies.

11. Tap View More to view more accessories in the Samsung Accessories or Partner Accessories category.

12. Tap the accessory in the list to open the device screen and view the device. Within the device screen you can also get more information from the company website and also register your device on the Galaxy S7.

What Must I Do to Register My Fitness Device?

Before you register your fitness device, you need to turn your device on so your Galaxy S7 can find your device using a wireless technology such as Bluetooth. The Galaxy Apps or the Google Play app may also open so you can install an app on your Galaxy S7 that is necessary to operate the fitness device.

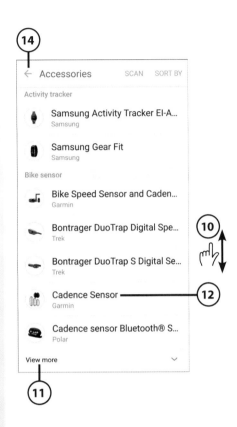

13. If you're in the device screen, return to the Accessories screen by tapping the Back touch button (not shown).

14. Return to the S Health screen by tapping the Back icon.

Setting Goals and Creating Running Programs

The S Health app has several preset goals, and each goal takes you step by step through setting daily goals such as how many calories to eat in a day.

If you're a runner, there are also several programs that you can initiate in S Health to prepare you to run up to 10 kilometers (10K), or 6.2 miles.

1. Tap More in the menu bar and then tap Manage Items as shown in steps 1 and 2 of the "Add and Remove Trackers" task earlier in this chapter.

2. Tap the Goals tab.

3. Select a goal from Be More Active, Eat Healthier, or Feel More Rested. If you're already working toward a goal, the In Progress text appears underneath the goal name.

4. The screen you see next depends on the goal you selected. You can follow the step-by-step instructions on the screen to set up your goal, or you can return to the Manage Items screen by tapping the Back touch button (not shown).

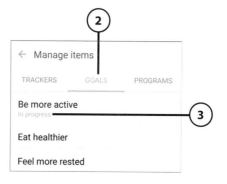

5. Tap the Programs tab.

6. Select the type of run you're looking for. If you're just getting started, tap Baby Steps to 5K.

7. The next screen you see depends on the program you selected. You can follow the step-by-step instructions for creating a workout program over a period of weeks, or you can return to the Manage Items screen by tapping the Back touch button (not shown).

8. If you decide you don't want to set a goal or program, tap the Back icon to return to the S Health screen.

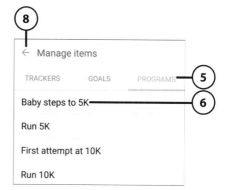

Index

D

H

I

J-K

REGISTER THIS PRODUCT
SAVE 35%*
ON YOUR NEXT PURCHASE!

How to Register Your Product

- Go to quepublishing.com/register
- Sign in or create an account
- Enter ISBN: 10- or 13-digit ISBN that appears on the back cover of your product

Benefits of Registering

- Ability to download product updates
- Access to bonus chapters and workshop files
- A 35% coupon to be used on your next purchase – valid for 30 days

  > To obtain your coupon, click on "Manage Codes" in the right column of your Account page

- Receive special offers on new editions and related Que products

Please note that the benefits for registering may vary by product. Benefits will be listed on your Account page under Registered Products.

We value and respect your privacy. Your email address will not be sold to any third party company.

* 35% discount code presented after product registration is valid on most print books, eBooks, and full-course videos sold on QuePublishing.com. Discount may not be combined with any other offer and is not redeemable for cash. Discount code expires after 30 days from the time of product registration. Offer subject to change.

quepublishing.com